Dedication

This edited collection is dedicated to the late Maggie Woodrow who strove tirelessly to improve the opportunities in higher education for students from less privileged backgrounds. She was an inspiration to many people working in access and widening participation, and a formidable and persistent challenge to those seeking to preserve elitist inequitious systems.

Maggie Woodrow
Founder member and EAN Executive Director 1991-2001.

Trentham Books Limited

Westview House	22883 Quicksilver Drive
734 London Road	Sterling
Oakhill	VA 20166-2012
Stoke on Trent	USA
Staffordshire	
England ST4 5NP	

First published 2002

British Library Cataloguing-in-Publication Data
A catalogue record for this book is available from the British Library

1 85856 280 5

Designed and typeset by Trentham Print Design Ltd., Chester and printed in Great Britain by Cromwell Press Ltd., Wiltshire.

Acknowledgements

The editors would like to thank Jo Astley and Lorraine Casey of the Institute for Access Studies at Staffordshire University for providing editorial support, and all the contributors who have patiently fulfilled the editors' requests in the preparation of the chapters for this book.

The editors would also like to thank the European Access Network (EAN) for organising the 10th EAN Anniversary Conference, June 2001, University of Glasgow, Scotland.

Trentham Books

Stoke on Trent, UK and Sterling, USA

Contents

Notes on the contributors • ix

Tribute to Maggie Woodrow • xv
Leslie Wagner

Introduction • xix
Michael Cooper

Part 1: National Approaches

Chapter 1
Pyramids or spiders? Cross-sector collaboration to widen participation. Learning from international experiences • 3
Maggie Woodrow and Liz Thomas

Chapter 2
Collaboration within and between HEIs in England: a review of policy and practice • 29
Liz Thomas

Chapter 3
Widening Access to higher education in Ireland • 49
Don Thornhill

Chapter 4
Government deliberations on widening recruitment to higher education: partnerships in Sweden with higher education institutions, schools and others • 71
Kenny Jonsson

Chapter 5
Collaboration to address equity problems in access to higher education in Lithuania • 79
Saulius Vengris

Chapter 6
Pathways to College Network: Collaborating nationally to improve college access and success for under represented students in the US • 85
Ann Coles and David Malcolm Roth

Chapter 7
Collaboration: the past and the future for higher education in South Africa • 99
Prakash Naidoo

Part 2: Case Studies

Chapter 8
Six years on: REACHOut® degree route – widening participation by collaboration with the community • 111
Martin Carey, Fiona Chambers, Margaret Mairah and Lyn Carey

Chapter 9
Ten years of access policy into practice through Partnership: a pragmatic approach to progression • 139
John Blicharski and Michael Allardice

Chapter 10
Developing progression to learning: building progressive pathways in the Tees Valley • 153
Margaret Noble and Pauline Lynn

Chapter 11
The role of Community Colleges in promoting access to higher education for low-income students: the University of California at Los Angeles transfer program • 171
Maureen Hoyler, Holly Hexter and Lorraine Casey

Chapter 12
Why collaborate? Initiatives for improving participation and completion for students with a disability in South Australia • 181
Ann Noble and Gerry Mullins

Chapter 13
**'College wouldn't touch me with a barge pole':
a collaborative educational development programme
for ex-offenders** • 199
Lucy MacLeod and Jan Tunnock

Chapter 14
**Academics and first-year students: collaborating to access
success in an unfamiliar university culture** • 213
Jill Lawrence

Chapter 15
Inter-university collaboration – a regional approach • 239
Algirdas Vaclovas Valiulis and Edmundas Kazimieras Zavadskas

Chapter 16
**Interdisciplinary collaboration: its role in widening
participation in Higher Education** • 247
Jocey Quinn

Chapter 17
Putting partnerships into practice • 257
Sarah Williams

Index • 267

Notes on the Contributors

Michael Allardice graduated from the University of Dundee as a mature student in 1997 and became involved with their Access Summer School the same year. Since then he has conducted longitudinal research on access students and helped in the expansion of access programmes at the University. He is also interested in the philosophical and social policy aspects of the widening participation agenda and is currently writing an MPhil dissertation on Access policy.

John Blicharski is Director of the Wider Access Study Centre and is responsible for nine access programmes offered by the University of Dundee. He transitioned to the access field in 1995 from a background in biochemical pharmacology and medical education. His main interest is successfully preparing and qualifying disadvantaged young people for HE, although his role in outreach work to all ages and stages continues to grow. He is a Specialist Consultant for the Universities UK Access Advisory Partnership.

Lyn Carey is REACHOut® Pre-Access Co-ordinator, (seconded from Liverpool City Council Parent School Partnership Service), Liverpool Hope.

Martin Carey is Executive Dean of Hope in the Community, Liverpool Hope.

Lorraine Casey is Research Support Officer in the Institute for Access Studies at Staffordshire University. She graduated from Keele University in 2000, with a BA Joint Honours degree in Sociology and Applied Social Studies, and is currently studying part-time for an MA in Social and Cultural Theory. She has carried out a number of research projects in the field of post-compulsory education, particularly with reference to student funding and is currently working in the first-year student experience and retention.

Fiona Chambers is REACHOut® Degree Route Co-ordinator (seconded from Liverpool City Council Parent School Partnership Service), Liverpool Hope.

Ann Coles is Vice Chair, Board of Trustees, The College Board, in New York City and Acting President of The Education Resources Institute (TERI) in Boston, Massachusetts. She has over 35 years experience working in programs to ensure access to higher education for traditionally under represented students of all ages in the US and serves as Director of the Pathways to College Network. She holds a doctorate from the Harvard University Graduate School of Education.

Michael Cooper is Director of the International Office at Karlstad University, Sweden. He holds a degree in modern languages form King's College London and a research degree in English from Göteborg University, Sweden. Previously he was head of the School of modern languages at Karlstad where he lectured in English, in particular language and linguistics. He is currently President of the Compostela Group of Universities and a member of the committee of the European Access network. He has worked extensively as a translator and language editor of scientific publications.

Holly Hexter is a consultant to the Council for Opportunity in Education and the Pell Institute for the Study of Opportunity in Higher Education in Washington DC. She has worked as a writer, researcher and editor and has helped develop the Council's international programs. Previously she was a research analyst for the American Council on Education, which represents college and university presidents, and served as co-ordinator of the Council for Inter-institutional Leadership, a group of university consortia.

Maureen Hoyler is Executive Vice President of the Council for Opportunity in Education and has been with the Council since 1981, where she is responsible for the governmental relations, professional development, communications and research units of the organisation. She has been involved in drafting legislative language a particularly as it relates to the Trio Chapter of the Higher Education Act of 1965.

Kenny Jonsson is Director, expert; Ministry of Education and Science, Stockholm, Sweden. He deals mainly with matters concerning recruitment to higher education and labour market questions.

Jill Lawrence is a Lecturer in the Faculty of Arts and Learning Enhancement Counsellor in the Student Services Centre at the University of Southern Queensland in Australia. She is currently completing a doctorate in communication and education which investigates how first year students learn to become successful in the new, and often unfamiliar, university culture.

Pauline Lynn is Co-ordinator of the Progression Pathways Project at the University of Teesside. She was previously a lecturer in History at the University of Teesside and has written articles and papers on her research into the political significance of female enfranchisement in the North East of England. Other research interests include access and equity issues, community education and gender experiences

Lucy MacLeod is Head of the Wider Access Unit in the Department of Lifelong Learning at Napier University, Edinburgh, responsible for driving forward the University's strategy on widening participation, including management of partnership projects between the University and other organisations. She has a background of research, policy development, evaluation and training in the voluntary and public sectors in Scotland, including equal opportunities and represents the University on significant bodies and networks relating to access to higher education and social inclusion. She has an MSc in Applied Social Research.

Margaret Mairah, as a mature returner to education, has a wealth of expertise in the field and has been closely involved in the REACHOut ® project since it beginnings. She has an in depth insight into the issues experienced by those who wish to resume study and supports the vision of REACHOut® and the process which allows for the development of a fully inclusive curriculum. She is Associate Director to Network of Hope.

Gerry Mullins is a Senior Lecturer in the Advisory Centre for University Education at Adelaide University, Australia. He provides professional advice on learning and teaching to academic staff at the University, particularly in the fields of curriculum review and development and in the use of online resources.

Prakash Naidoo was a former lecturer in Management Accounting at the Durban Higher Education Institute in South Africa. When he wrote this chapter he was the Dean of the Faculty of Management Sciences at the Vaal Triangle Technikon – The First University of Technology – and is now its Vice-Rector. His research focuses on costs of higher education and his PHD thesis, titled 'An Investigation of Cost Management in Higher Education Institutions in South Africa' will be examined in 2002.

Ann Noble is a Lecturer in the Advisory Centre for University Education at Adelaide University, where she provides learning assistance to undergraduate and postgraduate students. She has been convenor of the University's Advisory Committee on Students with a Disability, a member of the Equal Opportunity Board, and is currently a member of the South Australian Universities' Uniability Committee.

Margaret Noble is Director of Lifelong Learning at the University of Teesside responsible for part-time programmes, workbased learning, community learning and open and distance learning. She was previously Head of Education Development at the University of Lincolnshire and Humberside. She directs and manages a range of projects and initiatives in widening participation, lifelong learning and community learning and is chair of the widening participation management and steering groups of the Universities for the North East.

Jocey Quinn is Research Fellow at the Institute for Access Studies, Staffordshire University. She has a PhD from Lancaster University on the mass participation of women students and the Higher Education curriculum and is currently writing a book based on this research. Her recent research includes work for HEFCE on the role of partnerships in Widening Participation in Higher Education. She is Managing Editor of the *Journal of Widening Participation and Lifelong Learning*.

David Malcolm Roth is Deputy to the President at Occidental College in Los Angeles, California. He also provides direction to a national collaborative he co-founded, called the Pathways to College Network, an initiative designed to increase the number of under represented students who graduate high school and attend college and is Commissioner and Representative of the General Public to the California Student Aid Commission.

Liz Thomas is Director of the Institute for Access Studies at Staffordshire University, dedicated to widening participation, lifelong learning and social inclusion. She has recently completed research on behalf of the Higher Education Funding Council for England on the development and effectiveness of partnerships between higher and further education institutions and other groups to widen participation. She is author of the book *Widening Participation in Post-compulsory Education* and other books, and an editor of the *Journal of Widening Participation and Lifelong Learning*.

Don Thornhill is Chairman of the Higher Education Authority (HEA). Previously he was Secretary General of the Department of Education and Science from 1993 to 1998 and, before that, an Assistant Secretary in the Office of the Revenue Commissioners in Dublin. He has also worked in the Departments of Finance and Foreign Affairs and at Unilever. He is a member of the Royal Irish Academy, Honorary Treasurer of the Statistical and Social Inquiry Society of Ireland, Treasurer of the Irish Fulbright Commission and is a member of the Executive Committee of the European Cultural Foundation.

Jan Tunnock is a member of the Wider Access Team at Napier University responsible for development and delivery of community-based partnership projects. She has over twenty years experience in professional, personal and organisational development in both industry and education. For the past seven years, she has contributed significant projects across the University, whilst also researching and writing successful ESF applications and conducting project evaluations. She holds a counselling qualification and is an experienced group worker and facilitator.

Algirdas Vaclovas Valiulis is Vice-rector of Vilnius Gediminas Technical University and head of the department of Materials Science and Welding. He has received research scholarships from Prag Technical University, Moscow Bauman High Technical School, Engineering College of Denmark, Leuven University (Belgium), Glamorgan University (UK) and North London University. He is a member of the European Society for Engineering Education (SEFI), the European Association for International Education (EAIE), and is on the steering committee of the University Consortium in Science and Technology (BALTECH). He has written over 200 research, methodological, scientific and organisation study publications including books and textbooks.

Saulius Vengris is Vice-rector of Vilnius University. His field of expertise is the sciences and during 1992-3 he was Dean of the Faculty of Physics. He has many publications in this area, and also in work relating to legislation problems of higher education in Lithuanian and the international press.

Leslie Wagner is Vice-Chancellor of Leeds Metropolitan University, having previously been Vice-Chancellor and Chief Executive of the University of North London from 1987-1993. A former Chairman of the Society for Research into Higher Education and of the Yorkshire and Humberside Universities Association, he currently chairs the University Vocational Awards Council together with the Widening Participation and Lifelong Learning Group of Universities UK and also the Advisory Group of Leeds Common Purpose. He is a member of the Council for Industry and Higher Education and the Leeds Cares Leadership Group and also a Director of Leeds Business Services Ltd. He has written or edited four books on economics and the planning of education and is a regular contributor on higher education in the media. In June 2000 he was awarded the CBE for services to higher education and the Jewish community.

Sarah Williams is a Research Officer in the Institute for Access studies, Staffordshire University. She studied for an MA in Media and Cultural Studies at Manchester University, where she developed an interest in the impact of new technologies on social structures and has worked on a project that received European Commission funding to research ways of making lifelong learning more effective through using new technologies. She has written a number of reports on how people learn using new technologies and how new technologies can be used to inspire and develop learning communities.

Edmundas Kazimieras Zavadskas is Rector of Vilnius Gediminas Technical University, which is a member of the Lithuanian Academy of Sciences and of the Ukrainian Academy of Technological Cybertechnics. He has close academic links with the universities of Aalborg (Denmark), Salford and Glamorgan (UK), Poznan University of Technology (Poland), Leipzeig Higher School of Technology Economics and Culture (Germany) and Aachen Higher Technical School (Germany). He is also a member of many international organisations, and of the steering and programme committees of many international conferences and sits on the editorial boards of several research journals.

TRIBUTE TO MAGGIE WOODROW
– EAN EXECUTIVE DIRECTOR, 1991–2001

Leslie Wagner

It is fitting that this volume is dedicated to the memory of Maggie Woodrow, a formidable champion campaigner for wider access to higher education in the UK and abroad.

Maggie's career following her undergraduate studies at Southampton University moved from school teaching to further education and on to higher education. Her involvement with wider access began in the unlikely setting of Harrow College of Further Education in Hatch End. There, with Gareth Parry and others, she devised one of the first access courses to higher education. This was in partnership with the Polytechnic of Central London and the Polytechnic of North London.

Through the 1980s, coinciding with her work for the Open College of South London, she began to move from running access courses to engaging in the policy issues, becoming involved increasingly at a national level. I was pleased when, in 1989, she joined the Polytechnic of North London to lead our access work there. Subsequently, she moved on to the University of Westminster and eventually created the European Access Network, of which she was the Executive Director.

It was through her work here, over the last decade, that she came more into public prominence. The post gave her the freedom to research, write and campaign and Maggie always saw these three activities as interrelated and indivisible. Not for her the dry research paper languishing in an unread journal. Research and writing had to have a social and a political purpose. They had to change the way things were done. This didn't mean biased or sloppy work. On the contrary, Maggie knew that it was the very thoroughness of her methodology and empirical research which made her conclusions compelling.

The work of the European Access Network was the focus of her activities in recent years. The EAN currently represents 22 countries. It seeks to influence policy and practice in respect of widening participation by under represented groups, through sharing problems and solutions, and providing contacts, research partners and information through its Annual Conference, its newsletter and its international journal. Through Maggie's work the EAN now has close links with the European Union and the Council of Europe, and is developing good contacts with UNESCO and the OECD. Indeed, Maggie was consultant to the Higher Education and Research Committee of the Council of Europe. Her recent international research included: *Lifelong Learning to Combat Social Exclusion: the Role of HEIs. A comparative study of five European countries*; and work on the participation of under represented groups in HE in both Western and Central and Eastern Europe. At the time of her death she was in the process of launching an international comparative study of retention, progression and completion of students from under represented groups (with the Institute for Access Studies, UK and the Council for Opportunity in Education, US).

At home her work was influential too. She undertook research for the UK National Audit Office, the Higher Education Funding Council for England, the Scottish Funding Council and Universities UK. Her work on good practice for the latter, embodied in the volumes *From Elitism to Inclusion*, helped influence government policy on student funding. Her earlier work in the 1980s should not be forgotten either. It was here, reflecting on her experiences with the students on her access courses and seeking to change national priorities, that she was at her most radical. Some of her best work was done unseen in the invisible world of committees and working groups where the outcomes are collective and only the committee members know who were the main influences.

Maggie always challenged conventional wisdom. In the early days of access, she promulgated the then radical view that it wouldn't work without curriculum change within higher education. And when curriculum change occurred, she argued that it didn't go far enough or moved on to the support, financial or pastoral, which non-traditional students required. She was adept at pointing out the discrepancies between rhetoric and reality, whether in national policies or institutional practice.

Maggie was not the easiest person to work with. She did not suffer fools gladly, and hated mediocrity: she was no respecter of power and she hated humbug. Weasel words and the dissembling which is sometimes required from those in authority were not for her. She had the gift of making you feel uncomfortable, even guilty, in her presence because both of you knew that you couldn't live up to her high standards. She was focused entirely on what policy meant for the students.

Her energy and enthusiasm at the end of her life were, if anything, greater than twenty years earlier. I'm not sure how many people knew how old she was but most of us thought she would go on forever. Her sudden death came as a great shock and has left a great void. As we try to fill it collectively and to hold aloft the torch of wider access which she lit so brightly, we will be inspired by the memory of her dedication, enthusiasm, integrity and sheer cussedness to do even better.

Introduction

Michael Cooper

It is now widely accepted that if societies are to continue to develop and to be able to offer their citizens the opportunity to realise their potential then access to education, including higher education, is an absolute necessity. Over the past decade or so many policies have been put into place and practices introduced to enable those who would not have thought of going on to higher education to make the transition. Governments have called for measures and institutions of higher education have responded, but many of the policies and practices that have been adopted, although successful, have tended to be restricted to individual institutions. In numerous fields, however, even in higher education, key words in activity plans and mission statements are networking and cooperation, underlining the belief that more can be achieved if we pool our strengths and resources. There are many reasons why this might also be the case with regard to widening access to higher education. One very obvious one is that the concept of higher education or university often raises negative responses in those who may be considered potential non-traditional students and in those who see university education as something far removed from the needs of everyday existence. If institutions of higher education could, for instance, work together with institutions providing further or vocational education at a post-secondary level, the pathway could be smoothed and some of the obstacles removed. At another level, international cooperation can also result in widening access but in a somewhat different perspective.

Considering the issue of cooperation primarily from two angles, the present volume seeks to answer the questions of whether and how it could contribute to widening participation in higher education. Part 1 examines a number of national approaches. What is interesting is that they reflect and comment on the situation in widely divergent societies at different stages in their development. Part 2 presents a series of case studies, which, although they mainly discuss initiatives at English-speaking institutions, cover many different forms of collaboration. The volume concludes with a consideration of the lessons that may be drawn with regard to collaboration.

The first contribution provides an excellent platform for a discussion of national approaches, based as it is on a comparative study of collaboration in four different countries. It is an edited version of a fascinating study, coordinated by the late Maggie Woodrow, which examines four models and attempts to draw up some recommendations for collaboration. It is obvious that, although all the models are concerned with widening participation in some sense, they each have a different focus and so cannot strictly be compared with each other. Nevertheless, the material has provided enough substance to underpin a series of recommendations for both practitioners and policy-makers. However, as always, whether one should adopt an approach to collaboration in the form of a 'pyramid', 'spider', 'bridge' or 'marriage' has perhaps rather more to do with the social and cultural context than pure educational considerations.

Directing the focus to England, Liz Thomas discusses the approach adopted in a country where access has a strong foothold, particularly in the newer universities. She looks at ways in which the Higher Education Funding Council (HEFCE) is promoting collaboration as a means of widening participation. As HEFCE sees it, this may involve at one level collaboration within a single institution, where teaching and learning policies, recruitment policies and other aspects of an institution's activities are linked together to form a strategy for widening participation. At another level, however, the funding council is keen to promote regional partnerships as a way forward.

Moving from England to the Republic of Ireland, the third chapter gives a thorough survey of the Irish perspective. Don Thornhill, who is chair of the Higher Education Authority, sets the framework by providing a statistical background regarding transfer to higher education and discussing the main statutory provisions relating to the issue and to equality in higher education. This is followed by an overview of the actions to promote these aspects and comments on studies and policy documents. The final section of the chapter describes in some detail the statutory review of university equality policies being undertaken by the Authority. His conclusion is that, although achieving equality in higher education is no easy task, the goal is more than justification for the effort involved.

Widening the circle, the next chapter looks at initiatives in Sweden. Kenny Jonsson presents and comments on a bill before the Swedish Parliament which is intended to create what is termed the open university. This does not refer to a distance university of the UK's Open University type, although it includes what the Swedes term a cyber university. What is implied in the wording is the idea that there should be a university that is open to everybody. Sweden funds its universities through taxation and thus there are no tuition fees; it also provides a system of state maintenance grants and loans so there are no real economic barriers to higher education. However, transfer to higher education in Sweden is still not much more than 30% of an age cohort and the government is therefore keen for universities to put in place measures to increase recruitment and to attract non-traditional students. These include an extension of the university preparatory year, college/access programmes, introductory courses and Swedish language courses, as 20 per cent of the population does not have Swedish as its first language.

A short voyage across the Baltic Sea brings us to Lithuania which, like the other Baltic countries as well as other members of the former Soviet Union, has had to restructure their societies, including higher education. As Saulius Vengris notes, when the country was part of the Soviet Union socio-economic inequalities were officially fairly minimal in Lithuanian society and access to higher education was basically only limited by the physical capacity of the universities and the political loyalties of families. With the independence of Lithuania came rapid social changes particularly as regards income differentiation and the current legislation regarding higher education relates access to ability but does not envision financial support for under represented groups. One obstacle to access lay in the complicated method of gaining entrance to higher education where each institution had its own entrance examination. A first step towards reformation has been taken through the establishment of a National Examination Centre to provide a common high school graduation exam. Further, a number of institutions of higher education have formed an association to organise common entrance to all universities. Finally there are a number of recommendations to Parliament regarding measures to facilitate access to higher education for students from low-income groups.

Where Lithuania is a small and fairly homogeneous country, the US is highly fragmented as regards education and other aspects of society. Taking as their point of departure a series of statistics showing that low-income students are under represented in college enrolments, that over half those enrolled never complete their degrees and that a much smaller proportion of African-American and Hispanic high-school graduates succeed in gaining a bachelor's degree as compared to white students, Ann Coles and David Roth present a model for improving college access and success for under represented groups termed Pathways to College Network. This is a network of major educational institutions and organisations, national foundations and federal funders whose aim is to collaborate to promote college access and success for under represented groups. Their methods include identifying research-based effective policies and practices which have an impact on student achievement, disseminating what works, highlighting and addressing what is missing and encouraging collaboration. The authors maintain that with their ambitious programme, the Pathways to College Network has tremendous potential for improving access to and success at college for under represented groups.

The final chapter in this section discusses the situation for higher education in South Africa. Prakash Naidoo maintains that the higher education system in South Africa has so far failed to overcome the fragmentation of the apartheid system, to achieve economies of scale and to enhance governance, administration and management structures. He discusses the national plan for higher education in particular with respect to collaboration, concentrating on issues such as establishing institutions that are truly South African – that is moving away from traditional dominant English or Afrikaans-speaking institutions to encourage diversity in student enrolments. Other topics he considers important include developing programme and infrastructural collaboration among institutions to make the use of common resources more efficient, achieving greater access and equity, and also merging institutions. His chapter concludes with a consideration of a case study relating to the proposed merger between two institutions.

Having examined a number of national approaches, Part 2 of the book contains a series of case studies which show various approaches to collaboration of an inter-collegiate, interregional or interdisciplinary nature in action. The studies are mainly but not exclusively drawn from the English-speaking world.

An interesting example of what can be achieved in collaboration with the community is provided by a programme developed by Liverpool Hope University College working together with the Liverpool City Council Parent School Partnership. The programme, REACHOut® (Routes into Education through Access in the Community and the Home), is designed to promote flexible learning and overcome barriers to learning which have been identified over a period of years in consultation with parents, community workers and parent educators. It provides access and degree provisions and also now pre-access in inner city primary schools and is designed to enable students who are unable to study full-time to take their degree on a part-time basis. With the first cohort graduating in 2001, the chapter focuses on what has been learnt on the basis of a wide range of evidence, including students' experiences, qualifications, reasons for part-time study together with measures of their academic performance and retention. The key lesson would seem to be that education is likely to be really successfully designed when learning is taken to people both physically and culturally.

Another approach to collaboration is provided by the University of Dundee, which, in partnership with the Local Councils, local careers companies and others, has been running an Access Summer School for ten years to assist disadvantaged young people gain access to higher education. John Blicharski and Michael Allardice provide insight into how an effective educational partnership with cross-sector collaboration can be developed. They outline the key successes and avoidance of failures, and show how a plan to increase inclusiveness has been converted into provision that benefits about 200 candidates per year. They describe the impact of the physical and emotional environment on young people deterred from seeking higher education and demonstrate how the partnership has made a real difference.

Working with the community has also proved a useful model in the Tees Valley in northern England, which has one of the lowest participation rates in post-16 and higher education in the country. Margaret Noble and Pauline Lynn discuss a range of initiatives put in place by the University of Teesside with the object of raising aspirations among young learners and also encouraging adults to participate in learning. They examine the development of a set of holistic and coordinated approaches to facilitate progression where the university is working with a series of education providers at many different levels to achieve a number of clear routes to higher education for both young people and adults. The chapter debates the challenges, issues and impacts faced in the establishment of such partnerships, including the criteria for successful partnerships, meeting diverse partner needs, maintaining coordination and sustaining impact. Their conclusions may, to some extent, be valid for all the collaborative projects presented in this volume: that the challenges to be faced and overcome lie very much in the issue of sustainability. It takes considerable effort if initiatives are to be maintained over time and many of those who become engaged in learning through widening participation projects may need considerable support and encouragement to continue on a lifelong learning path. To provide this and also to take a broad view of outcomes beyond immediate and educational progression is one of the big challenges.

Looking beyond the United Kingdom, the next chapter considers what has often been considered a specifically American phenomenon, community colleges, and how these can work together with universities to widen access and retention for low-income groups. This case study, which formed part of the empirical material on which Maggie Woodrow's research was based (see above), has wider implications in that a number of UK institutions are following the US example. The study focuses on the University of California Los Angeles (UCLA), which in 1999 set up an office dedicated to community college outreach to increase the number of community college transfer students. The outreach scheme has a number of core components all designed to facilitate transfer from community college, traditionally the point of entry to higher education for low-income groups, and is intended to provide a means of tracking students from secondary to post-secondary education. It is without doubt a highly interesting initiative and although it has not been running long enough to provide any definite conclusions, it would seem that the initial results are positive.

Whereas the case studies up to this point have concerned the whole range of non-traditional groups in higher education, the next two are more limited in scope but nevertheless of great importance since the specific groups under consideration are not often a focus in the debate. Following the introduction in Australia in 1992 of the Disability Discrimination Act, Ann Noble and Gerry Mullins discuss initiatives designed to improve participation in higher education of students who have a disability. Their comments are restricted to South Australia, where initiatives designed to improve both access and retention rates involved collaboration between staff in a range of tertiary institutions: academic staff developers, student welfare staff, equity personnel and disability liaison officers, and resulted in a whole series of resources for both staff and students. These included web-based guidelines and training programmes. Surveying these initiatives and assessing their impact leads the authors to raise a number of questions with no easy answers. However, they conclude that the collaborations described and the policy and pedagogical issues raised represent both an achievement and a challenge.

The specific group targeted by Lucy MacLeod and Jan Tunnock of Napier University involves ex-offenders, and the university, together with Jewel and Esk Valley College and APEX Scotland, a voluntary body supporting ex-offenders put together a pre-access course to address the barriers facing ex-offenders, wishing to enter college or university. Like many similar programmes, it is designed to raise awareness of educational opportunities, develop personal and study skills, and increase self-confidence. The authors argue that the programme has, in general, been successful although it has raised a number of issues that need to be resolved. Their conclusion is that it could not have recruited so well and provided the range of learning experiences or had such positive outcomes without collaboration. Echoing many of the case studies, they claim that 'collaboration does make a radical difference to widening participation'.

Collaboration in the final three case studies is more concerned with inter- or intra-university cooperation. In the first of these Jill Lawrence of the University of Southern Queensland argues that contemporary Australian universities and, I would maintain, most universities in the western world, represent a new and unfamiliar culture for a growing number of students. She maintains that the traditional view has been to regard the problem in terms of academic deficiencies, that is there is one academic discourse and that students who lack this discourse are deficient and are thus faced with problems. She argues that, instead, by applying an alternative approach utilising Critical Discourse Analysis, it is possible to re-conceptualise the university as a dynamic organisation with a multitude of diverse discourses and cultures, with which the student must come to terms. She maintains that academics have an important role to play here, collaborating with students to assist them in this process.

Unfamiliar discourses may also be said to be the topic of the next chapter. The need for the Baltic states to modernise their educational systems and provide their societies with an educated workforce that has the most up-to-date theoretical knowledge has led to the establishment of a consortium of technical universities in Lithuania, Latvia, Estonia and Sweden under the umbrella name of BALTECH. Universities in Finland and Denmark have recently joined the consortium. The main objective is to create a virtual Baltic Sea

University of Science and Technology, which can offer students co-operative programmes. The authors of this contribution from Vilnius Gediminas Technical University describe the first successful pilot project, a master's programme in industrial engineering and management. They maintain that this consortium will provide better access for all types of students although they are aware that much remains to be achieved for people who have a disability. They conclude that academic networks of this type help to promote democracy and intercultural contacts and to educate students for the better utilisation of the resources in the individual countries.

The final contribution in this section argues that the field of widening participation may, in fact, sometimes be rather narrow, with a tendency to concentrate simply on what seems to work, rather than the deeper issues which access raises. The author, Jocey Quinn, maintains that instead we need to find new ways of conceptualising widening participation and fostering its development. One way to achieve this is through interdisciplinary collaboration at a theoretical and pedagogical level. She illustrates her arguments by considering collaboration between educational research and human geography as a means to assist us in understanding the meaning and potential of university space and the learning opportunities it presents. Collaboration with feminist pedagogy may also make a significant contribution to the project of teaching a more diverse student body, she claims.

How then does collaboration work in practice? Do partnerships really help to widen participation for under represented groups? In the concluding chapter Sarah Williams discusses the findings of research that has been commissioned by HEFCE. Although this research is directly concerned with only England, I feel that many of the lessons and recommendations that emerge are largely relevant to other systems of higher education. One general point that is worth noting is that, although individual partnership initiatives are often successful, it is important that central bodies who have influence over a country's higher education really play an active role to ensure sustainability, a point referred to in several of the case studies presented in the other chapters of the volume.

Having surveyed the whole range of initiatives, one cannot but be impressed by what has been achieved. It is fairly obvious that, as in other fields of activity, collaboration and cooperation have a major role to play in widening participation. In Friedrich Schiller's version of the story of the Swiss hero, William Tell, Tell maintains that a strong person is strongest alone whereas the leader of the citizens opines 'wir könnten viel wenn wir zusammenstünden' (we could do much if we stood together). I think that the present volume clearly demonstrates the latter philosophy.

Karlstad
January, 2002

Part 1
National Approaches

1

Pyramids or spiders? Cross-sector collaboration to widen participation. Learning from international experiences

A comparative study to identify the most effective ways for post-compulsory education institutions to work together to widen participation

Maggie Woodrow and Liz Thomas

Introduction

> Collaboration is widely perceived as an essential component of policies to widen participation by under represented groups, but evidence on the relative merits of different forms of collaboration is not easy to find. Almost there is an impression that to collaborate at all is the important thing and that how it is done is largely incidental. Hence the structures and strategies employed sometimes appear to have developed almost accidentally, rather than as the result of any conscious and informed choice between alternative patterns of collaboration (preface, Woodrow *et al*)

In the year preceding her death Maggie Woodrow co-ordinated an international study to examine approaches to collaboration between educational providers to widen participation to under represented groups. The research was commissioned from the European Access Network by the Scottish Funding Councils for Further and Higher Education. Allen Barlow, Marese Bermingham, Bert Eggink and Maureen Hoyler assisted Maggie in this study. The Scottish Funding Councils for Further and Higher Education have kindly agreed to an edited version of the report, based on Maggie's analysis of the case studies, being included in this book in recognition of her work on collaboration.

Overview of the research

This study of international experiences of widening participation is intended to examine collaboration between different types of tertiary level institutions, broadly equivalent to further education colleges and higher education institutions in the UK. Strategies to widen participation in Scotland place a strong emphasis on collaboration between different sectors of post-16 education. Such collaboration is generally perceived as being essential to their success. This comparative analysis, of very diverse international approaches to cross sector collaboration, intends to indicate the contribution of alternative approaches to widening participation; the forms and factors that make for the most effective collaboration and the applicability of this collaboration to other countries and contexts.

The research compares collaborative strategies from Australia, Ireland, the Netherlands and the USA and evaluates their contribution to widening participation. It will be used in Scotland, as stated by the Joint Group, 'to inform the deliberations of both Councils in terms of exploring possible strategies for joint action in widening participation'. It is anticipated that this report will also be of value to governments and institutions, and policy makers, practitioners and researchers seeking to widen participation in other countries.

In the research brief, the Joint Funding Councils Group summarises its interpretation of widening participation as follows:

> The Group regards widening participation as a process which seeks to increase and enhance initial access to, participation in and progression through further and higher education for under represented groups. There are many factors, often inter-related, which may constitute barriers to participation in post-compulsory education. These

factors may include, but are not limited to, socio-economic status, gender, ethnicity, age, disability and geographical location.

The research recognises that these barriers may be attributable to systems, structures and cultures in post-school education. It seeks to indicate the most effective ways in which barriers to participation can be overcome, and participation by these groups increased, by appropriate forms of cross-sector collaboration.

Collaboration is widely perceived as a key component of policies to widen participation, and is central to the access policies of the Scottish Executive. Yet there is nothing new about collaboration, and in many countries, progress towards increasing participation by low-income groups, disabled people and ethnic minority groups remains slow. There is thus a need to identify the impact of collaboration, to distinguish between the relative effectiveness of its different forms and to recognise that:

> ...at its worst, collaboration can be a time-consuming, resource-intensive stereotype-reinforcing, self-satisfying substitute for any real action to change higher education and make it more inclusive (*European Access News*. No 7. Spring 2001).

Collaboration clearly is not something to be viewed uncritically, although policy-makers frequently urge and sometimes fund post-school institutions to 'collaborate' as though it is an all-time good. Nor of course is collaboration a thing at all, but many different things, often bearing little resemblance to each other. These differences and their strengths and limitations as a means of widening participation are seldom discussed and there is a serious dearth of evaluative research on the impact of established policies and programme initiatives. In particular, there is:

> ...a lack of clear research findings about and understanding of why policy measures have not worked, notably in seeking to improve the ratio of low socio-economic groups in upper secondary and higher education (Skilbeck and Connell, 2000).

This research has been undertaken in recognition of this gap in information and understanding. It seeks, by adding to the limited evidence base, to inform policy and practice about what works in collaboration to widen participation by under represented groups. Questions asked include the following:

- What is the precise purpose of the collaboration?

- What are the barriers to participation that it is seeking to overcome?

- Is collaboration more effective than competition for overcoming these?

- Who should be included in the collaboration and why?

- What are the areas of collaborative activity?

- What are the advantages and disadvantages of particular forms of collaboration?

- What are the main components of effective collaboration?

- What are the criteria for monitoring the effectiveness of collaboration?

- What is its 'value-added' contribution (as against that of individual institutions)?

- How *cost*-effective is the collaboration and who pays?

- Will the collaboration help to transform or to perpetuate current systems and sectors?

- How can it be improved?

Four Models of Collaboration

This research identified four distinctive models of collaboration to answer these questions. They illustrate four distinctive approaches to collaboration to widen participation, each set in different countries and contexts, but seeking to resolve similar problems. They represent a brief typology of collaboration, which includes vertical, longitudinal, all-embracing and integrated versions. They are based on examples of initiatives from Australia, Ireland, the Netherlands and the USA to widen participation among groups that have remained persistently under represented.

The Los Angeles 'Pyramid', US

This simple triangular model involves the University of California at Los Angeles (UCLA) in multiple direct links with local community colleges in disadvantaged areas of Los Angeles, for the purpose of increasing recruitment and improving retention, particularly among low-income and other under represented groups. While this is a UCLA scheme, it also provides a recognised transfer route into California State University.

Key characteristics:

- partners over 30 'lower-transferring' community colleges

- has high transfer rate to UCLA and to California State University (CSU)

- seeks to strengthen the curriculum of the community colleges

- links to post-entry support in UCLA

Key activities:

- The Community College Transfer Programme (CCTP), which provides assistance to prospective transfer students at designated community colleges, with special emphasis on historically under represented students, during the academic year

- The Transfer Alliance Programme (TAP), an academic honours programme at 33 community colleges that allows students completing a rigorous curriculum at the community college to transfer to UCLA as juniors

- The Transfer Summer Programme, a summer bridge programme for community college transfer students who already have been admitted to UCLA, administered by the university's Academic Advancement Programme

- The Transfer Student Centre, an office that provides special support services for transfer students

- The Summer Intensive Transfer Experience (SITE), an intensive one-week programme that brings high school students who have been admitted to community colleges to the UCLA campus

- Dual Admissions – a process of simultaneous admission to a community college and a university programme at UC.

For further details see Hoyler, Hexter and Casey, in this volume.

The Utrecht 'Bridge', the Netherlands

The bridge has been built between three key, but distinctively different, educational providers in the region to create a new infrastructure which will meet the individual needs of ethnic minority and refugee students, often from lower socio-economic groups. The aim is to give them a better chance of success in employment and society by offering a continuous learning experience from secondary education through to society and the labour market post-graduation. The collaborating institutions are: the Regionaal Opleidingen Centrum Utrecht, which provides secondary, vocational, adult and further education, the Hogeschool van Utrecht, which offers higher vocational education, and the Universiteit Utrecht, a traditional university specialising in academic education and research. The Multicultureel Instituut of Utrecht acts as an advisor.

Key characteristics:

- encompasses secondary, further, adult, vocational, higher vocational and higher academic education, and employment opportunities, and so offers access to a 'non-stop' learning process all the way from secondary education, through bridging courses, through higher education, into society and employment

- consists of three equal partners, the key educational players in the region

- involves co-operation with autonomy for the partner institutions

- and it is built on the concept of meeting individual needs by the provision of a flexible, continuous learning path. Students are able to enter the process at different stages and

8

levels, and course programmes are designed to meet individual needs.

Key activities:

- Establishing joint assessment and accreditation facilities
- Establishing joint bridging and preparatory courses
- Adapting course content to the multicultural society
- Sharing expertise, know-how and good practice
- Staff development programmes
- Organising joint mentor and tutor programs
- Retention and student service programmes
- Clearinghouse web sites

For further details see Duvekot, 1999.

The Cork 'Spider', Ireland

This is a multi-dimensional, multi-player approach to collaboration. It seeks to widen participation, primarily for young people from lower socio-economic groups, by a long term collaboration and consultation involving all regional stakeholders. It encompasses collaboration on two sides of the supply/demand equation – creating a demand, while changing the nature of supply. The focus here is on the process of collaboration as a means of effecting attitudinal and systemic change, as much as on its immediate outcomes.

Key characteristics:

- Multi-partner, multi-level, multi-dimensional collaboration
- High level of commitment to the collaborative process by senior management of institutions involved
- Intergenerational focus, targeting both young people and their important centres of influence simultaneously – aspects of the project target younger students at primary level (age 11-12 years) together with parents

- Long term vision – a focus on widening horizons and opening up options, aiming to create/encourage demand for higher education six years from now

- Joint development/delivery of new courses specifically located in area of disadvantage

- A commitment to innovative actions which aim to simulate demand from a target group where expectations are generally low, eg Exploring Education through Art, Exploring Education through Music.

Key activities:

The aim is to share expertise, experiences, contacts, knowledge and resources to develop pilot and mainstream collaboration projects, such as:

- Awareness raising activities

- Targeted outreach

- On campus taster programmes

- Information workshops

- Third level orientation for students and their parents

- Supplementary tuition programmes

- Development and delivery of courses

- Preparatory courses and access routes

- Retention programmes

- Transfer mechanisms

- Staff development activities

- Evaluation

- Research activity

- Currently planning a new HE campus to be situated in the Northside of Cork City, a joint initiative of Cork Institute of Technology and University College Cork.

For an example of the work of this partnership see Powell, 1999.

The Melbourne 'Marriage', Australia
This 'marriage' model involves amalgamation – in this case to create a 'dual sector' university, by combining a former technological university with an institute of technical and further education. Marriage between these two institutions has provided a balanced and stable parentage for the birth and rearing of Victoria University of Technology's widening participation offspring, the Personalised Access and Study Scheme (PAS).

Key characteristics:

- A single post-school institution, with the infrastructure and systems to create new entry mechanisms, and support a range of learning needs post-enrolment.

- PAS provided the opportunity to link all TAFE courses into a comprehensive pathway framework, via a range of alternative entry mechanisms into higher education.

- There is a focus on meeting the individual learning and support needs of students: recruitment process recognises an individual's preparation for study, prior learning, work experience and motivation; and students are prepared for further study and for employment.

- The creation of this dual-sector institution is based upon the key premise that students can achieve their educational and vocational objectives best when impediments to access to study are removed and administrative systems are based on student expectations and needs.

Key activities of PAS:

PAS comprises a complex set of processes focussed around the inter-related issues of access (creating alternative entry mechanisms) and study (assisting them to stay in the institution once they arrive).

- Establishing alternative entrance arrangements, via learning pathways for individuals and communities with specific needs

11

- Transition framework has been developed to ensure articulation from TAFE courses into HE

- Interviews to assess point-of-entry learning requirements of each student

- Personal student compacts that detail how the institution will meet the learning needs of the individual student

- Comprehensive staff development programme, designed to embed the PAS strategy within the University.

See also Ronayne, 2000.

In each of these case studies, the regions appear to face similar problems in widening participation by those from low-income groups, and each has sought collaboration as the answer, but their collaborative strategies and structures are markedly different. This study explores these differences and identifies factors making for the most effective collaboration to widen participation. It is acknowledged that although there are differences in the post-school education systems between countries, there is also fluidity and change. The structure of post-school education provides no serious barrier to the transferability of the models of cross-sector collaboration outlined in this study. Indeed it is hoped that it will itself contribute, as earlier international comparative studies have, to the continued development of the structure of post-school education.

Comparative Analysis

The four models illustrate four very different forms of collaboration to widen participation. Yet each claims that their structures and strategies will travel and are applicable to a variety of systems and circumstances. In deciding which model would be the most appropriate for a particular set of circumstances, it is not necessarily advisable to opt for the one which appears to conform most closely to these. While some forms of collaboration may appear to slot more neatly into given situations, there may be a case for a more ambitious choice of 'best buy' which necessitates greater systemic change.

If then, all have transferability and all are designed to widen participation by lower socio-economic groups, what are the criteria for distinguishing between them and for selecting a 'best buy'? This section compares the four models of collaboration in terms of their: strategies for widening participation, structures for delivering these, activities to widen participation, achievements in widening participation and cost-effectiveness.

1. Collaborative Strategies for Widening Participation

All four models of collaboration aim to widen participation by those from lower socio-economic groups, but their strategies for achieving this are remarkably different, as indicated below:

The transfer model – single direct strategy. The USA 'pyramid' has a single, easily identifiable, direct strategy for widening participation. It is to be achieved by increasing the progression, or transfer to higher education at the University of California at Los Angeles (UCLA), of students from specified local community colleges where transfer rates are low. Numerical targets are set and progress towards them can easily be monitored. Changes in the community college curriculum, and support post-entry to HE for targeted students are included here, but are subsidiary to the main thrust of the collaboration.

This strategy offers all the attractions of a sharp focus with easily measurable and fairly immediate outcomes. It concentrates on university entry – always a crucial barrier to widening participation, and one which many access strategies fail to tackle effectively, if at all. It is a model which impacts on current generations of community college students. More recently it has begun to extend into longer-term strategies, involving low-income students in area high schools prior to community college entry in its new SITE (Summer Intensive Experience) programme.

The longitudinal model – a learning continuum. The focus of the Netherlands 'bridge' is much broader by comparison. This is a regional strategy which, instead of a sharp focus on higher education, takes a longitudinal approach from the start, seeking to achieve for its target group a continuum of cross-sector learning opportunities stretching from primary education into employment. Ethnicity is the main determinant of under-representation here (low socio-economic status being associated with this) and widening participation is perceived more as a strategy for social change. For the targeted groups, the strategy offers a blend of assimilation on the one hand and the prospect of a more culturally diverse society on the other.

The advantages for this strategy are less immediate, though it has the potential for greater long term gains. It also seeks to tackle under-representation closer to its source by reaching back into the primary school sector. Its targets however are less tangible than those of the 'pyramid' model, and the question here is what such a wide-ranging strategy can achieve without diluting its impact by diffusing its activities over a front which is too broad for its capacity.

The process model – stakeholder ownership. The strategies of the Irish 'spider' again offer a different formula for widening parti-cipation. Here the process is an essential part of the strategies, which are to maximise participation through an all-embracing, inter-generational collaborative approach, involving ownership by all stakeholders (including the targeted groups) at all levels in the education system. This is multi-partner, multi-level, multi-dimensional collaboration with its roots in regional regeneration. It seeks not only to create a demand, but also to change the nature of the supply. Both, it is emphasised, require a change of mindset.

At the heart of this strategy is attitudinal change on the part of all those involved, and this must be seen as essential to any in-depth approach towards widening participation. This is a complex strategy with the potential to make a significant difference, but how long will it be before it starts to change the pattern of participation in higher education?

The seamless model – abolishing the barriers. The Australian 'marriage' has the most radical of all collaborative strategies i.e. ending the barriers to progression between different sectors of post-school education by ending the separation between the sectors. The rationale here is that as long as further and higher education have reporting lines, standards and funding systems which are separate and largely incompatible, the seamlessness which is so vital to students from disadvantaged backgrounds cannot be achieved. Thus only a merger can provide the most favourable parentage and the most nurturing environment for the desired offspring of this collaboration, the Personalised Access and Study Scheme.

There is an inevitable logic in this collaborative strategy towards which the others make only tentative moves – no need for bridges where the chasms between institutions have been closed. The advantages, both immediate and long term, that it offers for widening participation are immense. The downside is perhaps in the scale of the initial operation required by such a strategy.

2. Collaborative Structures

Evidence on the relative merits of collaborative structures for widening participation is not easy to find. Almost there is an impression that to collaborate is the important thing – how it is done is largely incidental. Hence the structures employed often appear to have developed almost accidentally, rather than as the result of any conscious and informed choice between alternative patterns of collaboration. The four collaborative structures in this study are quite distinctive. While each of the four models has been devised to serve their specific purposes, their usefulness is not necessarily confined to these. They vary significantly as indicated below:

Vertical. The 'pyramid' involves collaboration between the University of California at Los Angeles and over 30 community colleges. Vertical collaboration recognises that pre-university institutions are much closer to the target group and have a greater understanding of their needs. While this pyramid is slightly flattened at the top by opportunities to transfer also to California State University, this is basically a very simple structure between a higher education institution and multiple colleges. Hence it is in keeping with its sharply focused objective. Its new 'Dual Admissions' scheme, with joint enrolment at college and university levels, however, gives this collaboration some activities which resemble the Melbourne marriage.

Tripartite. The Netherlands 'bridge' has the smallest number of partners, with power shared among only three institutions, which together link with local schools at one end and with graduate employers at the other. However neither schools nor employers are members of the partnership. This model has more elaborate bureaucratic formal structures than the UCLA 'pyramid', with co-operation at three levels: a Steering Group representing the three Boards of Government, a Managing Team consisting of the three Project Managers for each institution, and an Advisory Board of external experts. There is an unusually strong emphasis here on maintaining the autonomy of the three institutional members, which may restrict any close convergence. However there is encouraging insistence here that the 'bridge' will not develop an existence of its own, nor function as a separate body. Instead, all the collaborative widening participation activities will be delivered through the three institutions themselves, and will be seen as an integral part of their role.

Diffused. The Irish 'spider' has a more complex structure. It is also more indeterminate, seeking to operate in both formal and informal ways, and varying according to the task in hand. This multi-limbed structure is an exercise in genuine equity and power-sharing among its stakeholder members, who represent diverse interests, several of them from outside post-school education. The projected opening of a shared campus between the university and the institute of technology in a deprived area of the city, will bring this collaborative structure closer to that of the seamless model below.

Integrated. In the Melbourne 'marriage', the two partners have fore-gone their former separate single status to gain the advantages of shared entry procedures, enrolment, fee structures, student support systems, progression criteria, and to make pathways through the system easier. This model eschews the emphasis on institutional autonomy associated with the 'bridge' model above, and finds greater strength in widening participation where there are no separate cultures and institutional norms for students and staff to navigate.

3. Collaborative Activities to widen participation

Although the local and national contexts, and the strategies and structures of the four models of collaboration vary significantly, the activities they undertake to widen participation are remarkably similar. The impression is that, although governments in particular seem sometimes to be searching for a golden formula in terms of activities to widen participation (the Westminster government's recent enthusiasm for summer schools is one example of this), the particular choice of activities does not matter a great deal. The table below indicates the pattern of activities of the four case studies.

Table 1 Range of Widening Participation Activities Undertaken by each Model

Collaborative Activities to Widen Participation	UCLA	Utrecht	Cork	Melbourne
Activities with primary schools sector		•	•	
Awareness-raising pre FE	•	•	•	•
Changes in the FE curriculum	•	•	•	•
Advice/guidance on HE entry	•	•	•	•
Preparatory/bridging/foundation courses	•	•	•	
Accreditation of these		•	•	
Mentoring schemes	•	•		•
Taster courses	•	•	•	
Design of individual student pathways		•		•
Summer schools	•			
Automatic progression/transfer route to HE	•			•
Change in admissions criteria for HE entry	•			•
Support post-entry to HE course	•	•	•	•
Skills development	•	•	•	•
Changing the HE culture		•	•	•
Staff development		•	•	•
Employer links for targeted students		•	•	•

Notes in relation to the above table:

> Overall, the differences between the activities of the different models, as illustrated by this table, are less remarkable than their similarities.

> Only UCLA and Melbourne have strategies which affect HE entry requirements for targeted students.

> UCLA activities are the most heavily concentrated around progression to HE.

> In Melbourne, the formation of a dual-sector institution has reduced the need for bridging courses etc.

> Cork and Utrecht have the widest range of activities.

4. Achievements in Widening Participation

This section compares the achievements of each of the four models of collaboration in widening participation. Accurate assessment of their achievement is difficult, partly because it is too early to measure the long term outcomes of the collaboration – this is a particular problem for the Irish and Netherlands models with their emphasis on attitudinal change and longitudinal development. The other problem, which affects assessment of the achievements of all four models, is the impossibility of isolating the collaboration as the key factor in delivering change.

The indicators of success employed by each of the four models vary. In respect of *quantitative indicators*, they include: extent of widening participation activities undertaken; numbers of the targeted group participating in the activities; number of schools/FECs involved in the activities; changes in the number of target group applications to higher education; changes in the number of target group entrants to higher education; changes in retention rates among target group members post HE entry; numbers receiving student support post HE entry and numbers of staff participating in staff development programmes. *Qualitative indicators* include parti-

Table 2 Main Performance Indicators Specified by Collaborative Models

Performance Indicator	UCLA Pyramid	Utrecht Bridge	Cork Spider	Melbourne Marriage
Extent of widening participation activities		•		
Numbers of the targeted group participating	•	•	•	•
Numbers of schools/FECs involved	•	•	•	
Changes in no. of target group HE applications	•			•
Changes in no. of target group HE entrants	•			•
Numbers receiving student support post HE entry	•			•
Changes in retention among target HE entrants	•			•
Nos. of staff on staff development programmes		•	•	•
Student/staff responses to activities	•	•	•	•

cipant satisfaction/attitudinal change, as demonstrated by student and staff questionnaires, focus groups and feedback forms.

Variations in the pattern of performance indicators above are consistent with variations in the strategies and activities of the four models as specified above. It is the UCLA and the Melbourne models that have the strongest focus on expanding numbers of applications, admissions and progress within higher education. Both models are able to demonstrate significant success in these respects e.g. the UCLA reports a 23% increase in community college applications between 1998 and 2000.

5. Cost-Effectiveness of the Collaboration

Collaboration is often perceived as, and may well be, an unnecessarily expensive process because of the additional bureaucracy it can create. Resources spent on the collaborative process itself may seem to be utilising resources which might otherwise have contributed directly to the widening participation strategies themselves.

As noted above, the widening participation activities in the four models of collaboration are very similar. A comparison of the cost of these activities is therefore likely to yield fewer differences (other than those associated with scale) between the four models, than a comparison of the cost of their strategies and structures, which vary significantly.

The most cost-effective form of collaboration is clearly the Melbourne 'marriage', which makes possible, year-on-year, significant savings as a single institution by comparison with the costs of two original institutions, formerly in separate sectors. None of the other three models of collaboration can claim similar economies of scale, with the exception (in respect of enrolments only) of the UCLA 'Dual Admissions' Scheme.

In each of the other three models overall, the collaborative process creates additional costs, not savings. This is because the collaboration is in addition to, rather than instead of, competition between the partner institutions. The costs of the collaborative process are borne in each case by the partner institutions themselves, and staffing costs are identified as the main item of expenditure. By contrast the widening participation activities undertaken through the collaboration are resourced by a mix of national, regional, and institutional funding, including in the case of Cork, support from European Union funding.

The more complex collaborative structures will spend the most on the actual process of collaboration. Of the four structures here, those of the Utrecht 'bridge' and the Cork 'spider' are the most elaborate and could be the most resource-intensive in terms of staff time. Overall collaboration through the Cork model with its multi-partner, multi-level collaboration is likely to cost the most. However, in the case of Cork, the costs of the collaboration itself are not perceived separately from those of the widening participation activities. This is because here the process of collaboration itself is seen as a means of effecting attitudinal change and hence as an essential part of the activities. The costs of the collaborative process cannot therefore be viewed separately from the costs of the other widening participation activities delivered through this collaboration.

Which Model? Overall Assessment
The preceding discussion has demonstrated considerable differences in key aspects of the four models of collaboration in this study. In conclusion and overall is there a preferred model? It is immediately clear that like is not being compared with like. Narrowed down, the choice is about:

- vertical or multi-dimensional collaboration
- specific or all-encompassing strategies
- short term and long term priorities
- institutional autonomy or integration.

1. Vertical or multi-lateral collaboration?
It is easy to see the benefits that vertical collaboration between institutions in different sectors of post-school education can bring, particularly in terms of removing the barriers to progression between the sectors, and establishing pathways between them. The virtues of horizontal collaboration between institutions of higher education as

a means of widening participation may be harder to grasp. HEIs involved in horizontal collaborations tend to seek the high moral ground and to deny emphatically that their purpose in collaborating is to increase their opportunities to recruit more non-traditional students. If this is the case, it would seem that competition might serve the interests of these students better than collaboration.

Of the four models in this study, the Los Angeles 'pyramid' provides a clear example of vertical collaboration, while the Melbourne 'marriage' represents its most extreme form. The Cork 'spider' offers the only multi-level, multi-dimensional model of collaboration here and is thus both the most inclusive and the most complex of the four.

2. Central or circumference priorities

Perhaps the main distinction, however, between the four models relates to their first priorities. Here the greatest similarities are between the Los Angeles 'pyramid' and the Melbourne 'marriage', and between the Utrecht 'bridge' and the Cork 'spider'. It is the difference between a centrifugal and a circumference approach.

The 'pyramid' for example goes straight for the centre – the main bottleneck between the post-school sectors – progression to higher education. Here it can demonstrate almost immediate success in widening participation by progressing more students from under represented groups, and backs this up by strategies on retention to support these students post-entry. Its basic structure with few bureaucratic layers provides an effective mechanism for delivering this focused strategy. From this priority point, it is now widening out from the centre in extended circles to deliver longer-term strategies involving students at the pre-community college entry stage.

By contrast, the Utrecht 'bridge' and the Irish 'spider' locate themselves from the start on the circumference of the circle, focusing on the broader picture and employing long term and longitudinal strategies, with a main focus on attitudinal change. This is admirable in that it recognises the importance of changing the system, and the power-sharing structures of these model provides from the start an appropriate mechanism for achieving this. The Cork model for example has multi-lateral partners for multi-lateral activities. However there is no indication here of the prospect of any immediate increase in the proportion of under represented entrants to higher education, nor any certainty as to when and to what extent this is likely to be achieved. Attitudes, whatever the process, are notoriously slow to change. Moreover seeking to progress across a broad front, from primary education through to employment issues, must leave fewer resources available to implement change at any specific point. The difference here is one of first priorities. The first target for Cork's collaborative activities is '*to develop long term regional strategies*'. In both Cork and Utrecht, the broad sweep of the collaborative activities to widen participation enables them to play a significant part in the long term regionalisation of higher education, and in the case of Utrecht to the achievement of a multi-cultural society.

3. Jam today or jam tomorrow?

These differences in strategy immediately impinge on the timing of progression towards widening participation to higher education. For example, UCLA strategies move outwards from a central starting point and Cork inwards from a circumference position. Which should come first? The logical chronological option would seem to be to begin with awareness-raising at primary school level, and to move on from there to entry to higher education. This is to opt for a long term strategy from the start. However, activities to raise awareness of higher education opportunities at an earlier age may only raise expectations which cannot subsequently be met, unless the entry barrier to higher education has first been breached.

There may then be a stronger case for opting initially for a model which concentrates on immediately increasing numbers of targeted groups in higher education and on improving their retention, and subsequently broadens out, as the UCLA 'pyramid' has, into widening participation activities at an earlier pre-HE application stage. With this model, the short term gains are apparent, and should contribute to longer term gains in changing attitudes and systems. Nothing it seems changes attitudes in higher education towards 'non-traditional' students as much as encountering these students on degree programmes and seeing them succeed. And nothing it seems changes attitudes to higher education among 'non-traditional' students themselves as successful role models with backgrounds similar to their own. The 'pyramid' may therefore be the best way of ensuring jam tomorrow as well as jam today.

4. Institutional autonomy or integration?

There is also a choice between a collaborative scheme, like that of the Utrecht 'bridge' which jealously guards the independence and autonomy of its member institutions (possibly because one of them at least is already the product of a recent major merger), and that of the Melbourne marriage, where in the search for seamlessness, the partners lose their separate existence altogether. The latter may indeed be the best buy for widening participation, but is one which will require major policy decisions, and hence a longer lead in time to achieve. Abolishing the barriers between the sectors by abolishing the sectors offers considerable attractions, but there may be some losses too. A large dual-sector institution may itself present a more formidable initial barrier to participation by those from under represented groups than a small, if lower status, institution of the community college type. In between these two options, the Los Angeles 'pyramid' and the Cork 'spider' which offer the potential for a gradual convergence between the sectors – UCLA through its 'Dual Admissions' enrolment scheme, and Cork with its projected shared campus – may provide the most acceptable short term solution.

In conclusion, there is no one model here that emerges as a 'best buy'. All four models are in the process of change and development and in some respects the differences between them look set to decrease in the future.

If the prime purposes of the strategy are significantly broader in scope than widening participation by low-income students, for example the development of a regional post-school infrastructure, or the promotion of a more equitable and culturally diverse society, then the Cork 'spider' or the Utrecht 'bridge' would seem to be the most appropriate models. If on the other hand, the prime purpose of the collaboration is to avoid further delay in increasing participation in higher education by those groups which have already been excluded for far too long, a model which focuses its energies from the start at the main blockage point of progression to higher education, offers the most immediate gains. It also, as demonstrated for example by more recent developments at UCLA, has the potential to achieve longer-term attitudinal and systemic change, the impact of which will be less immediate, but none the less significant.

It remains to say that each of the models of collaboration included here can demonstrate success in achieving their objectives, and each has the most important ingredient of all – a shared vision of a more inclusive post-school education and a determination to contribute to it. The Cork study emphasises the *'warmth and energy of the relationships'* which now exist between the partners in the collaboration, as a particular strength. In the end, and whatever model of collaboration is chosen, the key to its success is the quality of the link between the collaborators. To achieve this, as the Cork study notes, *'the people who span the gaps, their energy and commitment, together with that of senior management are what really counts'*.

Recommendations

Effective Collaboration: Recommendations for Practitioners
The above discussion explores key features of the four models of collaboration in this study, and examines their particular strengths. All four models can be recommended, all are about widening participation by lower socio-economic groups, and all can be adapted to differing national circumstances. Nevertheless there are significant differences between them, particularly in respect of strategy and structure. This makes producing guidelines difficult, since one set of recommendations will not meet all requirements.

In particular, there is a marked distinction between forms of collaboration which are for the direct, immediate and specific purpose of improving participation and retention rates in higher education, and those forms of collaboration whose first priorities are of a broader long term nature, for example the creation of a regional integrated framework for post-school education. These guidelines relate primarily to the former kind of collaboration to widen participation. They are designed for those whose immediate and prime purpose is to improve entry to and retention rates in higher education of students from lower socio-economic groups, while recognising the part that longer-term strategies need to play in this.

1. *Shared vision* among all partners, of the collaboration as a direct means of expanding the participation and retention rates of low-income students.

2. Agreed *collaborative strategy* for achieving this which focuses initially on the recruitment and retention of under represented groups, as the most difficult barriers to cross.

3. Direct, vertical *collaborative structure* to link post-16 education institutions with one or more local higher education institution for the purpose of increasing progression by low-income groups. Agreement on an inexpensive structure for the collaboration which keeps bureaucracy to a minimum.

4. Including as *partners* only those who are essential to the success of the scheme, in particular post-16 institutions with a significant proportion of students from low-income groups.

5. Formal *commitment* by the senior management of each of the partners in the collaboration to its structure and strategy.

6. An initial *focus on recruitment* and formal recognition by all partners of admission criteria and procedures by which partner higher education institutions can increase their recruitment of low-income students from partner colleges.

7. Joint agreement on numerical *targets* and timescales for expanding the number of entrants from this group in the participating higher education institutions, and a shared commitment to meeting these targets.

8. Agreement on and implementation of strategies for *retention* and successful completion in HE by the targeted students

9. *Success indicators*: measurement of the success of the collaboration in terms of changes in the number of targeted students

progressing to and succeeding in higher education, and in terms of student assessment of their experiences

10. Shared *delivery* of widening participation activities by FE and HE staff.

11. *Longer-term planning* which extends the collaborative activities to include awareness-raising at an earlier age at one end, and links with employers at the other.

12. The involvement of successful *role models* from the target group in these activities, with appropriate recognition for their contribution in financial and/or study credit terms.

13. A distribution of *resources* which recognises the shared institutional ownership of the collaboration and which concentrates expenditure on the widening participation activities, rather than on the process of collaboration.

14. A recognition of the importance of adequate *student funding* arrangements if participation by those from low-income groups is to increase, and of the responsibility and role of the collaboration in advocating this.

Policy Implications of Collaboration to Widen Participation
There is a tendency for the policy implications of cross-sector collaboration to be confused or combined with the policy implications of widening participation itself. In fact collaboration can and does take place without widening participation, and widening participation can and does take place without collaboration.

What are the particular policy implications of collaboration to widen participation? Such collaboration arises from the conviction that differences between the sectors creates barriers for under represented groups which makes progression between them difficult. The way to overcome these barriers is by moving towards a more seamless system of post-school education. Thus the present and future relationship between further and higher education has become internationally a strategic policy pre-occupation. Overall, crucial policy considerations for cross-sector collaboration include the following:

1. The separate and different funding arrangements for institutions and students.

2. Institutional autonomy and the role of the state in changing the relationship between the sectors, or the sectors themselves.

3. Quality concerns (however unfounded) about a seamless progression from further to higher education.

4. The justification (if any) of maintaining or reinforcing the distinction between vocational and academic post-school education.

5. The extent to which computer-based learning will make sector differentiation redundant.

Recommendations for policy-makers

All four models of collaboration in this study have received both support and funding from central and sometimes also from regional governments for their widening participation activities. Nevertheless, no particular model or pattern of collaboration has been recommended by policy-makers, and no new policies have been introduced which might make cross-sector collaboration easier or more effective. Recommendations for policy-makers arising from this study are as follows:

1. A review of what exactly is being achieved by cross-sector collaboration to widen participation.

2. An assessment from this as to which models of collaboration can demonstrate progress in terms of increasing participation and completion rates among students from lower socio-economic groups.

3. Adequate mainstreamed funding for the widening participation activities of models of collaboration which can demonstrate progress of this kind.

4. A clear directive as to how students from lower socio-economic groups are to be identified.

5. The development nationally of effective means of tracking students across sectors e.g. by the allocation of individual student numbers.

6. A single, coherent, consistent and adequate cross-sector system of funding for students from low-income backgrounds.

7. Combined or at least complementary and consistent funding formulae for widening participation across further and higher education.

8. Comparable arrangements for monitoring and reporting progress in widening participation across both sectors.

9. The development of a nationally coherent policy on cross-sector collaboration, which seeks to narrow cross-sector divisions, and explores the option of cross-sector mergers.

References

European Access News. No 7. Spring 2001

Duvekot, R. (1999) 'Moving Targets: The non-stop learning process of 'The Utrecht Bridge'', *Widening Participation and Lifelong Learning*, 1:2 pp46-48

Powell, F. (1999) 'Adult Education, Cultural Empowerment and Social Equality: the Cork Northside Education Initiative', in *Widening Participation and Lifelong Learning*, 1:1 pp20-27

Ronayne, J. (2000) 'Creating a culturally diverse and inclusive higher education: an Australian example' in Thomas, E. and Cooper, M. (eds.) (2000) *Changing the Culture of the Campus: Towards an inclusive higher education.* Stoke on Trent: Staffordshire University Press

Skilbeck M. and Connell H. (2000) *Access and Equity in Higher Education: an International Perspective on Issues and Strategies*. Dublin: HEA

2

Collaboration within and between HEIs in England: a review of policy and practice

Liz Thomas

Introduction

This chapter examines aspects of collaboration to widen participation in English higher education (HE). In particular it considers the drive towards internal collaboration *within* higher education institutions (HEIs) through the development of widening participation statements which aim to link together institutional policies and practices into a more coherent strategy. Secondly, it examines the emphasis on regional collaboration *between* educational institutions, other agencies and training providers and the community. Before analysing the impact of these two policy thrusts, an overview of the English HE sector is offered; this is followed by reflection on two questions. Firstly, what is collaboration? Here, notions of collaboration are considered, and compared to alternative modes of working. The second question is why collaborate? Four possible motivations for collaboration are considered, and the tensions between collaboration and competition are noted. The discussion of these two questions – i.e. the type of inter-institutional relationship and the incentives for working together – are used as a framework to draw conclusions about the 'collaboration' *within* and *between* HEIs in England.

In the UK in the last decade there has been a very significant increase in participation in higher education, but this has not been accompanied by an expansion in the diversity of higher education students, so there has not been effective widening of participation. In particular, it is commonly acknowledged (CVCP, 1999; Woodrow, 1999; and Bekhradnia, 2000a and b) that lower rates of participation by students from lower socio-economic groups, i.e. by those with low incomes, is the most persistent failing of the higher education system in the UK. In an effort to overcome this disparity the government has used a 'carrot and stick' approach. The Minister for Lifelong Learning and Higher Education, Margaret Hodge, recently 'named and shamed' the HEIs that were performing poorly in relation to widening participation to students from lower social classes. Conversely, the various funding bodies with responsibility for higher education in England, Scotland, Wales and Northern Ireland have sought to encourage HEIs to widen participation, often via funding incentives.

Widening participation in England

The Higher Education Funding Council for England (HEFCE), the Learning Skills Council, government policy (e.g. DfEE, 1999) and high profile reports (e.g. Kennedy, 1997, Select Committee on Education and Employment, 2001) all provide a strong steer towards collaboration and partnerships to assist with widening participation. For example, HEFCE has commented:

> ... while individual projects can do excellent work, there are additional benefits if the work is co-ordinated and good practice is shared (HEFCE, preface in Harrison et al, 2000, p8).

This focus on collaboration is re-asserted in the recently published consultation document – 'Partnerships for Progression' (HEFCE 01/73) – which itself is a joint initiative between the Higher Education Funding Council for England and the Learning and Skills Council. This document notes:

> The Government has set a target that, by the year 2010, 50 percent of those aged between 18 and 30 should have the opportunity to benefit from higher education. That is an ambitious goal. To achieve it

we need to strengthen existing partnerships between higher education, further education and schools...' (para 1).

The document continues:

> The proposed joint initiative would build upon and encompass the extensive regional and local partnerships which already exist. It would link together into a more coherent framework the activities for successive age groups of school and FE students, and across different progression routes. It would build upon effective practice wherever this takes place, and be responsive to local needs. (para 4)

The HEFCE has sought to promote widening participation in a number of ways. Firstly, special initiative funding has been made available for widening participation projects. Secondly, the funding council introduced annual performance indicators in December 1999 (HEFCE 99/66), which attempt to measure the extent to which each HEI is performing in relation to recruiting students from lower socio-economic groups and low participation neighbourhoods. These latter 'postcode indicators' have been utilised to reward HEIs for recruiting students from these locales with a 'postcode premium' of an additional 5% for these students. In 1999 HEIs were asked to prepare Initial Strategic Statements (99/33), and, building on this process, in 2001 they have been asked to prepare a 'Widening Participation Strategy and Action Plan' for the next three years (HEFCE 01/29). Although there are contradictions within these policy strands, there has been an enduring and increasing emphasis on collaboration. In particular, two significant 'collaborative' trends within HEFCE's approach to widening participation can be identified. First there is the encouragement of greater collaboration *within* institutions and second, *between* institutions, especially at the regional or sub-regional level. These two issues will be reviewed, but first it is useful to discuss what collaboration is and why it is undertaken.

What is collaboration?
The post-war period in the UK witnessed the development of the public sector, and saw the State take far greater responsibility for the provision of education and welfare services than hitherto. This created debate about the role of other sectors, especially voluntary

activity, and in short, the public sector was not expected to replace voluntary action, but to complement it. The organisation of the public sector, and its relationship with the voluntary (and to a lesser extent the private) sectors was characterised by co-ordination.

The election of the Conservative government in 1979, under the leadership of Margaret Thatcher, marked the beginning of a new period in welfare provision in the UK; during this time contracts, rather than co-ordination, were the focus. The dominant ideology was neo-liberalism, which prioritised the role of the free market. This therefore required the role of the State to be minimised, and individual choice and responsibility to be promoted. Throughout all aspects of the public sector reform was introduced; this involved the establishment of competition (or quasi competition) between service providers, promoting the rights of 'consumers' to select the services they used (or 'consumed'). Also, far greater emphasis began to be placed on management, especially expertise from the private sector. Thus management and relationships *within* the public sector changed, for example New Public Management sort to stimulate competition between actors in different departments within one institution. The role of the state moved away from direct service provider to that of 'purchaser' of services (on behalf of users), and this was seen to necessitate greater accountability to ensure the quality of the services being provided.

In the 1990s there was a move away from reliance on markets to-wards the creation of alliances between service providers to meet the needs of users more effectively. This trend was continued and developed by the New Labour government, elected in 1997, which 'tied its colours firmly to the partnership mast, announcing its intention to move from a contract culture to a partnership culture' (Balloch and Taylor, 2001, p3). This approach does not rely on the public sector or the independent sector (i.e. private and voluntary sectors) to provide services such as education, welfare, health and social regeneration, but encouraged the interaction of 'interested parties' from all sectors, including targeted communities. This move away from the direct delivery of services by the public sector, or the independent sector, is encapsulated in the notion of 'public action' (e.g. Drèze and Sen, 1989 and Wyuts *et al*, 1992):

> Public action is not... just a question of public delivery and state initiative. It is also a matter of participation by the public in a process of social change (Drèze and Sen, 1989, p259).

Collaboration is therefore often viewed as an antidote to competition, but such a negative definition is of limited value. While it is now something of a necessity that different organisations and groups work together, this does not resolve the issue of what collaboration is. For example, working together raises a raft of issues about the nature of such a relationship, especially when agents have different values, modes of operation and so forth. Robinson *et al* (2000) in their discussions about 'inter-organisational relationships' consider that: 'there are three 'ideal types' or modes for structuring inter-organisational relationships' (p4) and these are competition, co-ordination and co-operation (or collaboration). Briefly discussing the characteristics of these three approaches to working together provides a framework with which to view collaboration *within* and *between* HEIs in the proceeding sections of this chapter.

In essence, a competitive relationship is predicated upon rivalry, and the introduction of the pro-market neo-liberal agenda in the 1980s viewed competition as a much more efficient means of meeting social need and public objectives than co-ordination, which was the main mode of organisation relied on in the preceding post-war period. Furthermore, markets are perceived as positive because they are seen to allow individuals freedom of choice. It may also be noted here that with respect to inter-organisational relations competition is something of a zero-sum game, whereby if one agent succeeds (e.g. recruits more students) it will be at the expense of others.

By comparison, co-ordination can be understood as a more harmonious, less antagonistic set of relations. It may, for example, involve dividing a task up along geographical or functional lines. It can be conceived as a rule-regulated and hierarchical mode of organisation, typical of the traditional public sector bureaucracy, and premised on the notion of the state deriving its legitimacy from a democratic system. 'Co-ordination is a way of bringing together disparate agencies to make their efforts more compatible (in the interests of equity, effectiveness and efficiency). Without co-ordination, the danger is of lapsing into chaos and inefficiency' (Robinson *et al*, 2000 p7). Such, bureaucracies are often criticised as being inflexible and inefficient, and reliant upon relationships of power, which may become corrupt.

Finally, collaborative relationships are not only harmonious, but actively strive for more lateral (less hierarchical) structures. There are a number of similar terms, neologisms and idioms, all of which imply collaboration. These include: partnership working, interagency and multiagency co-operation, synergy, holistic approaches and joined-up thinking (Ambrose, 2001, p17). Robinson *et al* note that:

> There are few common understandings of the term 'co-operation' beyond a rather broad notion of voluntarily working together based on consensus, camaraderie or solidarity, community or compromise...
>
> ...Co-operation is also often seen as the opposite of competition. On its positive side it is seen as a process of consensus-building and sharing in public action...
>
> ...co-operation as a concept offers the possibility for diverse interests to be brought together and to be built into a whole new idea or approach (2000, p8).

It is possible that the notion of 'synergy' can offer a helpful means of developing the term collaboration. Harold Geneeb and Brent Bowers (1997) define synergy as occurring when 'one entity that behaves in one way and another entity that behaves in another way merge into a third entity that starts behaving in an entirely new way' (p79). A similar idea is expressed by Peter Evans (1996) when discussing the collaboration of public and private sector actors: 'putting the two kinds of inputs together results in greater output than either... could deliver on their own'. Similarly, Mackintosh (1993) suggests that synergy is more than the sum of its parts.

Why collaborate?

Maggie Woodrow (in this volume) has suggested that there is a danger that to collaborate itself often is seen as the goal, rather than as a means to an end, such as widening participation. There is, however, a wide range of motivations for collaboration. Some collaboration may be an unreflective adherence to the current dominant discourse, while others may be seeking to gain the mutually beneficial effects from synergy created between partners. Robinson *et al* (2000) identify the following categorisation of 'perspectives on why inter-organisational relationships matter', which provides a useful framework for examining the differing motivations for collaboration.

> Evangelism: collaboration is a 'good thing', which should be aspired to for that reason...
>
> Pragmatism: in recognition of the fact that the world is becoming both smaller and more complex, and that societies and organisations are increasingly interdependent...
>
> Market imperatives: as the world of business organisations has become increasingly specialised..., inter-organisational arrangements are seen as key to efficiency and competitiveness (co-operation for competitiveness).
>
> Synergy: the idea that working with other organisations enables an organisation to better achieve its objectives; that is, the achievement of the whole is greater than the sum of the parts... (Robinson *et al*, 2000, p14).

Recent research on collaborative relationships between educational institutions (Thomas *et al*, 2001) found that partners had varying motives for working together, although these were less discrete than the above categorisation would suggest, and within the same partnerships, members would espouse different motivations. For example, for some more traditional universities, (who had been 'forced' to address widening participation issues, often for the first time), partnership was, perhaps rather pragmatically, viewed as an opportunity to learn from others who were more developed in their widening participation practice. Others however viewed collaboration as having benefits for all partners. For example, a senior manager from FE described a number of ways in which both the university and the FE colleges benefited from their liaisons:

> *Working together and being aware of developments is a learning process in its own right for the institute...You're meeting people at meetings and you're understanding their agendas and understanding issues at their meetings*

and there's development in terms of synergy about how you can tackle things together ...There are projects coming up where you think ... that particular college would be useful for us to work with in terms of this development and you wouldn't get that otherwise because you wouldn't necessarily know them otherwise or what they were doing. (Senior Manager, FE Institute)

The project manager based at the lead HEI reinforced these claims:

This is not just about outsourcing expertise but bringing in the expertise, that the partner institutions have. (Senior Manager and project manager, lead HEI)

For the majority of partners involved in collaboration the motivation to participate was closely tied to issues of recruitment within the locality in order to survive in the competitive market for students:

...we think it's got a lot of mileage, and to be quite honest, in the future, in order to get critical mass we have to collaborate because in the long term we're competing not just with universities in this country but also through new technologies countries elsewhere as simple as that, it's a global market for education, that's what e-university is also about. (Senior manager, post-1992 university which is the lead-partner in regional widening participation partnership)

Clearly then, there is a range of reasons for collaboration. Understanding the motivation for working together can assist with the development of partnerships, meeting needs of all partners and creating effective ways of working. Having addressed the questions 'what is collaboration' and 'why collaborate', I will now consider collaboration *within* HEIs and *between* HEIs in the English context. Each of the next two sections will include the policy context, evidence of collaboration, an example of collaboration and conclusions drawn in relation to definitions of collaboration and the motivations for doing so.

Promoting collaboration *within* HEIs

In the document 99/33 HEFCE requested every HEI in England to produce an initial statement regarding their widening participation strategies. The purpose of this task was, in part, to link together the different policies and practices within institutions, which I will refer to as 'internal collaboration'. In another document HEFCE wrote:

> We are keen to see the question of widening participation being addressed at the highest level, and for each institution to develop an approach that is in accordance with its mission, corporate plan and more general strategic development (HEFCE, preface in Harrison et al, 2000, p10).

The move towards a more strategic approach to widening participation was stimulated and informed by the policy climate of the time (Storan, 2000). For example, in the context of further education, the Kennedy Report noted the lack of a strategic approach to widening participation:

> The absence of a strategic dimension at local level, in our view, is a major weakness in the system which significantly reduces the potential for widening participation (Kennedy, 1997, p39).

Collaboration within HEIs is necessary as there are multiple barriers to participation in higher education, and these change over time, partly at least as students move between different stages within the student lifecycle. According to Thomas (2001) these 'barriers' to participation are perceived to be multi-faceted, and are categorised as emanating from the education sector, the labour market, the social and cultural background of students and from students own personal experiences. Drawing on this framework, I have argued for the importance of developing a strategic approach to widening participation, where 'strategic' is defined as an awareness of the inter-relationship between different barriers to participation, a need for coherence between different policies and projects and longer-term sustainability.

HEFCE has utilised the notion of a student lifecycle to demonstrate the need for a combination of widening participation initiatives throughout the different stages of being a student (HEFCE 01/36). This lifecycle is said to consist of six phases: aspiration raising, pre-entry activities, admission, first term/semester, moving through the course and employment. Aspiration raising is about raising awareness of higher education as a possibility, rather than about recruitment to a particular course or institution. Pre-entry activities tend to target groups of potential students to assist them in applying successfully to higher education; this phase may also include activities to prepare learners before moving into higher education. Admissions focus on the process of ensuring students can access courses through the acceptance of different qualification routes and developing alternative admissions processes (such as interviews and reviewing supplementary information). It is acknowledged that many students who withdraw from their studying do so in the first term or semester, therefore this is a particularly important time to induct students into higher education in general and the institution and course in particular. This suggests that induction should not just take place during the first few days, but should be an ongoing process. Students continue to need support after the first term/semester, although the nature of this may change. As students near completion of their programme of study they can benefit from preparation for employment or further study. Thus, there is little doubt that the barriers to participation in higher education by 'under represented groups' are multiple, reinforcing and change over time:

> ...Students experience disadvantage that is complex, compounding and dynamic. As understanding of its causes and nature has progressed, it has become clearer that simplistic responses to this disadvantage at the institutional level can have only a limited impact. (Ferrier and Heagney, 2000, p5)

The multiple and dynamic barriers to access and retention require a flexible and responsive HE system to meet the needs of all learners. Such an approach challenges the perpetuation of a traditional and elite model of higher education, and also rejects rigid and prescriptive 'blueprint' responses to widening participation. Robin Gutteridge (2001) seeks to adopt a new definition of the term 'additional needs' to encapsulate this idea:

> Additional needs is a term often used to describe students whose needs for extra support arise from a disability or health difficulty. It is suggested that this term could be used more globally to describe the needs of any student whose skills, academic baseline or experience varies from the normative expectation of the institution. Such re-definition may assist clearer analysis and understanding of the diversity of additional support needs and may support a classification of student by need rather than by minority group membership. This is important because analysis and understanding of the nature of the additional

need is crucial to the design of an appropriate action-plan to redress under-representation. It is a stereotypical assumption, for instance, that all students with disabilities will require study support, or that standard entrants will not have needs for additional study skills development. (p150)

Not only is it unhelpful and potentially counter-productive to assume the additional needs of under represented student cohorts, but it is also unwise to only offer a partial solution by providing support to overcome one limitation, while other difficulties remain unaltered. Simply changing the institutional structure will not ensure a diversity of students – it is a necessary condition, but it is not sufficient. Similarly, providing more information about educational opportunities will not, on its own, stimulate an increase in participation by non-traditional student groups unless there are structural changes to cope with the needs of these learners. Efforts to widen participation must therefore be 'joined up', and seek to overcome the range of barriers facing potential entrants throughout their engagement with the institution. This involves a collaborative approach to widening participation within institutions. HEFCE has encouraged widening participation strategies to make links with learning and teaching strategies, human resource strategies, estates and facilities, disability statements, marketing strategies, communication and information technology and childcare arrangements. (HEFCE 01/36)

Although the council noted that they 'intend to support diversity rather than prescribing any particular set of approaches or strategies for widening participation' (*op cit*, para 24), they provided 'generic guidance' for institutions' initial statements, which included this suggestion:

A summary of how the objectives for widening participation relate to the institution's corporate strategy and financial plan, and to other related strategies – for example, for learning and teaching. (*op cit*, para 26)

However, a subsequent analysis by Action on Access of the initial strategic statements for widening participation (HEFCE 01/36a) found that 'there is little cross-reference and linkage made between the teaching and learning strategies and the disability statement... It was disappointing that the statements may have been produced in isolation from other aspects of related activity... there is little evidence from the strategies of 'joined-up' thinking' (HEFCE 01/36a, para 14). The report continues in the same vein: 'Cross-referencing between initial strategic statements and areas such as teaching and learning policy, disability statements or financial planning, were uncommon. Most statements did not link their widening participation aims and objectives with their formula-funding allocation or their additional student numbers' (para 29). This document concludes that there is little evidence of widening participation projects making reference to the widening participation statement or the institutional plan, and there are no examples of projects relating to learning and teaching or disability statements (*op cit* para 35).

The HEFCE noted that: 'ideally HEIs should consider how they can link their widening participation strategy with the learning and teaching strategy' (01/36, para 55). But analysis of learning and teaching strategies shows that 'only 35 per cent of institutions made explicit reference to their widening participation statements in their learning and teaching strategies' (01/36, para 57). This discussion suggests that although internal collaboration and joined up thinking is desirable, when the 1999 Initial Statements were written it was not a strong feature within English HEIs. In a preliminary review of the 2001 Widening Participation Strategies Geoff Layer reported a much stronger link to learning and teaching strategies than in 1999, and medium and intermittent links to other strategies (Layer, 2001). Although the situation has improved, Layer still suggests that internal collaboration is limited.

An example of an institution where such collaborative organisational structures are more developed is Victoria University, in Melbourne, Australia. The aim has been to create a 'culturally inclusive university' by linking together internal policies and practices to meet the needs of the diverse student population. The University has also sought to develop partnership relationships with different communities in its locale, and this has led to the development of the Personalised Access and Study (PAS) policy:

PAS comprises a complex set of processes focused around the inter-related issues of access (creating alternative mechanisms for students to enter the institution) and study (assisting them to stay in the institution once they arrive). (Ronnayne, 2000, p149)

Access initiatives include developing alternative entry arrangements, interviewing students to assess their point-of-entry learning needs, and developing a 'personal student compact', that details how the institution will attempt to address these requirements. 'The 'study' elements of the policy have been addressed through a re-working and enhancement of institutional policies relating to the design and delivery of the curriculum: student progress procedures, study pathways between the vocational and academic components, and student learning support at course and subject levels' (*op cit*, p149).

To sum up, the need for and potential benefit of collaboration within HEIs can be understood to be particularly efficacious in relation to meeting the multi-faceted and changing needs of new student cohorts. There is however, comparatively limited evidence of such 'joined up thinking' in English HEIs. This approach to partnership working can, I think, be described as collaboration or co-operation, as the aim is joint operation in order to create a greater output than either could achieve on their own. The aim is more creativity and linkages between policies and practices, and not just better co-ordination of them. The motivations for collaboration are difficult to identify, and probably vary between institutions and individuals within them. There appears to be a danger that collaboration is simply believed to be a good thing (evangelism) both by the funding council and the institutions themselves. If this is the case there will only be limited understanding of the benefits of collaboration and thus the best ways to achieve this. In other words, institutions may (cynically) surmise that a collaborative internal structure will allow them to become more competitive externally. Alternatively, it may be perceived as the best way to meet the needs of students. There is therefore a need for greater reflection on the reasons for collaboration to assist HEIs to link their policies and practices together.

Developing regional partnerships to widen participation

Integration of policies is beneficial not only at an institutional level but across a broader dimension too. This is one reason why HEFCE has been concerned to promote regional collaboration to widen participation. Hence the introduction of a series of funding strands specifically for special initiatives (98/35, 99/07, 99/33 and 00/35) to promote inter-institutional working. In particular, the Council's intention has been to promote collaboration between HEIs and further education colleges and other education institutions, community groups and regional agencies, with the broad objective of widening participation in HE. Thus, in 1998, 25 regional or sub-regional partnerships were funded. The remainder of this chapter draws on evaluative research undertaken by the Institute for Access Studies at Staffordshire University, in relation to these regional and sub-regional partnerships (Thomas, *et al*, 2001). A survey of all partnerships was undertaken, adopting a case-study approach employing various qualitative methods and document analyses.

The research found that in general collaboration was welcomed by participants, but there were a number of tensions that some times made partnership working problematic. In particular, it was commonly acknowledged that there is a tension between collaboration and competition for those involved in partnerships, which is far less likely to exist within an HEI.

The nature of the competition could vary: for example institutions might be in direct competition with some but not all of their partners. In one partnership, the fear of competition came from other HEIs; in other partnerships competition is perceived between HE and FE. At a management level there were sometimes attempts to gloss over the competitive element, but a healthier approach was to acknowledge and work around this issue recognising that competition for students need not be a bad thing if it encourages institutions to be more inclusive in their overall approach.

Perhaps a more constructive way of addressing competition is associated with the type of activities undertaken. Many partnership initiatives are targeted at young children rather than those at HE entry age and this can take the competitive edge off the proceedings.

It was where projects targeted the point of entry to HE that there was likely to be significant conflict of interest. One partnership, involving more than one HEI (which may be viewed as similar institutions in terms of their recruitment profile) is developing a range of regional activities with younger children. The aim is to develop pupils' awareness of and aspiration towards post-compulsory education from a very young age. But this is seen as a long term process, which is best done collaboratively, as this reduces the amount of work each institution has to undertake, and there is no competition because there is '*no institutional label to that at all*'. The aim is not to 'sell' particular institutions, but to promote the idea of post-compulsory education.

As has been noted, another approach to overcoming competition is via co-ordination. Succinctly, co-ordinated approaches are less divisive than competitive relationships, but less integrated than collaborative methods. Thus, on one level, they can be understood as somewhat oligopolistic. For example, one partnership member commented: '*Well once we establish this database we can see who is getting who and what our patch is, this will help us to establish what each other does*' (Senior manager, non-lead HEI). This suggests that each institution will have a clearly defined and discrete geographical area in which to operate, and thus can effectively co-ordinate actions in order to avoid overlap (and thus reduce competition).

The discussion so far has highlighted the potential tension between partners. The following very brief analysis demonstrates the ways in which further and higher education institutions can work together at the sub-regional level to widen participation. The aim of the partnership's activities is to create progression pathways for students studying at different levels and at different institutions. The partnership consists of a post-1992 university, a number of FE colleges and some specialist HE colleges. Within the sub-region there is also an elite pre-1992 university, and on the edges of the sub-region there are other new universities with a keen interest in widening participation and recruiting local/regional students. The lead HEI now has approximately 4,000 students studying HE in FE institutions, and this accounts for 15% of its total student body. HE provision in colleges includes HNDs, full programmes and joint programmes. Shortly, these will be complemented by Foundation degrees.

The lead HEI works with its FE partners to enable students to move from community provision, through FE and ultimately into higher education. For example, when colleges promote their City and Guilds courses or diplomas, they do not 'sell' the course on its own, but promote the idea of the course leading to an HND. This helps to raise the aspirations of students, and assists colleges to promote their courses, as potential students interested in progression are attracted by the fact that there are structured links to degree courses within HE. This view is supported by the colleges themselves, who are keen to provide progression pathways from lower levels right through to HE. For example, a manager from one college commented:

> ...the whole college is geared towards progression. It's not enough now just to give someone the qualification, they have to be able to see that they can go forward. It's to our advantage if we get students coming in to the college onto level 1 or whatever to move them on if we can but if they want to move onto another college or university we would be happy for them to do that.

Within the partnership, continuous progression pathways are facilitated by:

- Ensuring linkage between each stage of the curriculum, irrespective of which institution is providing the course, to create a better match between articulated courses
- Improving staff awareness that previous course content may differ, and students cannot be referred back to previous course notes
- Provision of advice and guidance to students before they transfer
- Visits and open days to the university by students, and visits to the colleges by university staff
- Progression agreements with all partner colleges that recognise FE qualifications as agreed entry requirements
- A letter to each student from the Faculty at the University informing them they have a place if they complete the course successfully reinforces progression agreements

- The introduction of top-up degrees that are designed specifically to map onto college programmes
- Providing an induction for new students, irrespective of when they join the institution
- Providing a (informal) peer mentor
- The creation of a university HE centre within an FE college site.

The approach to working with FE partners exhibits elements of co-ordination, as well as collaboration, in order to overcome the potential problems of competition. Most of the colleges within the partnership work only with the one university. The emphasis therefore is on co-ordination in the first instance. The lead HEI has an agreement with the other university in the sub-region, and their subjects are largely complementary. In addition to co-ordination, the scheme involves collaboration built on synergy – a mutually beneficial arrangement, the outcomes of which are greater than a sum of the parts. For example the University feels that they have been able to draw on FE expertise to develop and move into new curriculum areas they could not have developed on their own. The colleges also feel that the relationship is mutually beneficial. For example, one FE institution was emphatic that the partnership is cost effective, and that there is a degree of autonomy and independence but also of synergy in the way they are operating. This has developed over a period and has come from a small number of courses and students and grown progressively. Now they have a *'critical mass'* of HE students and are collaboratively developing an HE centre within the college. A senior manager in another college commented: *'We don't think we are in competition with this university … I think it would frighten us if universities, they just had foundation degrees, and we weren't able to get involved in that because we would loose that angle'*. This suggests that co-ordination and collaboration is working, but there is always a threat of competition.

In summary, the overwhelming response from the partnerships that participated in the research is that collaboration is an effective way to widen participation, (although there are some provisos). In addition, survey respondents were asked if they felt collaboration was an effective use of funding. Only one respondent felt that it was not effective, describing collaboration as '*costly and time-consuming*'. Other respondents felt that collaboration '*avoids duplication of effort*', facilitates '*shared good practice*' and '*provides better quality output than if FEIs get funding direct*'. Indeed, the evidence we found suggests that regional partnerships have the *potential* to widen participation.

It is clear however that there are very real tensions between collaboration and competition, and at times co-ordination offers a much better approach to structuring inter-institutional working. The necessity of institutions to retain or improve their market share of students from the locality seems to imply that one of the main motivating reasons for partnership working is market imperatives. Institutions are largely engaging in regional work for self-interested reasons, rather than for wider social goals. This is inevitable, but needs to be borne in mind when policies for promoting collaboration are developed.

Conclusions

Throughout this chapter, and perhaps the entire book, there is a tension. We have elected to discuss 'collaboration', and yet this term itself is only ever loosely defined and a more in-depth examination of the issues involved suggests that collaboration is not always occurring. Perhaps this lack of clarity results from unclear and muddled motivations for working together. Is it viable for groups to collaborate (i.e. have shared values, equal status, etc), when their motivation is to improve their position relative to their competitors, including those who are their partners? It seems apparent that collaboration should take place *within* institutions, but there is comparatively little evidence of this occurring. But this should come as no surprise considering the continuing insidiousness of neo-liberal discourses.

For effective collaboration it is necessary to know what collaboration is and to be clear about the reasons for doing so, otherwise how can we hope to structure effective co-operative partnerships which utilise strengths, compensate weakness and create something more than the individual partners could do on their own? Furthermore, 'collaboration' can often mask power relations, especially when the motivation for working together is to improve one's market position. Our research found that both further education colleges and community groups are rarely full partners in 'collaborative' endeavours, and tend to be used to provide access to target groups. They are seldom granted equal status, and are excluded from the strategic and research aspects of the partnership and confined to the operational realm. Ultimately, then, the most difficult yet simultaneously most pressing questions that collaborative approaches must address could well be about power.

References

Ambrose, P. (2001) 'Holism' and urban regeneration' in Balloch, S. and Taylor, M. (eds) *Partnership Working. Policy and Practice*. Bristol: The Policy Press

Balloch, S. and Taylor, M. (2001) 'Introduction' in Balloch, S. and Taylor, M. (eds) *Partnership Working. Policy and Practice*. Bristol: The Policy Press

Bekhradnia, B. (2000a) 'A national model for monitoring institutional progress'. Keynote speech at the ninth EAN conference *Access to Higher Education: The Unfinished Business: An Evaluation for the Millennium*. University of Santiago de Compostela, Spain, 3-6 September

Bekhradnia, B. (2000b) 'HEFCEs widening participation strategy'. Keynote speech at the conference *Action on Access: From Practice into Policy*. Nottingham: Nottingham Trent University, 6 October

CVCP (1999) *Briefing Note: Widening Participation*. Summer 1999. London: Committee of Vice-chancellors and Principals of the Universities of the UK

DfEE (1999) *Learning to Succeed: A New Framework for Post-16 Learning*. London: HMSO

Drèze, J. and Sen, A. (1989) *Hunger and Public Action*. Oxford: Clarendon Press

Evans, P. (1996) 'Government action, social capital and development: Reviewing the evidence on synergy', cited in Benson, L. (2000) 'Creating Synergy? VSO's contribution to a Juvenile Justice System in The Gambia', Final Report, MSc in Development Management, The Open University, p11.

Ferrier, F. and Heagney, M. (2000) 'Dealing with the dynamics of disadvantage: Options for equity planning in higher education institutions'. *Widening Participation and Lifelong Learning*, 2(1), 5-14

Geneeb, H. and Bowers, B. (1997) Excerpt from 'The Synergy Myth and Other Ailments of Business Today', in *Management Inc.*, vol. 19, no 3, p79

Gutteridge, R. (2001) 'Evaluating the role of life skills in successful participation', in Thomas, E., Cooper, M. and Quinn, J. (eds) (2001) *Access to Higher Education: The Unfinished Business*. Stoke-on-Trent: Institute for Access Studies, Staffordshire University and The European Access Network distributed by Trentham Books.

Harrison, R., Fraser, L., Braham, J., Davies, C., Robinson, G., Scott, B. and Ryley, P. (2000) *Ideas for Inclusion. An A to Z for Practitioners*. National Task Group for Widening Participation, with HEFCE

HEFCE 98/35 Widening participation: special funding programme 1998-99

HEFCE 99/07 Widening participation: special funding programme 1998-99. Outcome of bids

HEFCE 99/33 Widening participation in higher education. Request for initial statements of plans. Invitation to bid for special funds: 1999-2000 to 2001-02

HEFCE 99/66 Performance Indicators in higher education in the UK

HEFCE 00/35 Widening participation: special funding programme 1999-2000 to 2001-02

HEFCE 01/29 Widening participation in higher education – Funding decisions for 2001-02 to 2003-04.

HEFCE 01/36 Strategies for widening participation in higher education. A guide to good practice

HEFCE 01/36a Analysis of initial strategic statements for widening participation. Report by Action on Access

HEFCE 01/73 Partnerships for Progression. Proposals by the HEFCE and the Learning and Skills Council

Kennedy, H. (1997) *Learning Works: Widening Participation in Further Education.* Coventry: FEFC

Layer, G. (2001) 'Student Success and Widening Participation Strategies', Action on Access Conference *Supporting Student Success*, Moat House, York, 26th October 2001

Robinson, D., Hewitt, T. and Harriss, J. (2000) 'Why inter-organisational relationships matter' in Robinson, D., Hewitt, T. and Harriss, J. (eds) *Managing Development. Understanding inter-organisational relationships.* London, Sage Publications, in association with The Open University

Ronnayne, J. (2000) 'Creating a culturally diverse and inclusive higher education: an Australian example' in Thomas, E. and Cooper, M. (eds) *Changing the Culture of the Campus: Towards and inclusive higher education.* Stoke on Trent: Trentham, with the European Access Network

Storan, J. (2000) 'An analysis of HEIs initial statements on widening participation'. Keynote speech at the conference *Action on Access: From Practice into Policy.* Nottingham: Nottingham Trent University, 6 October

Thomas, E. (2001) *Widening Participation in Post-compulsory Education.* London: Continuum

Thomas, E., Quinn, J., Slack, K. and Williams, S. (2001) *The Role of Partnerships in widening participation in higher education.* HEFCE

Woodrow, M. (1999) Student finance: access opportunity'. Paper for the Independent Committee of Inquiry into Student Finance, October 1999

Wuyts, M., Mackintosh, M. and Hewitt, T. (eds) (1992) *Development Policy and Public Action.* Oxford: Oxford University Press in association with the Open University

3

Widening Access to higher education in Ireland

Don Thornhill

Introduction

Many forces have driven the development of Irish education policy in recent years. On the one hand, recent economic success has brought home in a very tangible way the direct return that investment in education can yield for the economy and society as a whole. Changes in Irish demography, and in particular declining levels of school leavers are now posing new questions as to how this economic success will be maintained.

On the other hand, education is also seen as a key means to address issues of inequality and promote social inclusion in the face of high rates of economic growth. In this context, it is no surprise that much of the debate in Irish education, and particularly in the third level sector, is concerned with issues of access and equality and in this respect the Irish policy debate and the evolution of education participation at third level parallels that in other OECD countries.

The ethical arguments in favour of increased access and the promotion of equality are, I think, well known to all with even a passing concern in educational and social policy. The economic arguments are also compelling. Higher levels of educational attainment improve life chances and earning power for individuals. Data for Ireland (HEA, 2000 and CSO, 2000) illustrates this point.

Higher education enhances labour force productivity and output. Many OECD countries are now experiencing skills shortages in economically critical areas – particularly in information technology. In my view there is a powerful synergy between the social policy arguments for improved access and the economic policy requirements for increasing skill and knowledge endowments in our populations. In some areas of social policy the promotion of equality and redistribution may constrain economic growth and there can be tensions or difficult trade-offs to be made between economic and social policy objectives. This is not the case for equality in education.

The approach to the promotion of access to third level education in Ireland is multi-faceted. The various means used are described below. However one recent and key development is worth noting here. Arising out of recent legislation, there is now a formal onus on the Universities to put in place their own policies on equality, and for the Higher Education Authority (HEA) (the national Government agency supporting third level education in Ireland) to review those policies and to advise the Universities on the development of these policies. This new approach, which brings together both individual agencies, and, through the HEA, Government, has recently commenced and is described further below.

The Irish perspective

In order to provide a full picture of the current actions being taken in Ireland to address issues of access and equality, this chapter considers a number of areas. Firstly, it sets out some statistical background to Irish participation at third level in general, and to provide some statistical analysis on patterns of access to higher education. Secondly, it sets out the legislative context governing issues of access and equality. There follows a general overview of actions in relation to access and equality, before considering the specific statutory review of university equality policies currently being carried out and it ends with some conclusions drawn from the Irish approach to the promotion of access to third level education.

The statistical background

Figure 1 charts the participation rate in third level education over the last 34 years.

Figure 1

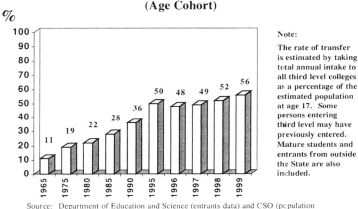

**Estimated Rate of Transfer to Third Level - Ireland
(Age Cohort)**

Note:

The rate of transfer is estimated by taking total annual intake to all third level colleges as a percentage of the estimated population at age 17. Some persons entering third level may have previously entered. Mature students and entrants from outside the State are also included.

Source: Department of Education and Science (entrants data) and CSO (population data)

The third level system is binary – the two main pillars being the universities and the institutes of technology. There is also a number of teacher training colleges and other smaller third level institutions.

The universities are essentially concerned with undergraduate and postgraduate degree programmes, together with basic and applied research. The main work of the institutes of technology is in certificate and diploma programmes, with a number of degree programmes and a growing involvement in regionally oriented applied research. However, within each sector and between the two sectors there is a diversity of institutions offering different types and levels of courses.

In 1982, the HEA published the first data on breakdown of participation in higher education. This was compiled by Prof. Pat Clancy of UCD in his publication *Participation in Higher Education: A National Survey* (Clancy, 1982). Subsequent reports have built on that empirical work. The most recent report, *Social Background of Higher Education Entrants* (Clancy and Wall, 2000) was published in 2000. Summary data is shown below.

Figure 2

Estimated Proportion of Age Cohort Entering Full-Time Higher Education by Fathers' Socio-Economic Group for in 1980, 1986, 1992 and 1998

Socio-Economic Groups	1998	1992	1986	1980
Farmers	0.75	0.53	0.42	0.30
Other Agricultural Occupations	0.35	0.24	0.12	0.06
Higher Professional	1.00*	0.85	0.72	0.59
Lower Professional	0.48	0.42	0.47	0.33
Employers and Managers	0.84	0.67	0.45	0.42
Salaried Employees	0.55	0.48	0.58	0.59
Intermediate Non-Manual Workers	0.33	0.27	0.28	0.22
Other Non-Manual Workers	0.31	0.26	0.11	0.09
Skilled Manual Workers	0.34	0.28	0.13	0.09
Semi-Skilled Manual Workers	0.23	0.19	0.11	0.09
Unskilled Manual Workers	0.22	0.12	0.04	0.03
TOTAL	0.46	0.36	0.25	0.20

* This is an overestimate. See Footnote 5, Page 70, Clancy Wall 2000
Source : 'Social Background of Higher Education Entrants' by Patrick Clancy and Joy Wall, HEA, 2000

This work focuses mainly on school leavers. The data includes comprehensive details of students' socio-economic, locational, gender and prior education characteristics. Over the next decade Ireland will experience a drop in the population of school leavers owing to declining birth rates. This 'demographic dividend' will provide an opportunity to increase participation rates among under represented target groups. Participation in higher education by mature students is low by international standards. (see HEA, 2000; OECD, 1997).

The legislative context

There are a number of statutory provisions that have a direct bearing on approaches to tackling the issue of equality. Over the past three decades a volume of legislation has built up which sets out State policy towards issues relating to access and equality. The Higher Education Authority Act of 1971 has been an important instrument in progressing change in this area, providing as it does for responsibilities on the HEA to promote equality of opportunity.

The universities have always enjoyed the traditional principles of academic freedom and institutional autonomy. Under the terms of the Universities Act 1997 there are obligations to promote gender balance and equality of opportunity among students and staff. A key component of the requirements under the Act is the duty imposed on the universities to prepare and implement statements of their policies in respect of

> *(a) access to the university and to university education by economically or socially disadvantaged people, by people who have a disability and by people from sections of society significantly under represented in the student body, and*

> *(b) equality, including gender equality, in all activities of the university.*

The Universities Act (Section 49) also requires the HEA to assist the universities in pursuing equality policies and empowers the Authority to review equality policies from time to time. Other education legislation with equality provisions include the Qualifications (Education and Training) Act, 1999, the Regional Technical Colleges Act, 1992 and the Dublin Institute of Technology Act, 1992.

Actions to promote equality and access – overview

The policy related actions relating to access to higher education include:

- The provision of student support mechanisms, including means tested maintenance grants. 40% of registered students are in receipt of grants but the level of the full maintenance grant ranging from between IR£710 ((902) to IR£1775 ((2254) has been robustly criticised by the Union of Students in Ireland and others as being too low.

- The Disadvantaged Fund, established in 1994, comprises two elements, the Student Assistance Access Fund and the Special Fund for Students with Disabilities. In the year 2000, the ESF Aided Student Assistance/Access Fund (formerly known as 'The Hardship Fund') provided IR£1.828m (€2.321m) discretionary financial support to disadvantaged students while the ESF Aided Fund to Assist Students with Disabilities amounted

53

to IR£1m (€1.270m). The overall administration of these funds is managed by the Department of Education and Science with the allocation to the University sector being made through the HEA.

- A variety of targeted initiatives supported by HEA for disadvantaged school leavers, mature age students and students with disabilities – see Figure 6.

Support for AHEAD and HEEU

Two bodies actively engaged in fostering equity at higher education level are funded by the HEA: the Higher Education Equality Unit based at University College Cork; and AHEAD (Association for Higher Education Access and Disability).

AHEAD (Association for Higher Education Access and Disability)

AHEAD is an independent, voluntary organisation working to promote full access to, participation in, benefit from and contribution to third level education by people with disabilities in Ireland, North and South. It is a registered charity and is funded by the Higher Education Authority, members subscriptions and European Union funding.

AHEAD undertakes research in areas relating to disability and third level education and acts in a consultative capacity to the Higher Education Authority, educational institutions and other bodies in the educational sector.

AHEAD lobbies to improve access to and increase the participation of students with disabilities in third level education in Ireland. It also strives to inform and change national policy in the areas of the education of students with disabilities and the employment of disabled graduates.

Further details as to the work of AHEAD are available at the web address: http://www.ahead.ie

HEEU (Higher Education Equality Unit)

Established in 1992, the role of the HEEU is to promote greater equality in Irish Higher Education Institutions for both students and staff. The HEEU aims to enable higher education institutions to develop effective equality policies and practices and to tackle discrimination against (potential and current) staff and students, having regard to issues of socio-economic class background, gender, race/ethnicity/nationality, disability, age, sexual orientation, family/care responsibilities and religious or political belief.

Further details on the work of the HEEU are available at the web address: http://www.ucc.ie/ucc/units/equality/

Publications, studies and policy documents

During 2000, the HEA published a number of significant studies:[1]

- *Social Background of Higher Education Entrants* (Clancy and Wall, 2000), the fourth national survey of entrants to higher education compiled for the Higher Education Authority by Professor Patrick Clancy and Ms Joy Wall. The work continues a series of research publications by Professor Clancy which began in 1982.

- *Evaluation of the Targeted Initiatives on Widening Access for Young People from Socio-Economically Disadvantaged Backgrounds* (Osborne and Leith, 2000). Professor Robert Osborne and Ms Helen Leith of the Centre for Higher Education Belfast were commissioned to conduct an evaluation of the programme.

- *Access and Equity in Higher Education: An International Perspective on Issues and Strategies* (Skilbeck and Connell, 2000). The report compiled on behalf of the HEA by Emeritus Professor Malcolm Skilbeck with the assistance of Dr. Helen Connell examines the evidence of gains made, of continuing weaknesses and of issues which feature in the international equity debate. This report has made a major contribution to the development of policy.

Other recent relevant studies and documents include the Report of the Commission on the Points System (Hyland) and the White Paper on Adult Education (2000).

One key theme highlighted in some of these reports – most particularly the recommendations contained in the reports by both Skilbeck and Connell and Osborne and Leith – is the need for a strategic and coherent national policy on access and equality to be achieved in collaboration between all relevant stakeholders.

With this end in mind, in October 2000, the HEA held a national conference to review the findings of these studies. The objectives of the Forum were:

- to provide an opportunity for third-level institutions, policy makers and social partners to consider the issues and strategies in relation to access and equity in higher education which have been raised in the reports; and

- to contribute to the development of strategies in relation to access and equity in higher education at national and at institutional level.

An HEA commissioned report on student retention – '*A Study of Non-Completion in Undergraduate University Courses*' by Dr. Mark Morgan, Ms Rita Flanagan and Dr. Tom Kellaghan was published in February 2001 and a follow-up National Seminar on the topic took place in May 2001.

The national non-completion figure of 16.8% for universities compares well internationally but there are worryingly high rates in some institutions and in certain fields of study. In tackling these and related issues, the approach is characterised by collaboration. Collaboration between government agencies and the institutions, and among the institutions themselves. There has to be a broad sense of ownership of this issue if meaningful progress is to be made.

Under the HEA's Targeted Initiatives Programme, the Authority is funding a number of schemes in institutions aimed at improving access and boosting retention. Particular emphasis is attached to increasing participation from disadvantaged school leavers, mature students and students who have a disability.

Disadvantaged school leavers – initiatives funded by HEA

- Development of links with schools designated as disadvantaged
- Direct entry arrangements
- Summer schools and mentoring programmes
- Co-operation with area-based partnership bodies
- Parents' programmes
- Supervised study
- Guidance counselling
- Supplementary tuition
- Orientation programmes
- Input to teacher education in relation to combating disadvantage

Mature students – initiatives funded by HEA

- Provision of outreach workers
- Training of adult tutors
- Development of courses and course materials
- Orientation programmes for mature students
- Guidance and counselling support
- Course in preparatory skills
- Information Packs
- Mentoring
- Development of on-line materials
- Promotional materials

Students with disabilities – initiatives funded by HEA

- Making existing buildings and facilities universally accessible (Capital Grant)
- The development of flexible assessment mechanisms
- Devising suitable examination arrangements

- Provision of assistive technology and services such as brailling

- Counselling and guidance support

- Campus transport

Evaluation of the targeted initiatives on widening access for young people from socio-economically disadvantaged backgrounds (Osborne and Leith, 2000)

In 1999, an evaluation was commissioned of the targeted initiative in relation to disadvantaged school leavers. The report by Professor Bob Osborne of the University of Ulster and Ms Helen Leith of Queens University Belfast was published in September, 2000.

While both detailing and commending the diversity of innovative approaches being pursued by the Universities, this report made a number of recommendations, including identifying the need for a coherent and consistent national strategy enabling policies and practices to be developed in a co-ordinated way towards improving the access of disadvantaged students to the entire range of third-level institutions.

Other key recommendations include:

- A national strategy must provide a broad policy framework within which individual universities and other institutions can evolve distinctive practices reflecting their diverse circumstances.

- A national strategy, funded by the State, should have clear objectives and measures available for progress to be measured.

- A national strategy should ensure third level access schemes are targeted at assisting disadvantaged students at each of the three key transitions – completion of second-level education, performance in the leaving certificate exam and transfer to higher education.

- The need for higher education institutions to develop a rounded and robust rationale for widening access activities and to place widening access in the mainstream of policy making and academic and resource decision making.

- The need to ensure that third level institutions give equal importance to targeting young people from disadvantaged backgrounds as to widening opportunities for mature students and students with disabilities.

- The need for national co-ordination with regard to the selection of disadvantaged schools to which third level institutions are linked and with regard to criteria governing the selection of individual students.

- The need to ensure not just the access of disadvantaged students to higher education but also the continued participation and benefit from higher education of such students post entry – in particular, the issue of financial penalties incurred as a result of experiencing academic difficulties such as having to pay fees as a result of failing a year.

- The need to consider individual student funding in light of the negative impact which combining part-time employment with second level studies may be having on the numbers of students progressing on to third level.

- The need to increase the level of student support to disadvantaged students so that they are enabled to participate fully in higher education.

- The need for a clear national definition of a disadvantaged student.

- The need to conduct appropriate statistical monitoring of all access activities on a common basis.

Future Action

The increased level of funding allocated in 2000 and committed for 2001 indicates the priority attached by HEA and the Department of Education and Science to the continuation of effective programmes to increase participation of groups in higher education, which are currently under represented.

Research and evaluation studies conducted for the HEA have pointed to the importance of mainstreaming initiatives funded under special programmes. Mainstreaming is seen as essential to securing the future success of these initiatives. The objectives outlined for such programmes must become core elements of the institutions' missions.

Proposals for Targeted Initiatives 2001 have already been requested to include information on planned commitment to the mainstreaming of access activities e.g. dedicated budget, long term planning, the status of posts and career development planning. Proposals for funding under the access initiative will be for a period of up to three years.

It is also anticipated that major co-ordination access policy will arise further to the report of the Action Group on Access (see below) and that this will feed into the future development and direction of the HEA targeted initiatives.

Action Group on Access to Third Level Education
In September 2000, Dr. Michael Woods TD, Minister for Education and Science set up an Action Group on Access to Higher Education. The three main groups identified in the terms of reference of the Action Group were:

• Disadvantaged school leavers

• Mature students

• Students with a disability

The work of the Action Group has been completed. One of the main recommendations of the final report was the establishment of a single co-ordinating administrative unit. The proposed activities of this unit would include drawing up policy proposals and overseeing the implementation of the national programme to promote access to third level education in liaison with the Department of Education and Science and other stakeholders. The full details of the report are currently being considered by the Minister for Education and Science.

Statutory review of university equality policies

The final section of this chapter describes the statutory review of the university equality policies which is now underway. In undertaking the review, the Authority is mindful of the steps already taken and initiatives already in place, the research findings, policies and views of stakeholders, and will wish to promote programmes and strategies that have demonstrated success in achieving equality goals.

As I noted in the introduction, recent legislation has set out clearly the respective roles of the universities and the HEA in the promotion of access and the development of policies on equality. The role of the Universities is to set out their own policies for the promotion of equality, while the HEA's role is to assist the Universities in this regard, and to review the policies prepared by the Universities.

As part of its role to assist the Universities, the HEA published a number of reports in 2000, and also convened a National Conference to review the findings of these reports. Details of the reports and the Conference are set out in Section 4 above.

Following the Conference, the HEA announced its intention to commence a review of the equality policies of the Universities, as provided for in the Universities Act, 1997.

In undertaking a review of equality of opportunity, the HEA drew attention to the reference in the Universities Act, 1997 to 'all activities of the university', to the object which relates equality of opportunity to employees as well as students, and to the definition of equity formulated by Malcolm Skilbeck in the study on *Access and Equity in Higher Education: An International Perspective on Issues and Strategies*. Used alike for students and staff, equity refers to:

(1) policies and procedures for enabling and encouraging groups at present under represented as students in higher education institutions and programmes or study areas, to gain access to and demonstrate successful performance in higher education, and transition to the labour market and

(2) extending opportunities for suitably qualified people, regardless of gender, ethnicity, disability or other extraneous considera-

tions, to achieve staff positions in higher education and to advance professionally according to merit and achievement and without discrimination based on these extraneous considerations.

The Authority recognises that achieving equality of opportunity for all is by no means simple or straightforward. As described by Skilbeck:

- There are structures and conditions, many in the wider society, which militate against achievement of equality of opportunity goals for members of under represented groups. These problems are not always susceptible to action solely within the domain of higher education; they require the development of broader educational policies and more cross-sectoral policy co-ordination.

- Difficulties in achieving equality of opportunity goals may be not only structural but also attitudinal or grounded in institutional norms and long-established institutional beliefs and assumptions. Thus attitudes, values and customary practice as well as rules and structures affecting admissions, advancement etc., require sustained attention along with specific, targeted initiatives to advance particular disadvantaged groups.

- Due to the complexity and scale of operations within large institutions, there may be a lack of co-ordinated, institution-wide action across all equity fronts.

- Implementation of policies and programmes to achieve equality of opportunity requires sustained action on many fronts: institutional leadership; sensitive management and decision-making; monitoring; good data; evaluation; analysis; a capacity to undertake systematic action of a supportive, remedial kind; and compliance measures.

- Limitations in the scope and coverage of research and evaluative studies and what appears to be relatively little funded support especially for longitudinal studies, mean that systematic knowledge about strategies that are effective is often lacking or unduly limited.

For such reasons as these, the HEA does not expect that institutions will as yet have a full repertoire of successful strategies in place for achieving the requirements of legislation and for meeting forward-looking policy goals. It will take time and considerable effort to achieve fundamental equality of opportunity for all designated categories and to ensure that all who can benefit from higher education actually do so.

This review has several purposes: to monitor progress; to advise and assist the institutions on ways of strengthening their equality of opportunity policies and procedures; and to indicate how the HEA can be of assistance in the future. Overall, the review should help to foster a climate in which there is a sound understanding of what equality of opportunity in higher education entails, and commitment to it throughout the system.

The equality of opportunity review – general strategy
This will be the first system-wide equality of opportunity review. Procedures are expected to evolve over time, particularly as universities may not, as yet, have either the necessary data sets or comprehensive policies and strategies in place. This initial review will assist in their development. The Authority will be seeking evidence of benchmarking and other procedures whereby institutions seek to determine their equality of opportunity goals and standards both nationally and internationally.

Equality of opportunity policies and procedures, although separately reviewed, are an integral part of a wide range of initiatives to strengthen tertiary education. Inevitably, there will be a balance among diverse goals and functions of higher education institutions.

A **five stage general strategy** for the review is planned:

First universities are at present in the process of preparing their institutional reports – a statement of policies – which addresses questions relating to equality of opportunity for both students and staff as regards all institutional activities with due regard for public policy in this area.

Second, HEA appoints a review team appropriate for the system-wide review.

Third, the review team meets and receives a brief before visiting each institution.

Fourth, the review team reports to the HEA within a period of two months of completion of the visits. The report will include recommendations to both the institutions and the HEA.

Fifth, the HEA prepares the report for publication following consultation with the universities and determines such follow-up action it regards as appropriate.

In line with the policy recommendations of Skilbeck and Osborne, – and the overall mission of the HEA in promoting equality of opportunity – a key feature of this follow-up action will be the achievement, in collaboration with all relevant stakeholders, of a coherent and consistent national strategy.

To this end the continuing development and refinement of **institution-wide policies and practices** should aim to encourage institutions beyond formal compliance with equality of opportunity legislation toward embodying a 'culture of equality of opportunity'. Key to this is fostering a positive attitude toward members of the various equity groups among both staff and the broader student population; also for all staff to develop knowledge and understanding of the needs of students and staff from the various equity groups and to act sensitively and consistently on the basis of this knowledge and understanding.

A number of **equity groups** relevant to the Irish setting are defined in line with the approach proposed by Skilbeck. While some difficulties attend the equity group approach (e.g. multiple membership; defining boundaries; operational definitions; alternative definitions for equity groupings, etc.), it is an approach which has proved helpful in other settings when initiating a process of equity reviews. It is important that the equity categories and their operationalisation be themselves kept under review, as well as the 'equity group' approach itself.

It will be necessary to define those equity groups most relevant to Irish higher education. While a smaller, rather than larger, number of groups is preferable for review purposes, there are at least six categories:

- Socio-economic disadvantage

- People with a disability

- Women

- Mature and part-time students

- Rural

- Minority groups, including travellers and refugees.

In reviewing each equity group, different considerations become important; for example:

a) **Socio-economic disadvantage**

This category is also associated with other equity categories. Special linkages with secondary schools seem important; provision of special support such as study and computer skills workshops for first year students can be beneficial. Evidence of such links and effectiveness of access programmes are to be sought.

b) **People with a disability**

Integration or 'mainstreaming' policies at school level in many countries have, over the past decade, enabled a significant flow-on into tertiary education of students with a disability. There is considerable variation in how broadly different countries define disability, particularly with regard to learning disabilities and certain medical conditions. Key concerns for institutions are in providing an accessible physical environment and providing inclusive pedagogic and social environments for people who have a disability. A major difficulty is knowing the number of students and staff with disabilities in an institution. Many systems rely on self-identification by students and staff with a disability, and act in a responsive mode to their requests for assistance.

c) **Women**

This equity category has shown most progress in many systems. Current concerns internationally are: women in non-traditional subject areas; women in post-graduate study; the balance of women staff among permanent (as against casual) employees; women in management positions in the university.

d) Mature students and part-time students

This has been identified in national policy as a target area, but there are disincentives and barriers to participation. Acknowledging these, are the institutions facilitating access and providing opportunities by providing for (a sufficient diversity of) part-time and off-campus study? Issues such as recognition of work experience and flexible study arrangements also arise. The Hyland Report on the Points system identifies a range of procedures needed, including alternative entry requirements. Staffing practices may also be reviewed for evidence of age discrimination.

e) Rural

Rural becomes an especially significant factor when combined with economic disadvantage. Are there initiatives to address rural disadvantage, e.g. linkage with targeted secondary schools?

f) Minority groups, including travellers and refugees

The disproportionately low second level completion rates for the traveller communities point to the need for such support as alternative entry requirements; flexible study arrangements; study skills and other support during initial year of tertiary study. Refugees have emerged as an equity category in recent years. Despite publicity, institutions may not have taken active steps to meet particular needs, for example English language support, recognition of foreign qualifications and alternative entry requirements.

Other categories identified in anti-discrimination legislation are: marital status, family status, sexual orientation, religion, race. A key issue here is the sensitivity of institutions, e.g. in inclusive language, curricula and teaching.

The Equality of Opportunity review – planning steps

a. Institutional equality of opportunity report

In line with legislative requirements, the institutions have been requested to submit equality of opportunity reports drawing on the above, but adding and modifying these in light of the individual strategies they have adopted and results that have been achieved. The reports should address both student and staff experience at institutions in respect of all institutional activities.

The **first** part should focus on the overall orientation of institutions to meet equality of opportunity needs. It should outline the institution's equality policy and draw attention to institution-wide strategies and procedures for implementation. For example: provision of accessible buildings and venues; use of inclusive language and curriculum practice; definition of institution-wide positions with equity responsibilities; recruitment and promotion policy; university council and committee memberships; strategies and procedures at the department/ unit level as well as whole institution level; and procedures for communication of policies institution-wide and for staff training.

The **second** part should report on the defined equity groups in turn. For each group, the report should address: institutional objectives; strategies; establishment and monitoring of performance indicators and experience of success/difficulties in achieving greater participation in the institution by students and staff in each of the defined equity groups.

In monitoring equality of opportunity for **staff**, it is important to take account of administrative, technical and general, as well as academic, staff, and to have data on seniority as well as the specific measures in place to recruit and provide career paths for equity group members, to provide professional development support, and to encourage them to apply for career positions, and to address the barriers encountered by people from these groups. For **students**, important considerations include admission, progression, retention, and completion of courses, as well as the level, length and nature of courses in which they are enrolled.

b. **Appointing a review team**
The HEA will seek to appoint a single review team to visit all relevant institutions.

c. **Review visit**
At each institution, the review team will discuss the institutional equality of opportunity report with the President and other university authorities, including one or more non-staff governing body members. It will also meet a sample of departmental, staff and student representatives. It should be empowered to seek information additional to that provided by the institution.

d. **Report to HEA**

The review team will submit a single consolidated report to the HEA within two months of its final visit. Particular attention may be drawn to successes and difficulties expressed by individual institutions.

e. **HEA follow-up action**

On completion of the review, the chair of the review team will be invited to prepare a report evaluating this exercise with recommendations for future review procedures. Institutions will also be invited to submit their own assessment of the exercise and to advise on adjustments that may be required for the future.

Conclusion

Achieving equality in higher education has many of the features of a long and difficult campaign. Structural change in education invariably takes a long time. Wider society, its attitudes and structures, have an enormous bearing on the capacity of third level institutions to achieve equality in their activities. This is particularly true of the influence of first and second level education and the success or otherwise of policies at those levels to promote equality.

However these are not reasons as to why those of us engaged in higher education should moderate our efforts. There are clear social and economic rewards in widening access to, and promoting equality in higher education.

Furthermore any approach must be co-ordinated and structured to take account of all the parties involved in third level education, to allow them to work in a consistent fashion to meet these goals.

Malcolm Skilbeck put it very well in his study *Meeting the Equality Challenge in Higher Education* which was published by the HEA last year and which I have referred to a number of times.

> But who is to do all this? Individual teachers and researchers will need to look beyond their disciplines to the moral purpose of education. Institutional administrators and leaders will need to provide encouragement and support for a wider vision than research outputs and specialised scientific and professional training. It is for public authorities and governments to provide the resources and ensure that the necessary policies and frameworks are in

place. It is only through shared responsibility and concerted action that there can be further progress towards a more equitable system of higher educa-tion.

The recent approach in Ireland to these policy issues is aimed at developing an appropriate framework to tackle these issues. The approach recognises that there are many different actors who at one level or another are involved in issues of access and equality. Ireland has adopted a collaborative approach to meet this need. Universities have a specific role to put policies in place, assisted by the HEA both through its general advisory role and its specific reviews of individual policies. The events of the coming years will demonstrate how far we have succeeded in using this approach to enhance access to third level education in Ireland.

References

Action Group on Access (2001) *Final Report* Dublin: Government Publications

Clancy, P. (1982) *Participation in Higher Education: A National Survey*, Dublin: Higher Education Authority

Clancy, P. and Wall, J. (2000) *Social Background of Higher Education Entrants*, Dublin: Higher Education Authority

Learning for Life: White Paper on Adult Education (2000) Dublin: Government Publications www.irlgov.ie/educ/pub/htm

Morgan, M., Flanagan R., and Kellaghan, T. (2001) *A Study of Non-Completion in Undergraduate University Courses*, Dublin, Higher Education Authority

Osborne, R. and Leith, H., (2000) *Evaluation of the Targeted Initiatives on Widen-ing Access for Young People from Socio-Economically Disadvantaged Backgrounds*, Dublin: Higher Education Authority Commission on the Points System, (1999) Final Report Dublin: Government Publications

Skilbeck, M., and Connell, H., (2000) *Access and Equity in Higher Education: An International Perspective on Issues and Strategies*, Dublin, Higher Education Authority

Skilbeck, M. and Connell, H., (2000) *Meeting the Equity Challenge in Higher Education (A short version of Access and Equity in Higher Education: An Inter-national Perspective on Issues and Strategies)* Dublin: Higher Education Authority

Acknowledgements

I wish to acknowledge the assistance of the HEA Executive, particularly Orla Christle, Brian Dennehy, Sheena Duffy, John Hayden, Jacintha Healy and Gerry O'Sullivan, in the preparation of this chapter.

Note

1. (HEA published reports are available at: www.hea.ie/pub_rep/index.htm)

4

Government deliberations on widening recruitment to higher education: partnerships in Sweden with higher education institutions, schools and others

Kenny Jonsson

Introduction

The Swedish Government is planning to introduce a bill aimed at widening participation in higher education. It intends to lay the bill before the Swedish Riksdag (parliament) in the autumn.

Officials in the Ministry of Education are currently discussing and analysing a variety of ideas and proposals. Discussions involving the State Secretary and the Minister have been initiated but there is still a great deal to be considered. Thus the bill's actual contents are still an open issue. Most of the ideas and proposals presuppose collaboration between university institutions and schools and central and local authorities.

Recruitment to universities today is biased and socially unequal; 60 per cent of pupils in upper secondary schools whose parents have pursued post-secondary or university studies go on to higher education, compared to 15 per cent of pupils with parents with a compulsory school background only. In order to broaden recruitment to higher education it is necessary to reach out to new groups in society, groups that are under represented at universities today:

people from homes where studying is not traditional, and people with foreign backgrounds.

Officials in the ministry believe that a large number of young people from under represented groups could well go on to university if they (and their parents) are given relevant information about what it actually means to study. Encouraging this untapped talent to enter higher education is a crucial task.

Two years ago, the Government appointed a committee, chaired by the Vice-Chancellor of the University of Lund with a view to eliciting ideas and stimulus for broadening recruitment to universities and thereby increasing social and ethnic diversity in these institutions. A project group was also established in the Ministry. These two bodies produced a significant number of ideas and proposals in the form of memoranda. The Ministry also received a memorandum containing proposals and comments on recruitment and admission regulations from the National Agency of Higher Education. These documents were circulated for comments to agencies and authorities, universities and other organisations and have served as a basis for the work of drafting the new bill.

Before discussing the ideas, which are now taken into consideration in the Government Offices, a few words about the Government's policy goals on recruitment to higher education would be useful.

According to the Government's long term goal, half a given cohort should have started higher education by the age of 25. The Government has also defined other recruitment goals; these include increasing social and ethnic diversity in higher education. The latter is aimed at reducing social bias and broadening recruitment through the addition of new groups of students. Another objective is to increase the number of young people who go on to higher education.

The Ideas
Active recruitment
To give this undertaking a formal basis, a provision should be introduced into the Higher Education Act to the effect that universities and university colleges should initiate and pursue an active recruitment policy.

The Government aspires to make higher education accessible to new groups of students and to obtain a more balanced student population from a social and ethnic standpoint. The aim is to ensure that the composition of the students reflects that of the population at large in these respects. This requires a more active and broader recruitment initiative vis-à-vis young people and others from non-academic backgrounds.

By definition, a broader recruitment initiative presupposes an increase in multicultural diversity and a reduction in social bias among the student population.

Active recruitment measures by universities and university colleges
Active recruitment initiatives are vital if we are to stimulate and attract young people to higher education. Many universities and university colleges now implement a wide variety of recruitment schemes. Examples include discovery clubs for children between the ages of 7 and 8, technology contests for 15-year-olds, invitations to pupils at upper secondary schools to attend lectures and seminars and take part in student life at a nearby university, training university students to act as 'ambassadors' to upper secondary schools, where they can inform pupils about and encourage them to go on to higher education.

Other activities include information days at upper secondary schools, recreation centres and military units, meetings of school and university teachers, participation in fairs and exhibitions, caravan tours in the region, homework assistance from students at universities to pupils at upper secondary schools, laboratory experiments, Swedish language classes, support measures for those with functional disabilities, sponsor or 'adoption' initiatives, mentor programmes, etc. Some universities arrange start and introductory courses to facilitate the transition to higher studies.

Many of these activities are based on cooperation with the staff of compulsory and upper secondary schools and with municipal authorities and companies. However, it has been observed that measures applied at one university may be unknown to others. It is therefore important to highlight good ideas wherever possible and disseminate information throughout the country.

Delegation on recruitment
A delegation (commission) should be established to stimulate recruitment activities at universities and university colleges. This presupposes collaboration with schools and other bodies.

The delegation´s task would be to help influence public opinion by disseminating knowledge, experience and ideas on ways of broadening recruitment. It should also initiate as well as promote and co-ordinate development and pilot projects.

Information can be provided at regional conferences, to schools, university and university colleges meetings, to municipal authorities, in contacts with working life, enterprises, the parties in the labour market and other organisations. The commission should dispose of the necessary financial resources to stimulate recruitment measures.

Action plans for broader recruitment
Universities and university colleges should draw up local action plans aimed at enhancing social, ethnic and gender diversity at the respective place of learning. These plans should contain measurable goals.

It is considered that the National Agency for Higher Education, acting in collaboration with universities and colleges, should develop uniform and sustainable indicators designed to facilitate follow-ups of measures to broaden recruitment. Examples include the parents' educational background, social class (from highly-placed officials to unskilled workers) and foreign background.

Improved study guidance
The need for study guidance has increased. A study and vocational guidance function with well-established links to the rest of the community should be developed in schools and universities as a means of supporting and promoting recruitment to higher education.

Success in stimulating the interest of new groups of pupils is contingent on providing encouragement early in their education – among other things by instilling the notion that the desire for knowledge is a positive thing – and continually providing them with relevant information about educational and career opportunities, professions, working life and roles in life throughout their school career. Teachers, head-teachers and other staff at compulsory and upper secondary schools, as well as day care and after-school centres, can play an important role in stimulating the interest of children and young people and encouraging them to study. Study and vocational guidance provided later on in life to students at universities and university colleges also plays a part in influencing their choice of studies and course of life.

This will be facilitated through contact and the exchange of information with universities and colleges, employment offices, the business sector, etc.

Extended preparatory year

Universities currently offer students the option of a preparatory year, aimed primarily at equipping undergraduates who have completed a social science programme at upper secondary school with the necessary qualifications to pursue technical or science studies.

In principle it would be possible to arrange a preparatory year for all university programmes for which the number of qualified applicants has proved to be low. As at present, this would be targeted at applicants who lack specific qualifications for the programme in question.

College/access programmes

Universities and university colleges should be able to offer a so-called college/access programme for recruitment purposes in co-operation with local authority adult education centres, upper secondary schools, independent adult education colleges (folkhögskola) or other providers of education. The aim would be to give certain groups an opportunity to supplement their previous knowledge and to pursue certain higher education courses. The programme would consist of an upper secondary school component of 20 weeks at the most, and a maximum higher education component of 20 academic credits (equivalent to 20 weeks of full-time study).

The propensity to pursue further studies among groups with the same basic potential varies depending on the individual's circumstances. For Sweden, these potential students represent a valuable untapped source of talent which should be made the most of. Special measures to encourage their entry into higher education are essential.

Introductory courses

Universities and university colleges should organise a voluntary academic-level introductory course for students who intend to take a degree either through a full study programme or through single subject courses, and who need extra support.

The introductory course should aim to introduce students to the university environment and to support those who feel unsure of their abilities or who find the academic environment so unfamiliar that they are hesitant to pursue studies at tertiary level. The objective here should be to bridge the cultural gap between the university and upper secondary school studies.

Swedish language courses

A sound knowledge of Swedish is crucial in both higher education and working life. It is essential to have the ability to follow courses and to communicate within universities and colleges. It should be mentioned that about 20 per cent of the Swedish population is of foreign extraction, i.e. at least one parent was not born in Sweden.

Academic level Swedish language courses should be made available in various forms at universities and university colleges to students and academics with immigrant backgrounds. Swedish language courses could, for example, be offered as part of the introductory programme mentioned earlier. The availability of special language support in the form of language workshops and language labs would be a valuable asset to students whose native language is not Swedish.

Selection

To be eligible for university studies, certain requirements must be fulfilled: students must possess basic qualifications, which are identical for all higher education programmes and courses, and special qualifications if a particular course of study has additional requirements.

It has now been proposed that both basic and special qualifications be regarded as met by people who by virtue of their education in Sweden or abroad, practical experience or other attainments, are capable of profiting from basic higher education. Methods for assessing proficiency in real terms in relation to higher education should accordingly be developed.

If the number of applicants for a course is greater than the number of places available, a selection procedure should be applied. The selection should be made on the basis of upper secondary grades or the result of the national university aptitude test or other tests. Work experience could also be taken into account in certain cases.

It has also been proposed that the governing board of each institute of higher education should be given the opportunity to apply locally determined selection criteria to a maximum of ten per cent of the places on beginners' courses.

Within the framework of the specified selection criteria, the university and university college should be able to target certain courses at applicants who fulfil certain qualification requirements. It should also be possible for the university to apply this provision if there is a clear need for staff of a particular gender or with a native language other than Swedish, or if there is a need to provide training to meet the demands of a local or regional labour market.

The governing board of a university and university college shall determine what form the selection procedure should take. In order to ensure protection of students' statutory rights, the university's governing board should draw up a special policy document for the selection procedure.

A Swedish cyber university

A Swedish cyber university should be established. The cyber university would consist of a voluntary association of the universities and university colleges in Sweden that provide courses and programmes with flexible distance learning methods, all connected to a common electronically-based network.

Increased access to education is desirable for several reasons. Accessibility facilitates broader recruitment and lifelong learning. Distance learning makes it possible to reach different under represented groups and individuals across the country. Many municipal authorities have set up special learning centres with a variety of educational purposes and these can cooperate and take part in this project.

Local and regional labour market demand for a relatively broad variety of skills argues in favour of a wide range of courses at universities and university colleges. The opportunities for making this range more accessible through distance learning courses via the cyber university should assist in promoting recruitment to higher education and help create opportunities for regional growth.

Mention has not been made of what is perhaps the most important measure for recruiting students to our universities, namely financial aid for students. A new improved study support system will be introduced this summer. A fundamental principle in Swedish higher education is that all students who need assistance in financing their studies should receive study support from the central government for this purpose. This is regardless of parents' incomes. Aid will take the form of student grants and loans. To be eligible for such assistance a student must fulfill certain requirements and show acceptable scholastic achievement. But that is another story.

Conclusion

To sum up, several of the ideas I have mentioned are based on co-operation between the universities and the community at large. This reflects the interest of different sectors of society in education and skills; they are, after all, the ultimate beneficiaries of such a development. I believe this cooperation will probably increase in the future because of the advantages to all the parties concerned.

In September 2001, the Swedish Government approved a draft bill on reforms in higher education designed to introduce a more open system. The bill, entitled *The Open University*, has been submitted to the Swedish Riksdag and will be debated in December. The Government has resolved to adopt all the ideas for widening participation in higher education presented and discussed above.

5

Collaboration to address equity problems in access to higher education in Lithuania

Saulius Vengris

The heritage of the past

Fifty years of life in the Soviet Union formed a Lithuanian society which had rather small social-economic inequalities (at least, officially). Access to higher education was limited by the physical capacity of the universities, as well as by the loyalty of students and their parents to the Soviet authorities. The entrance barrier to universities were not only the exams, but also the written and verbal characteristics of the candidates as judged by the representatives of the communist party who were always present in the admission committees. Moreover, during the course of studies some students were excluded because of 'behaviour inappropriate to the soviet student[1]'. The concept of 'under represented groups' did not exist at all.

Soviet citizens got into universities if they successfully passed entrance examinations. After being admitted, they were provided with low-cost lodging and access to higher education depended only on their efforts and abilities. Studies were free; furthermore, students who showed higher achievements received stipends sufficient to cover modest life expenses. Universities often faced problems with so-called 'perpetual students', who made minimum efforts to study and whose duration of study was much longer than initially applied for.

This historical heritage was the main reason why the statements concerning higher education were included in the Constitution of Lithuania adopted in 1992. They affirm that higher education is accessible to everybody based on their abilities only. Moreover, free education is granted by the state to students who achieve highly. Those not achieving good results are not mentioned at all; no statements are made about state support for poor or otherwise challenged families.

In the relatively short time since the Constitution was passed by Parliament, society has changed significantly. Based on the official income, during the period 1991-1999, differentiation has increased four-fold and the unemployed have emerged (7.3% of the total population in 1999). The fraction of population living below the level of poverty was 15.8% in 1999 (mostly the people living in rural areas).

Despite the attempts of all the governments to carry out various social support programs, current legislation does not consider the issues of already existent under represented groups. The new Law on Higher Education enforced at the end of 2000 relates the accessibility of higher education to the abilities of a person (which is completely in line with the Constitution) but does not envision any means of social support for the people from poor families who seek higher education. Moreover, the law even supports the rich in a way, because the universities are free to accept students who are ready to pay the full price for their studies, even if they fail to pass the competition for the state-financed places in a university. Institutions of higher education are also interested in accepting as many such paying students as possible, because state financing for higher education started to decrease in 1998. Due to this fact, the fraction of Lithuanian students who pay the full price for education was 30% in 2000/2001.

The road to higher education
Until 1999, graduates of high schools had to apply for specific study programs in specific universities and the number of study programs that could be chosen was limited to two. Then they had to take entrance exams organised separately by each university. Because the

prestige of a university is at least partly determined by the number of applicants, each university tried to organise the admission procedure earlier than the others did. In the end, graduates had to take entrance exams right after the graduation exams at the high schools. Those who failed the entrance exams could not enter the universities in the same year. Even though, theoretically, it was permissible to apply for several universities, due to uncoordinated entrance exams between different universities, this was hardly possible in practice.

Thus, the only hope was successful graduation exams at the high schools (the ranking in the competition depended on those as well) and, of course, the entrance exams. Graduation exams were held separately in each high school and evaluation was given by the teachers of the same school. This provided preconditions for corruption, both in the graduation and entrance exams, because the latter were carried out by the docents of the universities. The situation was worsened by the fact that given the strictly defined number of state-financed places at the universities, the students who failed to get access to free studies faced a dilemma: whether to reject higher education or somehow raise a substantial sum of money to finance their studies. This amounted to around 100 USD/month, when the average monthly gross earnings in 1998 were around 230 USD and in agriculture only 132 USD. It was obvious that higher education was more accessible to the rich than to the gifted.

The solutions to the problems

Addressing the crucial factor of maintaining objectivity in assessing the abilities of students, an important step towards equity was the reform of graduation exams in the high schools. The reform was carried out by the National Exam Centre (NEC), founded by the co-operative efforts of the Ministry of Education and Science and EU PHARE programme HERIL (Higher Education Reform In Lithuania). The partners of the programme were the Scottish Examination Board (SQA) and RIC (National Exam Centre of Slovenia). SQA and RIC were chosen because they offered different but complementary experiences and expertise. SQA incorporates the former Scottish Examination Board and therefore builds on the experience of offering national examinations for over one hundred years in a country of approximately five million people. By way of contrast, RIC is a relatively new organisation, having run its first Matura examinations in 1995. It serves a national population of two million, comparable to that of Lithuania. Besides the expertise and management experience provided by the foreign partners, international co-operation enabled Lithuania to apply for EU PHARE funding (0.7 million €) for the infrastructure and establishment costs of NEC2.

The principle of the reform is that graduates of high schools take graduation exams in the NEC, they are evaluated by independent examiners and the exams replace entrance exams. The modest experience of three years convinced both the graduates and the universities that the abilities of people seeking higher education are assessed more objectively. Moreover, with the reduced number of entrance exams, the procedure of accessing the universities has become simpler.

The second step in enhancing the accessibility of higher education has been made by the universities themselves, by establishing the Lithuanian Association of the Institutions of Higher Education to organise common entrance to all the universities (LAMA) in 1999. The principle of this initiative is that the members of the association establish the conditions to apply for all the member universities at once. Then should a prospective student fail to access one university or one study programme, he/she is not ejected out of the higher education system, because the possibilities to enter another university (or study program) remain open. In 2001, LAMA encompasses half of the universities. It is expected that in 2002 the vast majority of the universities will join in. The successful co-operative initiative started by the universities finally attracted the attention of the Ministry of Education and Science; thus it is expected that the support of the Government will convince all the universities of the benefits of this idea.

Unfortunately, crucial issues of poverty and social exclusion have yet to be addressed. Politicians are still avoiding recognising the increasing economic differentiation in Lithuania. Moreover, investigations of social development and economic inequality are carried out by non-governmental organisations (such as UNDP), and Parliament is still hesitating over when to pass the Law on Universal Income Declaration.

As already mentioned, the new Law on Higher Education relates accessibility to higher education only to the abilities and knowledge of a person, without considering social differences. The Education Committee of the parliament elected in October 2000 has started an initiative to facilitate (at least partly) access to higher education for the representatives of poor families. It is important to note that even though there is no direct support for under represented groups envisioned in the project proposal of the Committee, accessibility to higher education would be especially facilitated for them if the project were implemented. Furthermore, the project seeks to eliminate the obvious inequality which exists when there are two sorts of students at the universities: those who do not pay for their studies at all and the others who pay the full price.

The project is based on two recommendations of the European Council (EC). One has been prepared by the European Access Network (EAN) and is entitled 'Recommendation R98(3) of the Committee of Ministers to Member States on Access to Higher Education and Explanatory Memorandum'. The second was prepared by the Higher Education and Research Committee (HERC) of the EC and entitled 'The Position of Students' (Vilnius, 7-10 June 1995). The development of the project can be regarded as the fruit of co-operation between the Lithuanian Parliament and the HERC of EC, and in particular the European Access Network. In line with the above mentioned recommendations, the project envisions:

- In state-financed institutions of higher education, all the students are equal in terms of tuition fees

- The tuition fee constitutes only a limited student contribution to the cost of higher education. It is established by the law rather than by the management of the university

- All students are supplied with state warrants for the credits to finance their studies

- First semester studies are free for all accepted students.

Although the project is not sufficient in itself, considering the wide-spread evidence of under-representation in higher education affecting people of low socio-economic status, it has already made significant progress. In December 2001 the projected amendments to the Law on Higher Education were adopted by Parliament. Furthermore, in 2002, 13 out of 15 Lithuanian institutions of HE have already agreed to participate in the common entrance procedure. This makes further co-operation with EAN especially important to build on this initial success. The role of the EAN would be the further dissemination and discussion of the equity problems relating to higher education, not only among the universities, but also pointing them out to the people, policy and decision-makers of Lithuania.

To summarise, all the steps made so far towards greater equity in accessing higher education in Lithuania were achieved in close co-operation between universities, national authorities, and foreign organisations The design and implementation of some of them would not have been possible without the participation of foreign partners. Greater participation of the national authorities in international co-operation concerning widening participation in higher education would certainly assist in managing these issues more efficiently.

Notes

1.   Examples of such behaviour could be the singing of Lithuanian national songs in public, participation in ethnic-cultural unions, loss of the Komsomol membership card etc.

     For some time, admission to the universities was forbidden to people whose family members were convicted of anti-soviet activities.

2   For details see: George Bethell and Algirdas Zabulionis. *Examination Reform in Lithuania. Background, Strategies and Achievements.* (2000) NEC.

6

Pathways to College Network: Collaborating nationally to improve college access and success for under represented students in the US

Ann Coles and David Malcolm Roth

Introduction

According to the US Department of Education, National Centre for Education Statistics (www.nces.ed.gov), persistent inequities exist in the access of students in the United States to higher education by income and race. The data is dramatic in terms of students' high school graduation rates, readiness for college level work, and college completion rates. While 75% of all high school students in the US enroll in college immediately upon graduation from high school, only 47% of low-income students do. Over 30% of students enrolling in college need to take remedial, or high school level, courses at the beginning of their college experience because they are not college ready. Over 50% of students who enroll in college never earn degrees; a third of these students never reach the second year of college. Only 18% of African Americans and 19% of Hispanic high school graduates earn bachelor's degrees by their late twenties, compared with 35% of white students. Such statistics underscore the urgency of preparing much larger numbers of under represented students in the US, including low-income, African-American and Latino students, for entry into and success in college. Aggressively tackling this problem is especially critical for the increasingly knowledge-based American economy, which requires much higher literacy levels than were needed in a manufacturing-based economy in order to earn a living wage.

Enabling many more under represented students in the US to enroll and succeed in college will require far more substantial and co-ordinated efforts at all levels of American education than currently exists. While the need for far more coordinated efforts to improve college access seems obvious, the practice is in fact revolutionary. The US education system is highly fragmented and, historically, there has been a great emphasis on local control. The federal govern-ment has never had a strong role in education, and individual states have emerged only in the last decade as drivers of school reform. Each education level in the American K-16 system has developed independently, with little if any alignment from one level to the next.

Michael Usdan, former executive director of the Institute for Educa-tion Leadership, describes higher education and secondary educa-tion as living in 'splendid isolation' with different cultures, different publications and different networks. School superintendents and college presidents, and their counterparts on the state level, rarely speak to one another, let alone work together. Such a fragmented system means that there is little continuity of expectation for the per-formance of students from one level to another and that many students, except those in highly affluent communities, are inade-quately prepared for the next level of their education. For example, students can gain top grades in high school courses required for college admission to American universities, and perform poorly once they get to college because the high school courses they took lacked rigor.

To successfully prepare students for college, there must be collaboration among public schools, higher education institutions, and the thousands of college outreach programs spawned to compensate for deficiencies in the schools attended by most under represented/low-income students in the US. Practitioners, policy-makers, community leaders and parents of under represented students must collaborate in new ways. Collaboration must be based on a shared belief in the importance of ensuring that *all* students are able to enroll and succeed in college, and a common understanding of the preparation students need in order to move successfully from one level of education to the next, along the pathway to a college degree. Practitioners and policy-makers must work together to make needed changes: to adopt policies and practices proven to improve students' readiness for college studies, while also enabling them to successfully overcome social and financial barriers to college enrollment.

Pathways to College overview

The Pathways to College Network is an innovative approach to promoting college access and success for under represented students, involving unprecedented, large-scale collaboration among major educational institutions and organisations, national foundations and federal funders. With funding commitments expected to total over $2.5 million over its first three years, the Pathways partners are pursuing four major objectives. They are identifying and prioritising research-based effective policies and practices that impact on student achievement and college access and success, determining barriers to college access that are not being addressed through specific interventions, and identifying gaps in research on effective policies and practices. They will disseminate what works to high-poverty schools, college outreach programs and policymakers, and stimulate efforts to replicate effective policies and practices on the local, state and national levels. They will spotlight and address what is missing, including bringing together organisations to study the gaps in research, developing and field-testing promising interventions, and developing policies and practices to address these issues over the long term. Finally, the Pathways partners will encourage collaboration and system building across all levels of education, K-16 to eliminate policy and programmatic barriers to college going and make readiness for college success a fundamental goal of public education in the US.

Origins of Pathways to College Network

Pathways resulted from a group of foundation, federal and educational leaders seeking to strengthen and focus the effectiveness of efforts across the US to improve college access and success. Foundations in the US frequently provide funding to address critical social problems that might be funded by the government in European countries. The Pathways founders believed that the effectiveness of existing college access initiatives could be greatly multiplied by deliberately building policy and practice using research-backed evidence of effectiveness, as well as by linking college outreach programs and school reform to deepen, extend and sustain their successes. It also was clear that traditional boundaries had to be transcended, and that local, state and regional policy making bodies and researchers had to work together to focus resources on student impact and achievement.

Through a 'request for proposal' process, the group identified an alliance of nationally recognised organisations interested in working collaboratively to support the combined efforts of school reform and college outreach programs in order to increase opportunities for under represented students to enter and succeed in college. The alliance members, who form the Pathways to College Network, represent rich diversity in terms of experience, expertise and the constituencies they reach. Previously each had been working independently to develop policies and practices to improve college opportunities for under represented students. By pooling their expertise and resources, alliance members believed they could have substantially greater impact collectively on college access issues and could add value to their individual efforts. The Education Resources Institute (TERI) in Boston, Massachusetts, manages the project in collaboration with Occidental College in Los Angeles, California.

The mission of Pathways is to focus research-based knowledge and resources on improving college preparation, access and success for under represented populations – low-income students who are the first generation in their families to attend college, and students of colour, including African-American, American Indian, Asian-American and Latino students. Through their collaborative efforts, the Pathways partners expect to change perceptions, practices and policies about academic preparation and college opportunity; eliminate policy and programmatic barriers to college going; and make readiness for college success a fundamental goal of public education in the US

The work of Pathways is clustered into five program components. One component is researching and promoting effective policies that address college access, preparation, and success among under represented students. This work focuses on state policies and practices that affect student achievement and college access and success, including financial aid. Policies and practices are being identified, disseminated, continuously monitored, and used as a springboard for discussion in multiple ways. Case studies are being conducted of five states working toward a K-16 model, and the findings will be disseminated to assist other states interested in this approach. Pathways partners also will convene regional policy forums and state roundtables for the purpose of developing and assessing approaches to expanding and improving college access in their respective states.

A second component focuses on building the capacity of schools to better prepare under represented students for higher education. This work involves disseminating relevant research and information to secondary school leaders and practitioners. In addition, partners are building linkages between secondary schools and college access programs to encourage collaboration and alignment between college access programs and schools. Promising interventions will be field-tested, and funding sources will be identified and cultivated to take promising practices to scale.

Compiling and disseminating research on effective college outreach programs and practices used by programs for preparing students for college success is the focus of the third program component. Work in this area focuses on reviewing the literature and compiling a data-base of research on effective intervention and outreach programmes and practices that promote college access and success for under-served students. Linkages between secondary schools and college access programmes will be developed to encourage collaboration and alignment between college access programmes and schools.

The fourth component of the Pathways work emphasises the involvement of parents and families and engagement of community leaders in advocacy efforts to improve and support opportunities for under represented youth. Work in this area is based on the premise that successful pathways to college are the shared responsibility of students, parents, families, schools, and community and business leaders. Activities include developing a long term action plan that links student achievement to family/community engagement. Using existing research and data, a centre will be created to assist families and communities with engaging school and higher education leaders in work to improve students' likelihood of enrolling and succeeding in college.

Creating and coordinating a national social marketing campaign to promote early awareness of college opportunities constitutes the fifth component. This component focuses on creating a sustained multifaceted campaign that promotes college access as an important option for under represented students by changing the attitudes and actions of students and their families. It also is working toward the creation of broad-based support for making the promise of higher education a reality for all students through a series of targeted messages that advocate college for all students. Media audits and focus groups have been conducted to obtain baseline data and establish campaign benchmarks. Communications experts are identifying the most effective methods, strategies, and tactics for bringing messages to the targeted audiences in powerful ways.

A lead partner is taking responsibility for each programme component, working with other partners to compile and disseminate research based effective polices and practices, identify gaps in research and unaddressed barriers, and stimulate the use of effective polices and practices at local, state and national levels. A panel of nationally recognised research scholars is advising the lead partners in their research compilation and dissemination activities, and is helping to identify those areas in need of greater research. The scholars have experience and knowledge in the areas of pre-college access, school reform and system change, youth development, financial aid, diverse populations, college retention and persistence, and school-to-work. They are working with the lead partners and staff to select and vet the research studies and findings to be disseminated by the Network. The scholars' panel also is assisting with the development of a research agenda that accounts for gaps in knowledge and unaddressed barriers to college access and success.

Research findings and outcomes are disseminated through the Pathways to College Network clearinghouse, staffed by a user services specialist who assists practitioners, community leaders and policymakers with locating and incorporating relevant policies and practices into their work. In addition to the Clearinghouse, Network partners disseminate research findings through conferences, publications and other activities targeting their members.

Pathways' theory of action
The Pathways' theory of action is deeply rooted in collaboration. By bringing together leading organisations with broad-based experience and expertise in different areas related to college access, and by providing them with a structure through which to pool their expertise and resources, these organisations will be able to identify the most effective research based policies and practices and determine gaps in research across the K-16 education continuum. Collectively they will have the capacity to disseminate these findings to a broad array of practitioners, community leaders and policymakers working at local and state levels, which in turn will utilise these findings, to improve students' preparation for college and remove barriers to college enrollment. The outcome of these collaborative efforts will be much larger numbers of under represented students attending and succeeding in college.

Ensuring the effectiveness of the collaborative model
A primary challenge facing the Pathways partners is ensuring that such a large-scale collaboration is able to effect the changes needed to expand college access for under represented students, especially given the fact that the Network is several steps removed from its target population. To address this issue, Pathways has engaged an external evaluation team from Social Policy Research Associates in Oakland, California, to monitor the work of the partners closely, providing continuous feedback and assisting the partners with necessary adjustments in their action theory in order to ensure the success of the Network's collaborative efforts. The evaluation team is working with the partners to formulate and build consensus around a strategic framework detailing how all the parts work together as a whole and within what period.

Based on their experience with other large-scale collaborations, the evaluators also are working with the partners to ensure that Pathways incorporates elements that are key to successful collaboration. Social Policy Research Associates has identified the following elements as critical to the success of Pathways:

Flexibility to respond to contextual opportunities and the need to shift goals mid-stream.

Inter-partner communication to discuss progress and changes for the Network as a whole.

Deliberate *involvement of practitioners* who bear primary responsibility for implementing needed changes.

Active involvement of local affiliates of national partners that will serve as main engine for building nationwide capacity and realising sustainable local effort.

Development of a *learning community among collaborators* to provide feedback to help collaborative modifies priorities and activities as needed.

Early development of the Pathways Network

Launched in January, 2001, the first year of the Pathways Network involved putting into place the organisational and management structures required to accomplish the Network's objectives and implementing activities in the various program components. Six of the Network's partners assumed leadership for planning and carrying out activities to achieve the Pathways objectives. Each 'lead' partner organisation designated a nationally recognised senior staff member with extensive experience to oversee the work in that area. The lead partners also committed significance in-kind contributions to Pathways, including staff, overhead costs, and support services. A full-time project manager was hired to oversee day-to-day operations and coordinate work with the lead partners and members of the research scholars' panel. Occidental College worked closely with the funders and lead partners in the areas of strategic planning, public relations, fund-raising and evaluation.

An executive committee consisting of the lead partners, Occidental College staff and representatives of several funders provided oversight and general direction for Networks activities. Working with the Network director and manager, committee members defined the roles and responsibilities of partners, approved work plans and resource allocations for each programme component, selected the research scholars panel, and approved operational policies and procedures. Individual members also worked on the development of a quality assurance plan to ensure that Pathways documents met high standards and a government relations plan that focused on engaging federal officials in the work of the Network. In addition, the executive committee convened two meetings of all partners and funders for the purpose of securing their input and advice and developing plans for their engagement in the Network's dissemination activities. First-year work in each program area focused on gathering research data and evidence of effective policies, models, and practices that facilitate the college preparation, access, and success of under represented students. Research findings are being catalogued, synthesised and disseminated in ways that will inform the work of practitioner and policy makers at national, state, and local levels.

First year formative evaluation findings

SPR, the evaluation group employed to provide assistance to the Network, participated in all executive committee and partner meetings, interviewed the key stakeholders and at the end of the first year of Pathways prepared a written report of formative evaluation findings. Their report identified challenges and recommendations, related goals, outcome and impact, and organisational structure; communications and collaboration. In relation to goals and outcomes, the evaluation team found significant differences among stakeholders' interpretation of the Network's goals, particularly with regard to the impact that the Network can reasonably have within its first three years, which is the commitment made by funders. The majority of partners saw Pathways as institution-centered in terms of impact, that is, building capacity to change policies and practices related to college access. A few, however, defined impact as student-centered, that is the effect that the Network will have on students directly. People also differed on whether the impact of Pathways should be causal or relational. A number of partners emphasised that it would be difficult to determine that the Network had actually caused a change, because of the many intervening variables affecting what policy-makers and practitioners do. Rather they viewed impact in relational terms, that is, serving as a catalyst for people rethinking about the college potential of under represented students and what must happen for students to realise their potential.

A related issue identified by the evaluators was the underrepresentation of students, school and outreach practitioners on advisory groups or formalised feedback loops. Currently, the only way that practitioners have input into Pathways work is through the national organisations of which they are members and which are Pathways partners. As for student input, while it is their educational experience that Pathways ultimately expects to make an impact, the Network has no mechanisms, nor provided any opportunity for students to offer their perspectives on problems they encounter in preparing and planning for college. To address this issue, the evaluators recommended that Pathways form mini-advisory panels of practitioners, youth, parents and community leaders in order to ensure that the interests of these groups are represented.

The evaluators also stressed the need for channels to be established in order to ensure a strong link between research and action. Currently the mechanisms through which research findings are to be disseminated include a Web site, short papers and policy briefs, regional forums, conference presentations, professional development workshops and journal articles. The problem with such mechanisms is that they provide no assurance that practitioners, policy makers and community leaders will utilise applicable research in their work. Specific plans need to be developed, creating a process to ensure that research gets applied in order to produce needed changes. The evaluators noted that the Network's broad-based partners give it a competitive advantage over other collaboratives and proposed that Pathways use this advantage to distinguish its research and products from those of others.

Issues regarding the Network's organisational structure, communications and collaboration largely involved managing a collaborative of eighteen partner organisations covering the entire US, including the Pacific territories. Facilitating communication, coordinating meeting logistics and making decisions are challenges for such a large network. Particularly because of the distances among partners, the Network relies extensively on email communications. While email was effective for information sharing, it did not work well as a means for discussing important substantive issues or promoting collaborative work across the program components. As a result of these communications difficulties, some duplication of activities occurred that could otherwise have been avoided. Inefficient decision-making was another problem related to the organisational structure that the evaluators identified. Originally, the Network's executive committee chose to use a consensus approach to decision-making in order to foster a sense of ownership for the collaborative among the partners. Decisions about policies, resource allocation and other key issues were made by the executive committee as a whole. Such a model proved cumbersome at times, however, and so the evaluators recommended moving toward a governance model in which an individual such as the director of Pathways or small group is empowered to make decisions for the larger group.

Social context of Pathways

Although the Pathways to College Network represents a unique and historic partnership of organisations with the focused goal of increasing the numbers of American students who successfully enter and complete college, it was neither conceived to be nor is it perceived by any Network partner as an educational panacea. The issues and challenges faced by urban communities in the US and their schools are pernicious and perennial, and have stymied generations of those who consider themselves education reformers. Simply stated, the economies, educational systems and infrastructures of America's inner cities are paying the price for a society that does not judge all its members to be worthy of equal investment. The public primary and secondary schools that are located in US cities are regularly judged the worst performing in the nation – a fact that is worth careful analysis given the equalising power of education in the American social system. Not surprisingly, those communities whose public schools are failing are often also bereft of the human and social capital needed for effective engagement with the educational, political and economic processes that surround them. Residents of inner cities are disempowered and disaffected — conditions that manifest in myriad social dysfunction.

The Pathways partners are keenly aware of the social context of their work, and do not expect that their labours will mitigate decades of the social and political marginalisation of so many Americans. However, it is their hope to bring, for the first time, the combined resources of the nation's most effective and influential educational organisations to bear upon its most under-served communities and their schools. If Pathways is successful in this endeavour, the partners' hope is that that they will have begun the creation of an educational system that places equal value on every child, and invests equally in each of them.

Long term impact of collaboration

If the Pathways to College partners successfully achieve their short term goals and are able to engage educators and leaders on the local and state levels in changing policies and practices, the long term impact of this collaboration will be a substantial increase in under represented students not only going to college, but also successfully completing college degrees. The vision for change established by the Pathways partners is ambitious. By 2011, if the partners are successful in engaging educators and leaders at state and local levels to bring about needed changes, Pathways will have served as a catalyst for education from pre-school to college in the US beginning to function as an integrated system and for all school systems making the preparation of all students for college success an explicitly stated goal. All students entering high school will have completed Algebra I and will be reading at the 9th grade level so that they are academically ready to succeed in college preparatory courses. In addition, all families will have the information they need to actively encourage their children to pursue higher education, and lack of family financial resources will not be a barrier to anyone interested in going to college. Finally, because of these collaborative efforts, the college attendance and completion rates for under represented students will match the national rates for all students in the US.

The collaborative efforts of the Pathways partners and funders provide tremendous potential for improving college entry and success for under represented students. Many individuals and organisations with outstanding records as leaders and change agents are involved. Because of the high profile of its partners and their collective experience, Pathways has the capacity to focus public will in the US on college access issues in far more substantial ways than organisations working individually would be able to. Pathways can be a catalyst for change in many different directions and on many different levels, and can transform the possibility of college into a reality for large numbers of under represented students throughout the US.

Additional References

Henderson, J. (2001), *Proposal to Evaluate the Pathways to College Network*, Oakland, California, Social Policy Research Associates, Inc.

Kleinman, N. S. (2001), *Building a Highway to Higher Ed: How Collaborative Efforts are Changing Education in America*, New York, NY, Centre for an Urban Future

7

Collaboration: the past and the future for higher education in South Africa

Prakash Naidoo

1. Introduction

Thirty-six public institutions landscape the South African Higher Education System. These fifteen technikons and 21 universities are the product of apartheid that was structured along racial and ethnic lines. A host of state teacher training colleges, nursing colleges and technical colleges were also engineered on a racial and ethnic basis by the apartheid government. White universities and technikons were highly advantaged in the provision of infrastructure and funding whilst black institutions lived on the frivolous handouts of the apartheid-designed system. This has been revealed by institutional inequities reflected in historically white institutions (HWIs) and historically black institutions (HBIs). Academic development in the past was dictated by economic and political priorities of the apartheid government's separate development programme.

Democracy crowned in 1994 meant the hope of change. Change in Higher Education implied a process rather than an event that could make things different overnight. An agenda of transformation was adopted through the *Higher Education Act of 1997* and the *White Paper 3 of 1997, A Programme for the Transformation of Higher Education.*

The National Commission on Higher Education of 1995 set in motion specific policy goals and initiatives for the higher education system. These goals and initiatives have in the past five years been discussed and debated with a range of stakeholders. *The National Plan for Higher Education in South Africa* (NPHE) released in February 2001 is a result of these discussions and debates.

The NPHE sets out strategies for achieving the following:

• Producing the graduates needed for social and economic developments in South Africa

• Achieving equity in the South African Higher Education System

• Achieving diversity in the South African Higher Education System

• Sustaining and promoting research

• Restructuring the institutional landscape of the higher education system

2. Higher education collaboration in South Africa

In the apartheid period collaboration was unthinkable. Since institutions were developed on racial and ethnic lines, collaboration was unnecessary. Even English-speaking and Afrikaans-speaking white institutions existing next door to each other operated differently from each other.

The *White Paper 3 of 1997* focused on the 'importance of institutional collaboration and partnerships as a means of achieving a range of social, educational/academic, economic and political goals.'

The higher education system failed to break away from the apartheid-created institutions or reduce programme overlap and duplication, although this would have saved institutions and the state millions of rands and, more importantly, management and governance in higher education institutions were not totally improved.

Mergers in South Africa have not been common. An enforced merger of Medunsa and Onderstepoort Veterinary Faculties has met with great resistance and has created problems, which are still being resolved. The mergers of a number of teaching colleges has been enforced more through the drop in demand for teachers than the need to address past inequalities.

In technikons and universities the only collaboration that seems to have been initiated since 1997 has been the introduction of shared electronic library systems and expensive research equipment. This may have not happened if sponsors had not made it a condition of their contribution.

3. The national plan for higher education with respect to collaboration

3.1 Programme collaboration

Programme and infrastructural collaboration will lead to efficiencies for institutions within a region. The apartheid shape of higher education has been such that some institutions are within close proximity of each other and can share resources to their mutual benefit.

The Ministry of Education is hopeful that institutions will achieve this voluntarily and the minister could place embargos on institutions failing to move towards such cooperation.

One extensive development of the previous higher education system has been the establishment of satellite campuses of institutions in areas which have been seen as having growth potential. This has resulted in a number of institutions setting up satellites in the same area of demand. Satellites have also been established by institutions on the doorstep of existing institutions.

3.2 Infrastructural collaboration

The Ministry of Education encourages joint sharing of resource-based course material, library services and expensive equipment.

3.3 Provision of Higher Education in areas that do not have Higher Education Institutions.

The Province of Mpumalanga and the Province of Northern Cape do not have higher education institutions. A host of established institutions have created satellite campuses in these areas. The Ministry will establish a National Institute for Higher Education to oversee the provision of higher education in these areas.

4. The plan to reduce the number of Higher Education Institutions in South Africa

The ministry agrees with the Council on Higher Education in South Africa that the 'sustainability and transformation of the higher education system requires a reduction in the number of institutions' (NPHE, 2001:77).

In order to ensure that this reduction takes place, the minister has decided that some institutions will be merged.

Although the decision that institutions will be merged will not be reversed, the ministry has embarked on an investigation *into* how the number of institutions can be reduced and the form that the restructured institutions should take.

This investigation will ensure that it would promote the goals proposed by the Council on Higher Education (2000, 58-59). These goals include:

• Social and educational goals for the region and nation

• Access and Equity goals

• Quality and efficiency goals

• Institutional sustainability and viability goals

• Institutional identity and cultural goals in terms of overcoming the legacy of apartheid

A National Working Group has been appointed by the minister to carry out its investigation and submit its recommendations to the minister by December 2001.

4.1 Proposed Institutional Mergers
• **Natal Technikon and ML Sultan Technikon**

These two institutions arose as the result of the separate development of the country. They exist next to each other and actually share a common boundary. The courses offered at the institutions are virtually the same.

A feasibility study has been done and different models have been proposed.

I will discuss this as a case study later in this chapter.

- **The Qwa-Qwa branch of the University of the North as part of the University of the Free State**

As part of the separate development of the country the University of the North established a branch for black students, some 500 kilometres away from its central campus. This branch lies in the heart of the Free State where the University of the Free State, formerly catering for white Afrikaans-speaking students, exists. In 1998 the previous minister and the two institutions agreed that this branch in Qwa-Qwa would be incorporated within the University of the Free State. This has not materialised as yet. The current minister will re-initiate this process.

- **Vista, University of South Africa and Technikon South Africa**

Vista also arose out of the need to provide access for blacks to higher education since 1981. The institution has seven satellite campuses in the three large provinces of Gauteng, Free State, and the Eastern Cape. Approximately 32% of its headcount enrolment is for teaching programs. With there being a decline in the demand for teacher education programs this institution may not be viable as an independent institution.

Whilst the ministry recognises the role Vista can play in developing teacher education, the minister is positive that Vista can be un-bundled to be included as part of a single coordinated distance education system.

The expected advantages of a single distance education institution are:

- A well strategised distance education plan for the country

- The development of a national network of innovation centres which would enhance quality higher education

- The development of a national network of learning centres enhancing access and the coordination of learner support systems

- A contribution to human resource development within the SADC region

- Benefits of economies of scale

The minister has established a Working Group to investigate and provide recommendations by looking at international trends and at changes in information and communication technology.

5. Proposed strategies of the minister of education for collaboration

5.1 Programme and infrastructural co-operation

From 2003/4 the ministry will fund student places in small and costly programmes based on a regional framework for the rationalisation of such programmes. This framework can be a joint offering by institutions or an offering by an institution within the region.

- In specialised postgraduate programmes the ministry will not fund places for new programmes that are already offered by institutions in the region. The ministry will provide funding if these programmes are on the basis of a 'common regional teaching platform'.

- In the underdeveloped higher education areas of Mpumalanga and Northern Cape, and where already established institutions have created satellites, the minister will establish a Working Group, which will 'develop a framework and implementation plan' so that a National Institute for Higher Education can be established.

- The ministry will 'leverage' donor funds for the funding of regional infrastructural projects.

- Student places at satellite campuses in 2002/3 must be part of the institution's approved plan. The ministry will look closely at the needs in the area, the niche areas and the opportunities that can be unlocked for collaboration with other institutions in the area.

- There will be no government funds for capital development at satellite campuses.

- To ensure collaboration, higher education institutions will submit all new programmes for regional clearance to prevent any overlap and duplication within the region.

5.2 Strategies to facilitate mergers and new institutional and organisational forms

- The minister will establish a Working Group to investigate and advise on the mergers or restructuring of higher education institutions within regions. The Working Group will also take into account regional and national needs before arriving at their recommendations. This has to be completed by December 2001.

- The Working Group dealing with Vista, UNISA and TSA has been discussed. The plan is to be implemented by June 2002.

- The process with University of the Free State and University of the North Qwa-Qwa Campus will be re-initiated and completed by December 2001.

- The councils of ML Sultan Technikon and Natal Technikon have been requested to complete the plans for the merger of these institutions by December 2001.

6. The case of the merger between ML Sultan Technikon and Natal Technikon

These two institutions primarily offer the same type of programmes. Like all other technikons there is only a binary divide that currently separates these institutions from universities. As technikons strive to have their names changed to universities of technology, these two institutions have had the vision since 1998 to forge ahead with merger talks. The councils of both institutions have agreed to a vision of a 'single institution governed by a single Council'.

6.1 The merger vision of the institutions

The vision statements of the institutions are:

Technikon Natal:
'To be the leading technological education institution in Africa'.

ML Sultan Technikon:
'Will be a world class higher education institution of technology for entrepreneurial leadership'.

The above missions represent a considerable overlap in the ambition to achieve technological leadership in Africa. The merged institution will develop a single vision when the merger process is finalised.

6.2 Merger systems – the options
The following four strategic options were identified.

Co-operation and alliances – institutions undertake alliances and co-operate at different levels.

Shared services – when administration and support services are shared.

Federation – where merged governance takes over the governing of the two institutions.

Full merger – full amalgamation takes places in steps.The merger talks are in support of a full merger and the implementation of a six-step transition process illustrated opposite.

The detailed plan has been presented to a joint council meeting at which it was agreed that steps one and two should be implemented from 2002.

Concluding remarks
It has been stressed that the development of tertiary institutions that were predicated on the apartheid vision needs to be changed. The Association of South African Historically Disadvantaged Institutions (ASADHI) is strong in their view that much has to be re-considered by the state before these proposals are put into action. Vista University is currently in discussions with the minister to state their case against the minister's directive that they should be merged with UNISA and TSA. ASADHI further argues that the state needs to understand that some HDIs play an important role in higher education, despite their disadvantaged past. HDIs can 'provide life chances and mobility aspirations to large number of first generation (especially black, female, older and rurally situated) higher educa-tion students by offering high quality, relevant education and train-ing' (*The Star*, 2001:13)

Federation - where merged governance takes over the governing of the two institutions.
Full merger - full amalgamation takes places in steps.The merger talks are in support of a full merger and the implementation of a six-step transition process illustrated as follows:

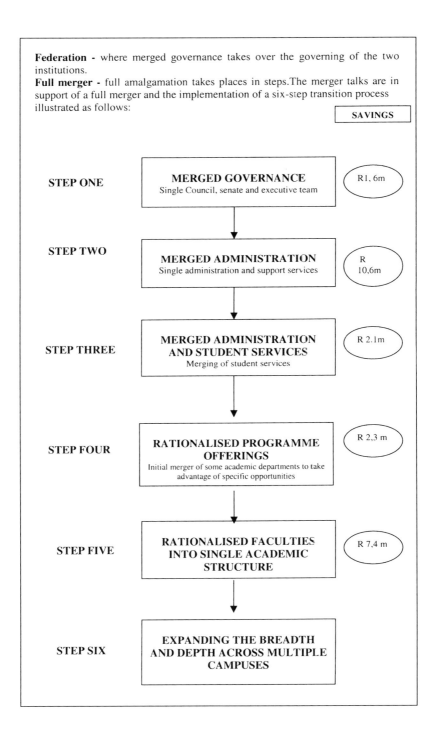

SAVINGS

STEP ONE

MERGED GOVERNANCE
Single Council, senate and executive team

R1, 6m

STEP TWO

MERGED ADMINISTRATION
Single administration and support services

R 10,6m

STEP THREE

MERGED ADMINISTRATION
AND STUDENT SERVICES
Merging of student services

R 2.1m

STEP FOUR

RATIONALISED PROGRAMME
OFFERINGS
Initial merger of some academic departments to take advantage of specific opportunities

R 2,3 m

STEP FIVE

RATIONALISED FACULTIES
INTO SINGLE ACADEMIC
STRUCTURE

R 7,4 m

STEP SIX

EXPANDING THE BREADTH
AND DEPTH ACROSS MULTIPLE
CAMPUSES

The ministry's strong decision with regard to mergers and collaboration has considerable merits when one considers the substantial savings that will flow from the economies of scale of relevant mergers and collaboration. A total initial saving of approximately R24 million in the proposed merger between two small technikons (ML Sultan and Natal) predicts the magnitude of savings if other institutions are merged or collaborate on different levels.

The positive side of the ministry's decision to direct mergers and collaborative measures is that the ministry does not intend to close programmes offered at institutions. It is envisaged that programmes will be 'centred' at particular institutions within geographical sites. It is also encouraging to note that the government is willing to facilitate merger proposals at a cost to the state.

References

Association of South African Historically Disadvantaged Institutions. 2001. Huge disparities mean massive funding vital. *The Star:* 13, February 28

Price Waterhouse Coopers. 2000. *ML Sultan Technikon and Technikon Natal, Phase II, Detailed Merger Investigation.* November-December 2000.

South Africa, Department of Education. 2001. *National Plan for Higher Education in South Africa.* February 2001. Pretoria: Government Printer.

South Africa. Department of Education. 1997. *Education White Paper 3: A Programme for the Transformation of Higher Education.* General Notice 1196 of 1997. Pretoria.

Part 2
Case Studies

8

Six years on: REACHOut® degree route – widening participation by collaboration with the community

Martin Carey, Fiona Chambers, Margaret Mairah and Lyn Carey

Can collaboration widen participation? Examining the evidence

1. Introduction

This chapter provides an exploration of REACHOut®, a successful case study of widening participation and access, that has utilised the family as a framework for learning. Before outlining this model it is important to put it into a theoretical framework. This requires an exploration of definitions of widening participation, partnership and family as a framework for learning.

1.1 Widening participation

In relation to higher education, the recurring words, ion the lips of the British Government are those related to widening participation. It could be argued that the Government's commitment to widening access has been placed within a contradictory policy framework, with the introduction of student fees and student loans on the one hand and, on the other, financial inducements for higher education to adopt coherent and effective widening participation strategies. While it is true to say that the mechanics of the implementation of student fees and loans do not necessarily prohibit participation by traditionally under represented groups, the perception by many is that study in higher education comes with a major personal financial cost. In addition such a cost is likely to remain a debt for the individual for a number of working years. Nevertheless the government has prioritised widening participation and provided significant financial inducements for higher education to adopt meaningful strategies for widening participation and access.

Some still define widening participation in terms of an open door model, which focuses on admission and recruitment policies. You open the door so far and you attract just enough of the 'self-reliant' and 'able' students who would have not achieved entry under more traditional forms of selection. Such a model is relatively passive and likely to achieve a creaming off of the Government's participation target groups. Of course for many institutions this may well be the intended consequence of their own strategy. However for many, the notions of 'self-reliant' and 'able' cannot be detached from the socio-economic and domestic circumstances that individuals operate in. The introduction of designed student support systems based upon students' needs, preparatory and continued key skills elements into the curriculum and targeted marketing of non-traditional students are all key indicators of awareness that barriers transcend beyond admission procedures. An achievement of the Government's 50% participation rate is going to require a far more proactive approach beyond this if it is to seriously engage those target groups who face significant barriers. The task is made no easier either by the poor progression rate of seventeen-year-olds; the UK is fourth from the bottom in the world industrial league table. The massive under performance as a nation in literacy and numeracy all mean that progression and key skills are additional contributors to those of socio-economic and domestic reasons for non-participation, and of course all are likely to be interrelated. An effective pro-active strategy of participation needs to ensure that engagement starts from where the target groups are, both culturally and physically. This means addressing issues of progression, student support, teaching and learning environments and curriculum as well as admissions and marketing. Many of these issues cannot be tackled by individual institutions alone and may well require partnership working.

1.2 Partnership

There are partnerships of convenience, partnerships of compliance and partnerships based around shared vision and mutual benefit. However as many will testify most partnerships come with some pain as well as some joy. All require working at and all require management. There are few if any that simply evolve. The increasing funding requirement, particularly in competitive bidding areas, to secure a list of required partners has fuelled the number of partnerships of compliance. In theory each brings its own contribution, each brings its own area of specialism and delivery and collectively the partnership provides added value and new opportunities. In practice this is often the case but they also can bring different institutional focuses and agendas, very different organisational work structures and cultures and not least very different personalities. Nevertheless all these partnership factors can work if they are managed well. Of course the best kinds of partnerships are likely to be those that have a shared vision, mutual benefit, clearly defined roles, transparent financial and operational arrangements and trust.

REACHOut® has all these qualities and has been a special partnership between Liverpool Hope, Liverpool City Council's Parent School Partnership, BT, Liverpool Pathway Areas, Community Groups and Parents. All these partnership elements need constant managing and working on and can never be taken for granted at any given time. A change in key personnel can impact on the nature of the partnership. However partnership does remain a dynamic framework for change and if managed well will resolve all the difficulties. Together through the pain and joy the REACHOut® partnership has changed the lives of thousands of students who otherwise would never have engaged with higher education.

1.3 Family as a Framework for Learning

The REACHOut® model is founded on the importance of family as a dominant force for educational attainment and achievement. It would be difficult to dispute that family is one of the key social agencies and one of the dominant forces in most people's lives. The correlation between parent and child educational experience is well documented and patterns of intergenerational participation in higher education are frighteningly recurrent for those who never had a parent who went to university. Patterns of participation are also expressed in social class and ethnicity terms with social class IV and V and African-Caribbean and Bangladeshi young males still topping non-participation tables. Such patterns are themselves manifestations of family participation rates. It is not difficult to predict that a parent from social class IV and V who has had no experience of higher education is likely to have children who will not progress educationally beyond their 17th birthday, and in many cases not formally beyond their 11th. This correlation between achievement rates and social class, ethnicity and family can lead to a deficit model of working class and Black, Asian and other minority group family models. A 'common sense' assumption would be that such families have inherent features, such as low aspirations, low self-esteem, a lack of delayed gratification, which all contribute towards low achievement. However the REACHOut® model would seem to refute this and suggest it is the level of involvement of the parents themselves within formal education which is a key factor of success. REACHOut® has shown that where a parent becomes positively engaged this is likely to have a beneficial impact on the child's perception of education (Mufti, 2000).

The utilisation of family as a framework for learning can be a key vehicle for change and raising aspirations for achievement whatever the social class or ethnic background. This utilisation of the family can be undertaken through the curriculum, designed modes of delivery, through the participation of parents as positive role models and of course through the specific design of student support systems to meet the socio-domestic needs of parents with young children e.g. child care. REACHOut® has worked with all these and this chapter now outlines the details of the specific elements of provision.

1.4 Widening access and the REACHOut® model

Liverpool Hope has committed itself to a meaningful widening of access. Over the last ten years it has increased its intake of mature students to 33.3% of the student population. It has successfully established its own access course to teacher training degrees targeted at Black and other minority students. It has actively engaged in a number of collaborative initiatives aimed at lower socio-economic groups, to increase their participation in higher education and provide quality educational provision leading to employment.

The last fifteen years generally have seen many improvements in the widening of access to higher education to a range of non-traditional students. These achievements have mainly been due to the development of access courses that adopted a more student centred approach and placed greater emphasis upon competence-based learning than that previously incorporated in the traditional 'A' level route. These access courses also were often at the sharp end of new developments in teaching and learning methods. The utilisation of credit as a currency of assessment in particular provided a framework for valuing a wider range of learning outcomes than those previously recognised in traditional forms of assessment.

The introduction of local Open College Networks, such as Merseyside Open College Network, and the National Open College Network further provided the institutional framework for the local and national recognition and development of credit at pre-degree level. Many higher education institutions in turn responded to these developments by adopting more flexible and sympathetic forms of admissions processes for non-traditional students that were also supported by changing government policy and philosophy to widening access.

However, regardless of all that success some disadvantaged groups still remain vastly under represented, particularly those from social class V. Educational attainment levels at pre-degree are particularly low in Merseyside, 15% of school leavers have no educational qualifications compared with a national figure of 8%. The national figure for full-time education is 49%, while only 37% of 17 year olds in Liverpool go on to full-time education in either the FE or HE sectors (Merseyside, 2000).

A group extremely vulnerable to the institutional barriers of education are adults from social class V with young children and those employed in low-income occupations. Both groups have often had negative past experience of formal education. Both groups also have domestic and work circumstances that make participation in full-time education difficult.

In addition, the increasing hardship that students experience at present due to the various financial constraints placed upon the funding of full-time education is likely to have a disproportionate impact in the future on students from non-traditional backgrounds. Therefore if the increased participation of adults with young children from social class IV and V and those with low income is to be achieved, it is imperative that new forms of cost-effective provision are developed providing supportive, quality programmes. It also means that any new provision would need to take account of the circumstances in which such target groups work and live their lives.

In March 1992 the opportunity arose for Liverpool Hope to bid to the Granby/Toxteth Task Force for the development of an educational provision that would increase the participation in formal education of adults with young children. The main aim was to increase the attainment levels of this target group through a community Access to HE provision and ultimately increase its competitive position within the labour market.

As a starting point Liverpool Hope and Granby/Toxteth Task Force accepted that in order to ensure the widest possible participation in education and training it was necessary to design and deliver educational/training programmes where people work and live their lives. This involves taking account of the life experiences of the student, and recognising that to educate the parent will have a positive impact upon other members of the family not only in terms of education but also in terms of a wide range of benefits to the individual, community and the local/national economy.

The targeting of parents and the family as a framework for educational attainment and progression made the LEA's Parent School Partnership Service an essential partner in the process of development and delivery of the REACHOut® Access initiative.

The engagement of parents in social class IV and V would not simply be achieved by a passive model of widening access; it would require pro-active measures which involved both the institutions and the individuals themselves reaching out to ensure meaningful educational achievement. The pro-active model adopted under the REACHOut® initiative involved the following:-

- Locating the learning in a supportive community location (in this case Liverpool City Council's Parent School Partnership centres) located in schools

- Outreach academic tuition

- Utilisation of open learning techniques to ensure teaching and learning activity in the community and home

- Partnership approach between partners and the learners

This model has been developed into three progressive provision elements, pre-access, access and the REACHOut® Degree Route. The main focus of this chapter is upon the Degree route and the other elements are returned to briefly under the partnership section. Therefore nearly all data presented relate directly to undergraduate levels of activity.

2. Aims of the REACHOut® degree route

The REACHOut® degree is a proactive strategy which aims:

- to provide Higher Education in outreach locations

- to provide supportive community locations

- to support students through the provision of crèches and close tutorial support

- to provide supported distance learning materials and teaching and learning environments

- to work with colleagues in the university to prepare and teach BA/BSc combined Honours modules in an appropriate way

- to utilise a three hours of contact per week model of attendance

- to engage those who would not otherwise become involved in higher education

- to engage those who are unable to study full-time

- to engage those who have no family tradition of involvement in higher education

3. Locations of REACHOut® degree route

Since its inception REACHOut® has been provided in ten primary schools and one secondary school and more recently at the Liverpool Hope Community centre at Everton. The inner city school centres are all run in conjunction with the Liverpool City Council Parent School Partnership (PSP) Service, which provides rooms, facilities and the services of a Teacher Key Worker and/or an Outreach Worker. These workers ensure that student support (including crèches, self-supporting study groups and other pastoral activity) is available and that the learning environment is appropriate. In addition they liaise with the visiting academic tutors and contact students who have missed two sessions or whose study pattern is of concern to the academic tutor. These are key and distinctive features of the programme.

The courses run in locations where there are clusters of undergraduates across areas designated as European Social Fund (ESF) Objective 1 priority areas. Therefore the student should find the location accessible.

4. Mode of Study
4.1 The degree

All students following the REACHOut® degree route are registered for the University of Liverpool Combined Subjects BA/BSc Honours degrees. The provision is part-time and the degree is divided into three levels, each of which takes two years of study. Some students choose to progress less rapidly through the programme depending on their personal circumstances, and to interrupt their study.

Students follow two main academic subjects throughout the six years of the part-time degree. At Level One (normally year 1 and 2) one third of the programme, originally called Core Skills and Personal Development and now called Unique Learning, is studied. All assessments are in line with those for full-time students in form, weighting, scheduling, criteria, marking and moderation. The subjects available are indicated on the table opposite.

	1995	1996	1997	1998	1999	2000
Sociology	45		49			
Biology	8		6			
American Studies			15*			
IT		53		63		86
Psychology		41		22		37
Geography		14		18		16
Theology						20*
Family Studies						23*
Total	53	108	70	103		182
* new subject						

4.2 Mode of attendance

Students attend either daytime or evening sessions of three hours duration normally at their local primary school. Such limited contact time is offset by the provision of supported distance learning materials by the subjects. Daytime classes fit in with dropping off and picking up school schedules. In circumstances where a subject is available at more than one location, students with particular concerns e.g. shift work or child care may choose to attend different locations or at different times of the day in another centre in order to complete their studies. Some students, after successfully completing Level 1 and/or 2 part-time in PSP locations, opt to transfer to full-time study at Hope Park (the main campus of Liverpool Hope).

Whilst most students follow all their study at the PSP Centres, some subjects may transfer to other locations where more specialist equipment is available e.g. in the case of some locations where ICT facilities are limited.

5. The research data of the degree route

Data used in this chapter are derived from two main sources. The Hope Annual Monitoring Process, which applies the Guildhall Method of qualitative evaluation, is used for student experience, and in addition, a REACHOut® Degree Route Annual Student Experience Questionnaire is circulated and analysed. Both are administered at special sessions at the PSP centres, organised by the REACHOut® Degree Route Coordinator, and remain anonymous unless indicated otherwise. Data is available for each year cohort and tables in this chapter refer to this. In addition the first cohort of students who commenced in 1995 and are completing in summer 2001 are referred to as a subset (five completers of the 45 who started had initially indicated that they would be willing to be contacted about issues and therefore can be identified as completers in 2001; the remaining nine completers from this cohort are unable to be identified in this way).

Subject administered module evaluation by REACHOut® students is not referred to in this chapter but is recorded in the Schools' Annual Monitoring Reports.

6. Recruitment to the programme

Recruitment to the programme is both formal and informal. The formal route involves the Liverpool Hope Access Route accredited by the Merseyside Open College Network. Subjects offered include Family Studies, Living Arts, Science and Social Science, which are provided at PSP Centres and at a local secondary school (with full PSP support) in the case of Science where specialist provision is required. Most recently pre-Access courses have been developed in PSP and other community locations (such as a play group) to feed into the lifelong learning sequence.

Informally recruitment builds upon the general interest courses and contacts already existing in PSP centres. Adults attending courses such as hairdressing, yoga and Parents as Educators Courses may be encouraged to follow a more formal educational route (25%). Other groups are targeted through flyers in community locations and partner locations such as libraries, health centres, careers offices and adult guidance centres. Other forms of advertising are used, such as newspaper advertisements but the most effective is word of mouth (over 25%).

Data is obtained from students who are asked annually where they heard about the REACHOut® degree route.

7. Student characteristics
7.1 Age
The largest group of students is aged 30-40. This group ranged from 40-50% of each year's entry. It is also noteworthy that between 28 and 38% of students are between 40 and 50 years of age. Combined, the 30-50 years category represents between 70 and 88% of the REACHOut® group. Most recently students aged 21-30 have begun to be recruited to the programme.

It is of interest that the first subset of the graduating group has students from the 40-50 years age range comprising 60% and the 21-30 age group is also significantly overrepresented (20%). Conversely the students aged 31-40 years seem to be under represented in the cohort graduating, compared with their appearance in the recruitment statistics. Perhaps students of this age, possibly with teenage children, are most likely to interrupt their study.

7.2 Gender
The majority of REACHOut® students are women. The percentage intake varies between 76% and 90%.

7.3 Ethnicity
The percentage of students from ethnic minority groups ranged from 14-19%.

7.4 Status
Approximately 25% of all students are defined as lone parents. The proportion is constantly around this figure. It is of note that no lone parents are graduating in 2001 despite 20% of all students registering in 1995 being in this category.

7.5 Children
Over the years of the degree between 70 and 89% of all students have had children living at home. Interestingly, of the 2001 subset of graduates only 66% have children living at home, perhaps indicating

that the presence of children reduces the chances of completing the degree without interruption.

7.6 Admissions Profile

	1995	1996	1997	1998	2000 BA	BSc
Under 21				9	2.6	0
21-24				9	14.3	7.2
25+		88	78	70	90.8	87.5
Female	87	90	85	76	85.5	87.5
Male	13	10	15	24	14.5	12.5
Parent	76	76	89	71		
Lone Parent	20	23	26	29		
Disability	12	11	11	11	10.1	18.75
Ethnic Minority	14	19	17	18	10.5	10.5
Employment		49	85	66		
Pathway Resident		48	38	35		

8. Students' educational experience

Approximately one third of REACHOut® degree students left school without any qualifications. This proportion has remained constant throughout the six years of recruitment to the degree. Since leaving school on average over 80% and in one year 97% of students have gained some qualifications and in addition a high proportion of students (50-85%) had taken part in skills training associated with their employment. Clearly REACHOut® students have, after a poor start to formal education, rapidly adapted to a lifelong learning agenda.

8.1 Students' School and Post-School Qualifications

	1995 (%)	1996 (%)	1997 (%)	1998 (%)	1995 Completers (%)
No qualifications on leaving school	33	26	33	32	60
Some qualifications gained since leaving school	95	87	78	85	80
Received training in skills related to employment	77	58	85	50	80

8.2 Parental Experience of Education

Between 73% and 87% of the parents of REACHOut® students left school at the minimum leaving age. This was true for all the 2001 graduates.

After leaving school some parents followed other courses. The percentage of students with fathers not continuing education beyond the minimum age was lower than the comparable figures for mothers (51-74%: 60-80%). In other words the fathers of REACHOut® students were more inclined to follow further education courses after leaving school than their mothers.

Another indicator of parental experience of education is the percentage that engaged in further education as an adult. Here the number of both parents was high with 20 and 38%. There were no significant differences between the mothers and fathers.

Educational Profile

	1995 (%)	1996 (%)	1997 (%)	1998 (%)	1995 Completers (%)
Parents left school at minimum age	86	87	85	73	100
Father taking no further education	65	53	51	74	75
Mother taking no further education	80	70	60	75	100
Father taking further education as an adult	23	32	26	35	66
Mother taking further education as an adult	27	21	20	38	3.3

9. Employment

Since the earliest days of REACHOut® the percentage of students in employment has increased from less than half to over two thirds, a high proportion (30% in 1997) work part time and a decreasing percentage are working at home.

10. Typical student profile

The characteristic student is a 35 year old, white, female, parent with children living at home, who works as she studies. Her parents left school at the statutory age and took no further education. She left school without any qualifications but then followed a number of courses, some leading to qualifications and others enhancing job-related skills.

11. Reasons for choice of a part-time degree provision

When asked why they were studying part time rather than full time the responses were largely associated with the cost of full-time study (47-85%) and the family responsibilities (33-88%) of the students. These figures have both increased significantly since 1998. Up until 1998 the mean for each answer was 57% and 47% respectively; since 1998 they have risen to 85% and 88% respectively.

Interruption of career by studying full time was also cited as a reason for choosing a part-time route. This reason has averaged about 40% but the general trend is one of decreasing importance of this factor. (43% to 38%).

	1995 (%)	1996 (%)	1997 (%)	1998 (%)	1999 (%)	1995 Completers (%)
Could not afford to live on student grant	62	47	63	85	85	90
Family responsibilities preventing full-time study	57	33	50	88	88	80
Full-time study would interrupt career	43	46	37	38	38	80

12. Student aims on entering Higher Education

Students following the REACHOut® degree route report a wide range of aims for their study. Three aims have been consistently of highest significance since the start of the programme. Highly significant for all but the latest 1999 entry was 'to prove to themselves that they could do it'. This was placed either first or second over a four-year period, although in the most recent survey it was placed sixth in rank order of importance. The aim 'to improve career prospects' was recorded as the highest aim for the most recent two years. The third significant aim was to gain the 'satisfaction of having done a degree'. This has always been recorded as one of the top three aims in all surveys. Interestingly, the instrumental aim of enhancing career prospects has become more important in the last two years.

Intellectual aims are also important. The combination of 'to be better informed' (44-56%), 'subjects interest me' (56-73%) and 'to keep my mind active' (44-47%) indicate an intrinsic as well as extrinsic motivation for their studies.

Student Aims

	1995 (%)	1996 (%)	1997 (%)	1998 (%)	1999 (%)	1995 Completers (%)
To 'prove to themselves' that they could do it	66	51	79	88	50	80
Satisfaction of having done a degree	57	46	70	82	60	60
To improve career prospects	48	65	61	94	72	60
To be better informed	48	44	55	44	56	60
To gain confidence	48	33	48	32	42	40
To enter a particular career	43	37	52	79	44	60
Career progression				59	51	70
Subject interests me				73	56	60
Mind active				47	44	60
To make up for lack of opportunities in the past					47	70
To re-enter the job market					33	20
To move out of low paid work					19	40

13. Reasons for entering Higher Education at this time

When asked why they had chosen to enter higher education at this point in their lives, the students most frequently referred to the existence of the REACHOut® degree route. This was triggered by their involvement in PSP activities and on the recommendation of family and friends. Others commented on being inspired by previous courses to continue studying (29-39%) and others had been prompted by lifelong learning (32-50%). Over 20% had commenced the degree because they had more time because their children were older and almost 20% were concerned about their children's education and hoped the REACHOut® experience would enhance both their own and their children's experiences.

	1995 (%)	1996 (%)	1997 (%)	1998 (%)	1995 Completers (%)
Attracted by REACHOut® Degree Route	66	61	54	67	47
Prompted by PSP	38	25	17	32	14
Inspired by some previous course to continue studying	29	39	31	29	23
More free time now children are older		23	28	20	12
Own personal goals/ motivation			59	50	58
Prompted by life-long learning			50	32	21
Concern about their children's education			19	17	14
Course recommended by family/friends			31	26	21
Response to mid-life crisis!			1		

14. On course issues

14.1 PSP and academic support

A hallmark of both Liverpool Hope in general and REACHOut® provision in particular is the quality of the student support. As described above, the students receive personal support from the PSP centre staff (Teacher Key Worker and Outreach Worker). Within the PSP centre a wide range of support services are available to all students. For example the provision of crèche facilities is important. In addition to locally based PSP support, there is a central support provided at the University by the PSP REACHOut® degree route coordinator. She is responsible for liaising with the PSP centres and the students. In addition the students receive academic support from their academic tutors.

When asked to rank PSP, administrative and academic staff on a 1-5 scale for helpfulness and efficiency for each year, between 71 and 41% of academic staff obtained the highest rating of extremely helpful, but less (61-29%) were rated as extremely efficient. With regards to PSP staff a range from 81-55% were rated as helpful and efficient.

	1995 (%)	1996 (%)	1997 (%)	1998 (%)	1995 Completers (%)
Academic staff 'extremely helpful'	66	61	71	41	93
Academic staff 'extremely efficient'	50	47	61	29	80
PSP helpful and efficient	81	77	60	55	80

Most interestingly, the 2001 subset of graduating students recorded far higher degrees of positiveness for all criteria than the average. For example 93% of the completers thought academic staff were extremely helpful, 80% thought they were extremely efficient. With regards to PSP tutors 80% were rated as 'helpful and efficient' and 0% 'could be more efficient and helpful.'

14.2 Other Support

A wide range of people support the study of REACHOut® students. From a list of six (employers, colleagues at work, spouse/partner, children, parents and friends), students were asked to rank their support on a 7-point scale.

Support was identified from within the family (see opposite).

14.3 Course Related Problems

Students were asked to identify those factors, which caused them problems with their studies chosen from a list of twelve possibilities. Over the six years of the course three major recurrent problems were identified: *access to computers, finding time to use the library* and *getting down to study at home*. Access to computers became more of a problem during the survey period. This is largely as a result of the

	1995 (%)	1996 (%)	1997 (%)	1998 (%)	1995 Completers (%)
Partner	93	61		85	90
Children	69	47		95	66
Friends		65		100	80
Parents	73	46		95	60

increased use of computers required by the course tutors who are increasingly using IT resources and the College Intranet to enhance their teaching. The access to the library as evidenced by *'finding time to use the library'*, *'library opening hours'* and *'availability of books'* remains an important issue but one which is declining in importance (noted by 74 and 26% respectively in 1997 and 50, 20 and 47% in 1998). *Getting down to study at home* remains a highly significant issue for approximately 50% of all students, although it is important to note that of the 2001 graduates who have most successfully navigated the degree in the minimum of six years none reported any difficulties at all with studying at home. Balancing work and study commitments introduced as a factor for the first time in 1998 has remained significant (in 1998 it was the second most important factor).

Several factors that were originally of great importance have become less important during the six years of the degree. Childcare problems have disappeared completely, and transport to class is now only a problem for 6% of students. Less significant has been the decline in the concern about coping with the level of study. In the first year of the degree this was reported by 55% of the students, the following year it declined to 25% and the figure has remained at the 20-30% level subsequently (see figure on page 126).

15. Personal skills and characteristics

Students are asked to consider six skills and six personal characteristics at the end of each year and assess their degree of competence. They are invited to indicate that their level of competence is 'okay' or whether it 'needs to improve'.

	1995 (%)	1996 (%)	1997 (%)	1998 (%)	1995 Completers (%)
Coping with level of study	55	25	20	29	20
Child care problems	50	26	0	0	N/a
Getting down to study at home	50	37	57	47	0
Transport to classes	n/a	16	13	6	0
No problems	n/a	16	7	11	20
Finding time to use the Library			74	50	20
Library opening times			26	20	40
Access to computers			37	61	40
Financial problems			24	9	40
Availability of books				47	40
Lack of support from family/ friends				6	20
Balance work and study commitments				58	40

Consistently at the top of the 'need to improve' list are IT Skills and Public Speaking. Whilst the former remains around 65% each year, the concerns about public speaking have fallen from almost 80% to 50%. Time organisation and mathematical ability are other areas that are consistently in the top five of concerns although the degree of concern for each is falling annually from 66-44% and 58-38% respectively, as more presentations are built into the curriculum.

16. Conclusions: six years on, what has been learned and what has been achieved?

16.1 Widening participation

Higher education responding to community need can change its profile by working in partnership with agencies that respond to non-traditional students in terms of entry qualifications, age, ethnicity, gender, disability, and educational experience. Comparative data from the 1999/2000 cohort of students demonstrates the success in diversifying the student profile by proactive partnership.

	1995 (%)	1996 (%)	1997 (%)	1998 (%)	1995 Completers (%)
Public speaking	79	65	69	50	20
IT skills	n/a	63	70	51	40
Time organisation	68	39	51	44	40
Mathematical ability		58	41	38	40
Study skills	58	42	57	29	20
Reading ability and resourcefulness	0	23	4	11	0
Increase independence	16	7	15	6	0
Confidence				32	40
Persistence				17	20
Self-esteem				29	25

	BA	Full time at Hope Park	BSc	Full time at Hope Park
A Level	9	56	6.3	57.3
Access	26.9	8.2	31.3	4.5
A Level Equivalent	1.3	.6		1.4
GNVQ 4	1.3	.14		
HNC/HND	1.3	1.5		1.4
Not Known	57.7	25.3	50.0	29
ONC/OND	1.3	1.9		3.6
Other HE	1.3			
Professional Qualifications			12.5	

Student profile 1999/2000

	Hope Park Main Campus full time	REACHOut®
Male	38.5	13.5
Female	61.5	86.5
Age Under 21 Years	77.35	1.3
Age 21-24 Years	8.80	10.75
Age Over 25 Years	13.85	89.15
White	92.9	85.65
Bangladeshi, Indian, Pakistani	2.45	NDA
Black African, Caribbean	1.43	7.9
No Disability	91.0	85.6
Deaf/Hearing Disability	0.61	NDA

The mainstreaming of such provision is now ongoing. Expertise gained by the institution in learning and teaching and student support systems has led to confident partnerships commencing in 1998 with six Church sixth form colleges across the North West of England now delivering Higher Education in Manchester, Wigan, Preston, Bury, Blackburn and Stockport.

The evidence of this data would confirm that such pro-active measures do successfully engage specific traditionally excluded groups. The design of the delivery and support model almost determines the specific characteristics of the clientele. The REACHOut® Degree Route seems to address issues related to women from social class IV and V more readily than their male counterparts.

16.2 Student achievement
Student retention in terms of suspension and withdrawal is not the focus of this chapter. However, data available from 1995-99 demonstrates that this is below national average.

As mainstream data becomes available and the route has become more established, comparative figures for 1999-2000 demonstrate that students successful completion of initial assessment is higher than both levels one and two at degree level.

Analysis of end of session results 1999-2000

	Full-time	Part-time
Total number of students BAC Level I	602	244
Ineligible to progress to Level II	180 (29.9%)	63 (25.3%)
Total number of students BAC Level II	498	62
Ineligible to progress to Semesters 5 & 6	81 (16.3%)	11 (17.7%)

16.2.2   However, most importantly, fifteen of the first 1995 cohort of sociology students have completed their BA/BSc study this year (33%). Additionally, 20% are still on course having had periods of interruption in their study.

16.3 Partnerships

16.3.1   Partnership is a dynamic framework for development that clearly needs to be managed. The context in which each of the individual partners operates, let alone the nature of the partnership itself, never remains the same. The present restructuring of the Parent School Partnership by Liverpool City Council is a good example. However REACH-Out® has been a good and dynamic partnership which has also been strongly supported by the private sector with considerable investment of £0.5m by BT in the project.

16.3.2   The management of REACHOut® has been led in Liverpool Hope by the Deanery of Hope in the Community and strongly supported by the other Deaneries, particularly the Deanery of Art and Sciences as well as the Foundation and Education Deaneries.

16.3.3   The management by the Deanery of Hope in the Community has required it to deal with both the internal and external dynamics of partnership which often involve the constant need to secure new forms of external funding. Critical in all of this is the support of the College Rector and Chief Executive as well as the support of other senior managers.

16.3.4　Internal colleagues from Deanery of Arts and Sciences have rigorously debated, worked and produced research, teaching and learning environments which have enabled the delivery of the academic subjects curriculum, validated at all levels.

16.3.5　External colleagues from Liverpool Education Authority Parent School Partnership Service have had the opportunity of supporting students from informal pre-access educational contact in primary schools in their areas and, in partnership with Liverpool Hope, have been able to see students progress through Access to degree level if they require. Benefits in continuing professional development have been gained throughout the process. Some workers have had the opportunity of being seconded to co-ordinate the development of the degree and the pre-access levels by this two-way process between HE and community education within schools. The Authority is currently restructuring PSP and it is essential that dialogue is maintained to ensure as a priority the retention of such opportunities for progression and lifelong learning for parents who require it.

16.3.6　A BA/BSc pathway in Family Studies (funded through REACHOut® to Parents SRB) has been designed with academic subjects responding to the issues identified by the community in an inter disciplinary approach. The whole pathway being matched to employment opportunities researched by the Careers Department not only challenges the HE curriculum, but also has re-aligned it. REACHOut® to Parents Access level modules have been designed to explore these issues. The curriculum has been designed by a partnership between the parents and 'academics'.

16.4 Partnership and the other REACHOut® provision elements.

Critical to the REACHOut® strategy has been the development of a lifelong learning progression route from a basic level to graduate study. The development of access and pre-access stages have been crucial in the engagement of parents and families and some of the more innovative forms of inclusive curriculum development have taken place at these levels. Independent research by Mufti (2001) has shown that the impact of these programmes on children's expectation is radically improved in relation to higher education. His research identified that 86% of 7 year olds from a school with no tradition of higher education and no family member previously gaining entry higher education viewed University as a career target.

16.4.1 REACHOut® access

The REACHOut® initiative had its origins in 1992, the result of a shared vision between Granby/Toxteth Task Force and Liverpool Hope. The shared vision was the consequence of the combination of the two quite separate but intimately related objectives of two distinctly different organisations. On the one hand regeneration was the objective, whilst on the other widening access and participation within higher education. Clearly the driving force of this particular initiative was one which all those involved in education have become increasingly aware of, namely outputs. Each organisation entered into an agreement, the ingredients of which were the insubstantial qualities of a vision mixed with a tangible product such as data. The result was a dynamic experience for all concerned.

The embryo of this union was the REACHOut® Access programme which, following the features of the model, required a supportive community location in which to develop and deliver the venture, hence the inclusion of the third ingredient of the original partnership, the Local Education Authority through its Parent School Partnership Service. The REACHOut® Access programme was heralded as a success demonstrable through the numbers of students either entering Higher Education or gaining employment. Demand for the course always dictated that over recruitment was necessary. Retention levels, higher than the national average, rendered further funding an almost foregone conclusion.

However two factors became very obvious very early on. Firstly, for those who successfully completed the course, a realisation that the model which had supported them through their pre-degree work was replaced by necessity with the more traditional form of higher education provision. Casualties of this were inevitable, however funding from new partners including the DfEE allowed for the transferance of the model at undergraduate level.

Secondly, for some students who experienced difficulties coping with access levels, new and more building blocks were necessary and it was clear that the model, if applied at pre-access level, would create the right environment for those who needed longer to reach their potential.

REACHOut® as a model clearly demonstrated that if we alter the way we teach, it can have a profound effect on the learning and achievement of so many. *How* we teach matters. It must be acknowledged, however, that the curriculum offered was clearly dictated by the world of academia, an often prescribed and exclusive curriculum. If a vision is to be realised it must remain dynamic. Not content to become complacent with its success to date, REACHOut® began to develop and explore *what* we teach and it is within the pre-access element of the REACHOut® lifelong learning strategy that we see the greatest challenge to higher education, as the family as a framework for teaching and learning takes the major stand.

16.4.2 REACHOut® pre-access

Single Regeneration Budget (SRB) funding by North West Development Agency has provided a considerable investment in curriculum development and an opportunity to develop a special partnership framework with parents themselves. The Pre-Access element of the project has developed an inclusive curriculum development process entitled the Curriculum Development Advisory Group (CDAG). CDAG is made up of 50% parents and 50% academic tutors who, in partnership, identify and develop the key curriculum issues. The parents' involvement is structured and accredited in order to maximise on their potential for progression. Their involvement is also recognised in the publication of curriculum materials. These materials are designed and produced to the highest quality in order to sell and generate revenue for further curriculum development and delivery. All curriculum materials so far have focused upon family issues. There are two obvious advantages in adopting family issues in relation to this approach. Firstly it is a curriculum area that all learners have some knowledge of and, secondly, it is an area of study that will stimulate further work of parents with their children. So far there have been four pre-access modules developed under the banner 'Our Family Matters'. In addition, an on-line ICT module is near completion and work with families at risk and for whom disability issues are key, has also been drafted.

The involvement of the learners as part constructors in their own curriculum raises some fundamental questions in relation to teaching and learning in higher education. The whole question of the relevance and appropriateness of knowledge as well as academic standards has long been debated, particularly in relation to employability, vocationalism and academia. The development of Family Studies at undergraduate level explores these issues further and is certainly informed by the developments presently being pursued at Pre-Access and Access level. The first steps back into education at this level are probably as difficult and as crucial as those steps undertaken for our target group at undergraduate level. Getting these entry levels of engagement right and the nature of what is taught, are issues that are all linked to the issues explored in higher education in relation to widening access.

The nature of partnership results in a continued exploration not only of ongoing operational issues but also in relation to further developments and what is possible. There is probably no other area of educational partnerships that offers as many challenges and rewards as the widening participation agenda does. There is still much to be done.

17. Summing Up

This chapter has explored, in the main, the data produced through the six year experience of the REACHOut® Degree Route. It has demonstrated that partnership is a dynamic force in the development process and new opportunities will result from such challenges of partnership. At the centre of the REACHOut® experience have also been the students who themselves have been pioneers, aware that their own success is contributing towards additional opportunities for future students who have experienced similar and other forms of barriers to higher education.

A key lesson in the REACHOut® success has been the simple acknowledgement that education is likely to truly connect when it is designed to take learning to where people are, both physically and culturally. The concept of inclusion will always be limited in a passive model of widening access because it is based around the 'open door' notion which, to some extent, assumes that the 'excluded' are entering into an unknown room where few of their own life experiences will be reflected. The pro-active model requires ensuring that the world of higher education does reflect, not in the abstract but in a real sense, a wide range of life experiences and considerations, both in curriculum and in forms of delivery and support. In this respect the family as a framework for learning has much to offer in the support of the development of these multi-site teaching and learning locations, not least for the likely impact it will have on the children, our potential undergraduates of to-morrow.

Additional references

Alexander, T. (1997) *Family Learning* London: Demos

Alexander, T and Clyne, P. (1995) *Riches beyond price* Leicester: NIACE

Batey, C (1996) *Parents are Lifesavers* London: Corwin Press

Beattie, N. (1985) *Professional parents* London: Falmer Press

Cullingford, C. *et al* (1996) *Parents, Education and the State* Aldershot: Arena

DfEE (2000) *School Plus: Building Learning Communities* London

DfEE (1999) *Learning to Succeed: a new framework for post-16 learning* London

Flew, A. (1987) *Power to the Parents* London: Sherwood Press

Grant, C.A. and Sleeter, E. (1996) *After the school bell rings* London: Falmer Press

Hughes, M. et al (1994) *Parents and their children's schools* Oxford: Blackwell

McCormick, J. (1999) *Parents as Co-educators* Scotland: Scottish Council Foundation

Mufti, E. (2001) Unpublished research

Munn, P. *et al* (1993) *Parents and Schools* London: Routledge

Sainsbury, M. *et al* (1998) *Evaluation of the National Slough Literacy project* NFER

Topping, D. and Wolfendale, S. (1985) *Parental Involvement in Children's Reading* London: Croom Helm

Utting, D. (1995) *Families and parenting Conference Report* London: Family Policy Studies Centre

9

Ten years of access policy into practice through Partnership: a pragmatic approach to progression

John Blicharski and Michael Allardice

Introduction

The University of Dundee has been involved in the cross-faculty delivery of a targeted Access Summer School for non-traditional students for ten years. The introduction and development of this course required comprehensive support from all departments within the University, as well as many outside bodies. One of the most important features of this initiative, which has seen 433 additional students gain entry to higher education, has been the development of this partnership at a variety of levels.

This chapter concentrates on the development of the Access Summer School at the University of Dundee: the challenges faced by the partnerships which created it, known outcomes for students coming through the course, and the future development of access policy in the East of Scotland. This chapter is not intended to provide an in-depth discussion of concepts underlying this programme. Rather it outlines the reasons for adopting a pragmatic approach to the development of a partnership-based programme which we hope may inform and encourage others.

From the outset, all involved in the development of the Access Summer School were clear that the course must be much more than a 'back door' for traditional entrants. To make this possible, the criteria by which candidates are assessed for eligibility became the key – all those involved in the programme needed to agree on an index of disadvantage against which achievement could be observed. This factor shaped the partnership, as well as allowing us to identify and encourage those otherwise potentially excluded. As a result, the mix of social and ethnic groups that have utilised the Access Summer School has begun to compensate for inherent biases in the present admissions system of looking at grades without direct reference to ability, potential and circumstance. Through no fault of their own, many of those applying to the Access Summer School find themselves educational outsiders – the teenage mother, the refugee, the person who has a disability, the unemployed New Deal client, those who have had long absences from school. Thus the primary focus of the University of Dundee's Access Summer School is people within its region who face educational exclusion, live in the most deprived areas and for whom the opportunity of higher education is very limited. To meet these diverse needs, a pragmatic approach to widening access and participation has evolved in our regional situation.

Rationale for the development of a local access partnership

Plans for targeted access provision in the former Tayside Region began in 1991, when a former HM Chief Inspector of Schools was commissioned to investigate reasons for low progression rates into further and higher education from schools in the region. The solution proposed was the development of a network of courses to provide a range of provision across the region and encourage young people to fulfil their educational potential. The higher and further education partners, together with local council colleagues, accepted this proposal. In 1993, the Access Summer School began at the University of Dundee. The programme was aimed specifically at disadvantaged, mainly young people living in a region where many urban and rural problems of an economic and social nature exist. Without additional support, it was recognised that many would not otherwise consider taking their education beyond secondary school level, despite having the potential to do so.

In 1993, 43 students attended the first Access Summer School at the University of Dundee. By the end of the 2001 course, 601 students have had the opportunity to find out, at first hand, whether higher education is the right option for them. Research figures compiled for the period to the end of December 2000 indicate that 393 students have qualified and entered the University of Dundee as under-graduates, while another 40 have gone to other Higher Education Institutions (HEIs) to study (Allardice and Blicharski, 2000). Through the 2001 course, it is understood a further 59 students entered higher education. Overall, 492 students, the great majority of whom were not expected to enter higher education by any other route, have had the opportunity to prove they have the potential to succeed as undergraduates. By December 2000, 90 former Access Summer School students had graduated from the University of Dundee, including five with a First Class Honours Degree and 29 with an Upper Second Class Honours Degree. Seven students are already known to have gone on to postgraduate study.

Geographical aspects of the Partnership
Progression from school to higher education in Fife and the former Tayside varies widely. The main problem facing those concerned with improving the prospects of young people in the region is that some schools have progression rates to higher education of below 15% per annum. Many pupils have a semi-hostile mindset towards 'staying on' at school or going on to further study. There are also geographic reasons for some young people not considering higher education.

To the South of Dundee, Fife has a historic and geographic identity that is stronger than most in Scotland. Bounded by water on three sides, the Rivers Tay and Forth present surprisingly large psycho-logical barriers to Fife pupils wishing to access higher education. This, plus travel costs (including bridge tolls) isolates large parts of the population from the rest of Scotland. The traditional mainstay of Fife's economy, coal, has disappeared over the past two decades and, with the electronics industry in recession for much of the recent past, the economic and employment picture for many young people in the region is limited. Many positive things are happening in Fife, but a significant part of the population lives in small communities, isolated from the main transport infrastructure and dependant on government support. In the most recent count of Social Inclusion Partnership (SIP) areas in Fife, over 21,700 people were identified as living within boundaries that are defined as including the most deprived 10% of postcode areas in Scotland. Fife's problems are a mixture of rural and urban, thus adding another layer of complexity to the work being done to resolve some of the educational issues that affect the county. Our relationship with Fife Council has been nurtured over a number of years to the point where funding for Fife school-leavers attending our Access Summer School is now available through the Fife Wider Access Partnership (FWAP).

The break up of the Scottish Regions in the mid-1990s created a serious difficulty for the University. Instead of dealing with one authority north of the River Tay, three partners became involved. Not all of the new councils were aware of the rationale of the Access Summer School and a series of negotiations had to take place to recreate the partnership.

Dundee has even greater problems of social and economic in-equality. Around 47,000 people are estimated to live in the SIP areas identified within the City. The total population of Dundee is estimated at 145,000 therefore, a large part of the population lives in difficult circumstances. These, and other factors, are a very strong influence on the way young people perceive their educational chances and highlight the need for special routes into higher educa-tion. Often fear of student debt deters potential students from the idea of higher education, whilst ultimately students cannot be sure of employment at the end of their studies.

The specific problems pertaining to Perth and Kinross and Angus revolve around the rural nature of these areas, and while government defined deprivation is harder to find, great social and economic disadvantage does exist.

Moreover, those who do succeed in their studies rarely return to their community to encourage others to follow the same route. Universities and colleges often seem very distant and difficult places to get to if you live on a council estate, in a former coal village, on a farm or in a fishing village, with limited access to public transport. For all these reasons, the efforts of schools and local education authorities are frequently undermined. The need for employment, to provide an immediate income for the family, is often the paramount pressure, outweighing the desire for further or higher education.

The partnership in action

The partnership developed in Tayside in the light of the 1991 HMCI proposal meant that, for the first time, planning was co-ordinated across a number of colleges and universities, to address the needs of disadvantaged young people in the region. Ten years on, this shared goal has achieved far more than simply helping individual institutions reach recruitment targets, as some sceptics at the time claimed. Some of the decisions made along the way appear, at first glance, insignificant. Development of a common application form in 1997 was one sign of co-operation that aided potential students. A unified application form offered the economy of only one set of information being sent to each school, thus reducing the burden of paperwork on school staff promoting these courses. It also enabled young people to see options clearly in a single format rather than trying to compare the claims of institutions in brochures or prospectuses.

Another such decision, the early appreciation that a system of informal interviews might be the best method of student selection, now appears particularly insightful. This process, which allows each candidate to discuss with experts from school and college/university the best option for them also, brought partners together and built confidence between them. The development of the interview process, involving senior representatives from the partnership, meant that a fair assessment of all the circumstances concerning the candidate could be made by those with close knowledge of education at all levels. It also allowed the interviewers the chance to assess the candidate's level of commitment and motivation to continue their education and ensure that they were aware of the realities of study in new environments. It was also recognised at an early stage that these students would need additional guidance to determine whether the access course they had chosen was the right one for them. If a candidate turned out to be better suited to another course (access or otherwise) because of subject interests, qualifications or level of preparedness then, with their agreement, they would be commended to the appropriate institution without having to begin the whole process again. Thus, for people often used to disappointment, the process of choosing the right course was made as open and straightforward as possible and the likelihood of a positive outcome became much greater.

Definitions of disadvantage – the core of targeting

The development of criteria to define disadvantage has been an important element in the process of assessing the needs and eligibility of applicants. Through a process of consultation, partners agreed six disadvantage criteria, namely:

Little or no parental experience of education post-16

Limited family income

Unskilled, semi-skilled or unemployed parent(s)

Living in a neighbourhood or other circumstances not conducive to study

Educational progress blighted by specific family events at critical times (e.g. bereavement, illness or family break-up)

Other exceptionally adverse circumstances or factors specified by nominator.

Applicants must meet at least one of the criteria to apply, although research over the last ten years has shown that, on average, 2.5 criteria per Access Summer School entrant is the norm. Each year there is evidence that for a number of students, all six criteria apply. Linkage between criteria is unsurprising – a candidate whose parents have no experience of education beyond secondary school may well be living in a low-income household because their parents are in low-skilled employment or are unemployed. The candidate may also have little space available for study or may be constantly distracted by brothers and sisters sharing the same room. This very common example highlights three of the six criteria. Other equally disadvantageous circumstances such as bullying, abuse and other debilitating problems are common. Those applying with only one critical reason, such as family break-up, illness or the death of a close relative or friend are also considered, reflecting our view that disengagement from further study can be caused by a variety of factors, some immediate, others long term in nature. In all cases, criteria are verified and described by a nominator – someone who knows the applicant and can expand on the applicant's motivations for wishing to enter higher education and their reasons for applying to the Access Summer School. Nominators are often senior members of school guidance staff. Consequently interview panels can gain insight in advance into reasons for an applicant's apparent failure at school and can place that candidate's true potential and motivations in context at the compulsory selection interview. The panel aims to select candidates with untapped potential, regardless of social distinctions.

Outreach activities

Over the years, many collaborative outreach activities have been deployed, following careful negotiation with partners who may have similar aims but different perspectives. For example, initially councils did not see access summer schools as core social inclusion business, but when shown what could be achieved, the councils became supportive and asked to be involved. Partnerships with local education departments, Scottish Higher Education Funding Council (SHEFC) projects and other education providers have enabled outreach work to move forward and thus provide advice and role models to encourage and support those who have shown potential. Student Shadowing schemes, Student Tutoring and other activities designed to expose as many young people as possible to higher education options are progressing. Similarly, work with groups in communities to create an awareness that higher education is a viable option for those who have been out of education, is beginning to bear fruit.

Key partners and key ingredients

The Access Summer School depends on a large number of partners at a variety of levels both internal and external to the University of Dundee. This section concentrates on the nature of these partnerships, the major areas of partnership and the multiple links between partners.

Faculties and support services

All faculties of the University of Dundee offer places to Access Summer School students on successful completion of the course. This is a vital incentive for the students, who need to know that success will attract an immediate reward rather than just the hope of a place in the future. Each faculty allocates a number of places for Access Summer School students in advance but, based on the success of former access students, frequently expand numbers if more candidates pass the course. This advance planning on the part of the faculties, and the flexibility to take extra students if demand exceeds initial expectation, means that students can concentrate on their own efforts rather than compete for a limited number of places. The Access Summer School is not a competitive course. Rather, it was conceived of as a non-competitive opportunity for all to prove they had the ability if given the chance. To broaden outcome options, teaching staff from subject areas not offered as full subjects on the access course give guest lectures as one-off 'taster sessions' to develop the breadth of choice available for undergraduates in each faculty. Despite taking place during term four when most students are not on campus, all the University's support services are available to the students on the Access Summer School, including access to the Students' Association, the Student Advisory Service, IT Services, the Library, Careers Service, Institute of Sport, Chaplaincy and Counselling. Presentations are made to the students from most of these support services in week one of the Access Summer School, to ensure that all are aware of the range of activities and support in place for them during the summer and as undergraduates.

Councils and Local Education Authorities

Partnership with the local councils has always been a vital ingredient in the success of the Access Summer School. Not only do the local education authorities in Dundee, Angus, Fife and Perth and Kinross promote the course in their schools, but they also provide staff to serve on the interview panels. This source of direct expertise is particularly important when so many changes have occurred in the school system in recent years to qualifications and coursework. Councils also provide weekly bursaries and travel expenses for students from their area. As loss of the potential to earn through work is a serious deterrent for many, this support helps students to concentrate on achieving their ambitions. Although council funding is limited (£25 per week) it does help to reduce the need for part-time work while the course is running. In recent years, 90% of students on the course have stated that the financial support they had received from their council had been vital (source: unpublished exit questionnaires). In 2001, students aged over twenty living in Dundee received financial support from the Neighbourhood Resources and Development Department of Dundee City Council instead of the education department. This new development extends the partner-ships with local councils and may well lead to an increased number of older, disadvantaged students taking the opportunity to improve their educational chances. This in turn will make the age profile of access entrants more closely reflect that of the institution as a whole, and is expected to have a positive impact on the motivation of all students on the Access Summer School.

Changes in personnel and the political priorities of each of the local authorities often entails the re-engagement of a council in relation to their commitment to widening access. Moreover, the difficult finan-cial position many councils face means that access has to compete with other important local provision to maintain funding for the students. One of the pragmatic solutions to these issues has been to invite local education authority representatives to sit on the Board of Studies of the Access Summer School as part of the core decision-making process.

Schools
As already stated, all four local councils have been persuaded to take responsibility for the promotion of access in their schools. One council seconded a senior teacher for ten days per annum to work in schools giving presentations and advice to interested pupils. All four ensure that materials and advice are available in all schools and that guidance staff are aware of council support of these initiatives. Again, this process suffers from difficulties in maintaining strong

links when teachers change roles within a school or move to new posts. It is especially difficult to create strong links in schools when guidance staff are changing annually. One solution has been the recent involvement of staff from local careers companies who have a regular presence within schools and who can act as 'honest brokers' when highlighting all access provision in the area.

The private sector

In November 2000, a major Scottish bank announced funding for a number of access initiatives, including funding of students on the Access Summer School at the University of Dundee. This new funding began in 2001 and effectively doubled the income of students on the course, creating a realistic bursary to ensure that already disadvantaged individuals did not fall further into debt. This new partnership, offering £340,000 of funding over four years, will not just improve the situation of students on the Access Summer School, it will also provide £4,000 of funding for each of the 60 disadvantaged students who successfully apply for this help. In 2001, it was pleasing to note that twelve of the fifteen successful applicants were former Access Summer School students. It is worth stating that all the funding from the bank is being directed to students, not to the administration of courses or staff.

The PROGRESS Group

Through an organisation called PROGRESS (**P**lanning and **R**esources **O**perations **GR**oup for **E**qual **A**ccess **S**ummer **S**chools), all of the HEIs and FEIs in the local area are working in partnership with councils and careers companies covering the former Tayside and Fife. PROGRESS has become the body that oversees all access activities across the region and helps to co-ordinate the production of the common application form mentioned earlier, as well as visits to schools and the production of promotional material. Meeting approximately three times per annum, policy can be made in response to changing circumstances, and practitioners have an opportunity to discuss issues concerning all institutions. The recent inclusion of the careers companies on PROGRESS means that young people can receive information on access, in a co-ordinated manner, from all the sources of advice available in schools.

In terms of further outreach, the SHEFC funding for new initiatives has helped to establish the Discovering Degrees for Schools course. This 'taster course' gives disadvantaged school pupils the chance to experience higher education during a series of activities over four-days, designed to show them that university is for all who are able to take the opportunity, not just the socially or economically privileged. Aimed mainly at S.2 and S.3, the course targets groups that teachers are concerned would be 'lost to education' before access initiatives such as the Access Summer School could help. Since 1999 over 160 school pupils (each meeting the same disadvantage criteria as used on the Access Summer School) have attended this course. In addition a similar 'taster' initiative, Discovering Degrees for Adults, has been developed and proved successful in the short time it has been running. Approximately fifteen people have already entered higher education as a result of their four-day experience and others have taken places on part-time access courses with a view to continuing into undergraduate study. Through careful support, many attending these courses have used the opportunity to discover what they consider to be a previously hidden future.

Partnership within the institution
Another important component of the Access Summer School programme is that of partnership within the institution. Whilst the culture and content of degree-level study continues to evolve, access routes currently have to prepare students for the reality of a slowly changing higher education system (whilst simultaneously pushing the boundaries of modernisation).

In the past, suspicions about the acceptance of access students into academic institutions has been hard to overcome. It is all too easy for negative impressions to circulate that access students have a higher tendency to 'drop-out'. There is also criticism from some quarters of 'dumbing down' by accepting students who do not have traditional entry qualifications. To counter these criticisms, academic quality is closely monitored and access students are tracked throughout their academic careers and beyond to provide evidence of progression. Tracking has been a vital ingredient and has allowed information on non-completion to be disseminated to each faculty.

The quality of the teaching on the Access Summer School is another important factor in ensuring that academic standards remain high. University teaching staff chosen to work on these courses are well aware of the level that access students need to achieve in order to succeed. A number of the teaching staff themselves have come into higher education as mature students or by other non-traditional means. Indeed, one of the 2001 subject tutors was a graduate of the 1995 Access Summer School and, in turn, a first class honours graduate of the University.

Developing strategies for learning is an important part of the Access Summer School. For example, taking lecture notes is a potentially daunting prospect for any student. Learning the best way of tackling essay writing, report writing and developing presentational skills can be equally challenging. The study skills element at the beginning of the course aims to develop these abilities in a constructive, positive and non-threatening manner. By the time students are faced with tasks that are to be assessed, they have been encouraged to develop strategies to cope with academic demands and so produce work that demonstrates their intellectual abilities that otherwise might have been masked by adversity. These same study skill techniques, many of which were pioneered on the Access Summer School, are now being used by academic departments in the University of Dundee to develop the abilities of all their undergraduates.

Student Support
Complimenting teaching on Access Summer School are two layers of support for the students on the course: Student Leaders and Personal Tutors. It is clear that Access Summer School students require people they can relate to who are similar in age and background and, crucially, are already students at the University. The Student Leaders are, normally, students at the end of their first year, having themselves come through the Access Summer School the previous summer. Student Leaders act as befrienders and give the present Access Summer School students an insight into the realities of student life through conversation available throughout the course. Personal Tutors take on a rather different role, that of academic advisor and, to some extent, counsellor. Students meet each week

with their Personal Tutor to discuss issues they feel might be affecting their academic progress. These discussions are informal, confidential and normally held somewhere quiet to allow a relaxed discussion of issues. Often, discussions concentrate on very practical issues, but occasionally deeper fears will be aired, helping the tutor to understand the reasons behind behaviour or unexplained absences. The development of a strong relationship between tutor and student provides a unique insight into the constantly changing challenges some students face. Towards the end of the Access Summer School the additional support is progressively reduced, to allow students to adjust to the normal levels of support available within the University. It is frequently the case that students have, by that stage, had all their queries answered and are comfortable with the expectations that will be placed upon them as undergraduates. That said, an open-door policy remains, with four full-time staff available between 9.00am and 5.00pm weekdays, although this provision is seen as very much a backup for the University's main support infrastructure. The support mechanisms used on the Access Summer School have also been useful to the University in developing improved support arrangements for all students.

Overall, the high level of acceptance the Access Summer School has achieved within the institution has been dependent on the combination of quality teaching, assessment techniques, strong support and the development of appropriate learning skills for undergraduate study. Most importantly, all teaching and support staff aim to develop and improve the confidence of each student by giving them positive criticism and advice, and allowing them to develop.

Conclusion

Although a great deal has already been achieved, with 601 potential students undertaking the Access Summer School, 492 of them gaining entry to higher education and 90 already having graduated, much remains to be done. Partnerships at all levels, from institutional relationships through to links at national level, are at the heart of this work and power new methods of further broadening participation and access to higher education in the region. As indicated, some partnerships have not been easy or straightforward. Many involve extended discussion and the involvement of groups in the decision-making process who would not normally expect to be included. While this can be time-consuming and, occasionally, frustrating the end result has been a course which has far exceeded expectation at its inception. Furthermore, the development of these partnerships at a practical level and with tangible results has given local councils, schools, community groups and university staff the confidence to continue to support this initiative. The knowledge that all partners are committed to the access agenda allows those working in the field to concentrate on overcoming the geographical and psychological barriers potential students face, giving them the support they need when pursuing their particular ambitions. It is hoped that, through the pragmatism of developing partnerships and working in collaboration with so many others, the Access Summer School at the University of Dundee will continue to provide a route into higher education for many years, for those who have been socially or economically disadvantaged.

References

Allardice, M. and Blicharski, J.R.D. (2000) 'Tracking Students' Progression – 'Learning Their Lessons", in *Widening Participation and Lifelong Learning*, 2:3 pp32-36

10

Developing progression to learning: building progression pathways in the Tees Valley

Margaret Noble and Pauline Lynn

Introduction

The developing Widening Participation agenda places a particular emphasis on the importance of partnership and collaboration as a means of raising aspirations and attainment and encouraging increasing numbers of young people and adults to take advantage of learning opportunities available in both post sixteen and Higher Education. A range of reports on widening participation and lifelong learning highlight the significance of partnerships in developing participation and progression. For example the second report of the National Advisory Group for Continuing Education and Lifelong Learning (Fryer, 1999) states:

> Partnerships have a particular contribution to the development of learning cultures. They can help widen participation, increase demand for learning and link together measures designed to strengthen local capacity and democracy.

The CVCP report *From Elitism to Inclusion* (CVCP, 1999) also highlights the significance of partnerships in delivering widening participation and a number of HEFCE reports encourage HEIs to build partnerships with other organisations to widen participation in higher education. The recent HEFCE guide to good practice on *Strategies for Widening Participation in Higher Education* (HEFCE

153

2001) stresses the importance of strategic partnerships, particularly in relation to pre-entry activities.

The reasons why people do not engage in learning are many and varied and thus it is unlikely that any one organisation has either the capacity or knowledge to be able to meet the diverse needs of non-participants. Involving partners in delivery is arguably essential if real differences are to be made. Furthermore the number of widening participation initiatives and pathways to learning are diverse, involving considerable numbers of providers including Further and Higher Education Institutions, Sixth Form Colleges, training organisations, Local Education Authorities, the Worker's Educational Association (WEA) and voluntary sector organisations. The increasing range of government funded initiatives for lifelong learning through, for example, New Deal for Communities, the New Opportunities Fund, Learndirect (University for Industry, Ufi), Neighbourhood Renewal, SRB, and Non Schedule 2 has led to an arguably confusing and interrelated, although often uncoordinated, set of learning initiatives. Learners clearly need support in making sense of the myriad opportunities available and in being able to develop a pathway to learning that meets their individual needs.

Throughout the UK there have been a developing number of projects, which aim to encourage progression to further learning for both young people and adults. Among adults many learners may need to engage in learning for several years through a process of lateral progression before they have the confidence and skills to enter higher education (McGivney, 1999a). For young people the process often involves a process of longitudinal support throughout the years of secondary education. One of the challenges is to create synergy between initiatives and to take a view of the whole process of widening participation, not just its constituent parts. The often used expression 'from cradle to grave' thus assumes particular meaning and challenges institutions to develop holistic strategies if widening participation is to be more than rhetoric.

This chapter focuses on a number of progression initiatives that have been developed in the Tees Valley by the University of Teesside through working in partnership with a range of education providers.

The Tees Valley is an interesting case study due to both its political geography and generally low rates of participation in post compulsory education and training.

The Tees Valley

As part of the North East of England the Tees Valley emerged in the 19th Century as an industrial heartland with a major focus on the iron and steel and chemical industries. Politically the Tees Valley is a complex region comprising five boroughs: Redcar and Cleveland, Hartlepool, Middlesbrough, Darlington and Stockton-on-Tees, which together have a population of 650,000 people. The Tees Valley has a number of characteristics that illustrates its relative deprivation vis-a-vis the rest of Great Britain. As the following table shows, on a range of variables such as unemployment, the proportion of the population with poor literacy and numeracy skills, the number of pupils attaining five or more GCSES at Grades A to C and average earnings, the Tees Valley performs below the national average and in several cases below that of the North East.

Table 1 Characteristics of the Tees Valley

	Tees Valley	North East	Great Britain
Unemployment	7.6%	6.4%	3.6%
Population with poor literacy skills	27%	31.5%	24.0%
Population with poor numeracy skills	28.5%	-	24%
Pupils attaining 5 GCSEs grades A-C in 2000	40.8%	NA	49%
School leavers (16-19) entering continued education in college or Sixth Form	65%	-	
Proportion of population involved in training or education age 20-29	20%	-	
Education Attainment			
NVQ3	40.7%	-	45%
NVQ4	20.7%	-	26.2%

Levels of educational attainment are low not only amongst school leavers but also amongst the adult population. Currently almost 41% of the adult population of the region have attained qualifications equivalent to NVQ III compared to 45% in the UK as a whole. At NVQ Level IV almost 21% have gained qualifications at this level compared to over 26% in the UK. These differences illustrate the considerable gap that currently exists between the region and the rest of the UK. Other indicators of relative disadvantage are illustrated by the indices of concentration of deprivation. Three districts of the Tees Valley in Middlesbrough, Redcar and Cleveland and Hartlepool are among the worst ten districts in the whole country for concentration of deprivation (Joint Strategy Unit 2001). This relatively poor performance vis-a-vis national standards has led to a range of partnership initiatives being developed in the Tees Valley, many of which focus on raising aspirations and educational attainment and participation. Partnerships with a major focus on learning include the following:

- Tees Valley Lifelong Learning Partnership and five local borough Lifelong Learning Partnerships for Stockton, Middlesbrough, Redcar and Cleveland, Hartlepool and Darlington

- the University of Teesside Partnership, a consortium between the University, nine Further Education Colleges and six Sixth Form Colleges in the region

- FE Plus, a consortium between the seven Further Education Colleges in the Tees Valley

- the Tees Valley Informatics Partnership and in particular its Education Sub Group

- the Tees Valley Ufi Hub

- Excellence in Cities Partnerships.

The range of partnerships, and this list is by no means complete, illustrate the need for coordination in partnership activity if a real difference in progression to, and engagement in, learning is to be attained.

It is widely acknowledged that one of the keys to increasing engagement in learning is to develop clear progression routes (Baxter and Hunt, 1999, McGivney, 1999a). The University of Teesside has established a range of partnership initiatives for both young people and adults as part of a holistic strategy to increase participation in learning. A range of partnership initiatives have been developed from work starting with young pupils in years six to nine via the Meteor Scheme, through to mentoring schemes with secondary school pupils, Excellence in City Summer Schools, the Passport Scheme encouraging progression from post sixteen education to higher education and progression pathways for adult learners primarily focused on delivery of community learning (Centre for Lifelong Learning, 2001). Developing a holistic progression strategy is an integral part of the university's approach to widening participation and, as the following diagram illustrates, has resulted in a number of clear routes for both adults and young people, with strong interconnecting trends.

Fig 1. Developing a Holistic Progression Strategy University of Teesside

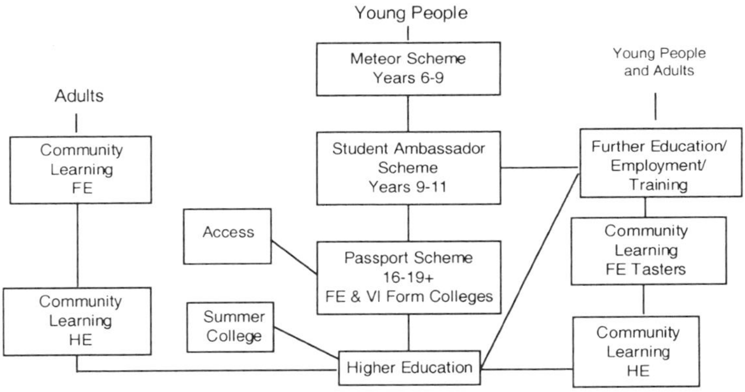

An integral aspect of the University's approach has been to recognise that if schemes are focused on particular age groups then it is important to develop both forward, backward and cross linkages with other initiatives. For example the University's innovative Meteor Scheme focuses on pupils in years six to nine (age 10-14)

with a particular emphasis on raising aspirations. If this programme stopped at year nine there would be a considerable gap with no particular support for pupils before they progressed into further learning, thus the emphasis has been on maintaining contact with pupils at each of a number of stages through a range of progression initiatives. For adult learners it is often easy to engage learners in initial 'short bites' and tasters but creating and sustaining progression to further learning through encouraging learners to take up the progression routes available is challenging. A major aspect of the University's work with adults has thus been to work in partnership with other organisations to provide initial learning at a level relevant to an individual's needs with clear progression pathways identified. It is also recognised, however, that learners have different aspirations and goals, some learners may wish to stop once they have reached a certain qualification level, others may wish to continue further study at the same level while a smaller number may initially progress through into further learning. Raising aspirations and developing progression is clearly a long term strategy and, whether dealing with adults or young people, it may be several years before clear progression routes and sustained participation is seen.

A focus on some of the particular partnership schemes developed by the University emphasises the importance of partnership working as one of the key critical success factors in delivering widening participation.

The Meteor Scheme

The Meteor Scheme is an innovative scheme aimed at raising aspirations amongst primary to secondary school children from years six to nine (aged 10-14). Currently it involves more than 460 year six pupils in twelve primary schools and over 700 pupils in fourteen secondary schools covering year seven to eight. The key aims of the scheme are to involve local children in higher education through linking University students with local children through mentoring and role models, to increase life chances through empowerment and awareness of opportunity, to raise achievement and to promote social inclusion and equal access to all. These aims are achieved through a varied programme of activities which include taster sessions, a summer school, student mentoring activities, ICT cross curricular sessions and sport and leisure activities. The major emphasis is on providing a range of challenging learning activities with a capacity to engage a large number of pupils with an enthusiasm for learning (Littlefair and Noble, 2001).

The scheme has been running since 1999 and has been hailed as a success through the pupil's enthusiasm for learning and their willingness to maintain links with education partners as they move from primary to secondary school. Critical success factors in the project have included the strong partnerships that have developed between the University and schools, pupils and their parents. Furthermore there has been an agreement on key objectives by all participants and an articulation of the benefits for all partners. There are clear benefits for University and student mentors, not only through developing further links with the local community but also through providing an opportunity for students to gain significant work-related experience and thereby enhance career opportunity. The provision of a wide range of innovative and stimulating learning activities has lain at the heart of the project and the response of pupils to the scheme has been extremely positive. Many have stated that they did not realise that 'learning was so much fun' and they have suggested that it has opened up their horizons (Littlefair and Noble, 2001). Other success factors include the links with parents through, for example, their involvement in celebrating children's achievement, the continuity of the programme from primary to secondary education, and the success of the project in gaining continuation funding to ensure that links are maintained. The success of the scheme means that it is currently being rolled out into new areas, and in particular into some of the more deprived rural areas in East Cleveland.

The Meteor Scheme is followed by the Student Ambassador Scheme, which has more recently been renamed Meteor Plus. This focuses on raising aspirations of pupils from year nine to eleven (age 13-16) through a structured programme of mentoring activities and University visits. The programme has been run in nineteen schools in the Tees Valley involving over 500 pupils and more than 50 student mentors drawn from both the University of Teesside and the University of Durham, Stockton Campus. The scheme works through schools identifying pupils who have the potential to progress to higher education but who for social and circumstantial reasons may be unlikely to do so without additional support. The pupils work in small groups with a student mentor on a range of aspiration raising activities, designed by the University in conjunction with schools, which include IT sessions at the University, games designed to help them to think about going to University and University visits and social events. The impact of the scheme has been evidenced through student evaluation and feedback; over 90% of participating pupils asked about whether their views of university have changed as a result of the scheme have indicated that they are much now more likely to go to university as a result of participation. One school stated 'the staff and pupils of the school who have been involved in the scheme are very positive about the effects this has had on pupil aspirations' (Baxter and Hunt, 1999). Now in its third year, the scheme is being rebadged as Meteor Plus, to provide the direct link through to the scheme operating with younger pupils in years six, seven and eight.

A number of critical factors are evident in the programme's success. These include the strong communication established between the project officer and partnership schools, the establishment of a steering committee, with senior representatives from participating schools, the University and parents, the carefully thought out set of motivational activities for pupils, designed to maintain their interest in, and enthusiasm for, finding more about progression opportunities to further and higher education and the production of a quality plan with staged and measurable targets. The careful recruitment and training of student mentors has been of particular importance; many students present themselves to be considered as mentors but the quality of mentors is of major significance in supporting pupils in learning attainment. Student mentors are recruited through the University's Students' Union Job Shop, Unitec, and through induction information packs. Selection is based on a range of criteria including, previous experience of work with children or young people, communication and interpersonal skills, a positive attitude and understanding of the demands of mentoring. Mentors are trained by the project co-ordinator and supporting staff.

Progression pathways

For adult learners one of the main widening participation activities has been provided by the Progression Pathways Project, funded by the higher and further education funding councils, jointly led by the University of Teesside and Middlesbrough College. The project involves more than seventeen providers of post compulsory education in the Tees Valley. The establishment of strong and robust partnerships and the creation of a sense of ownership of the project by all those involved lie at the heart of the project and a major aim has been to develop widening participation work as a truly collaborative activity able to meet the needs of the wide range of project partners (Lynn and Noble, 2001).

The project sees the development of outreach and community provision as a major vehicle through which new adult learners can be encouraged to participate in further learning. Existing experience in the Tees Valley suggested that many adult learners could be reluctant to attend formal institutions, but would be more willing to commence learning in their local community. An important aspect of the outreach work is to develop partnerships between further and higher education and the community and to adopt an inclusive approach which aims to involve all geographical areas and a considerable number of the project partners. A key aim of the project is to act as a catalyst to develop programmes in outreach centres across the Tees Valley to provide locally available learning and progression opportunities at a range of levels and to reach and work with groups who are under represented in formal education.

The strategy adopted by the project is therefore to provide a series of tasters and accredited short courses in outreach centres enabling participants to progress through from further education to the first level of higher education in the community. The programmes offered are designed to engage adults and second chance learners and were developed following focus groups and detailed discussions with local centres. Fairly modest targets were set for the development of outreach centres which involved five programmes and three centres.

These targets were well exceeded, with twenty new programmes, nine at FE level and eleven at HE level, offered in more than 24 locations to over 200 students in the first year.

Programmes covered a wide range of courses including arts and crafts, languages, women's studies, local history and English. The most successful FE modules, in terms of numbers attending and completing, were in Art and Design, Counselling, Languages, Local History and Women's Studies. While some students immediately progressed from FE to HE, others studied more than one module at FE level. HE modules were offered in Football History, Local History and Regional Writing, the most successful modules were in Family and Women's History with twelve and sixteen students respectively attending and completing.

A review of community based provision identifies that certain groups rarely participate. For older students the experience of Higher Education can often appear alien and the potential benefits of participation are not self-evident to the communities where there is no history of participation in HE. Taster modules are a widely accepted method of engaging learners (McGivney, 1999b) and new taster modules were therefore devised to meet their acknowledged interests and to promote engagement with other subject areas. National and local research (McGivney, 1999a and b), Lynn and Noble, 2001) demonstrates that individuals from manual working class backgrounds are under represented in both FE and HE and many projects are relatively unsuccessful in attracting men whose life chances have been damaged by a lack of skills and qualifications. Women appear to take more advantage of community learning opportunities, with more females enrolling on part-time and evening-only programmes; this was demonstrated during the first year of the project, in which 164 women and 49 men took part.

Recent surveys have found that the subjects men are more interested in are IT, Language and Sport (McGivney, 1999b). Research suggests that there are cultural, social and practical reasons for male non-participation and a lack of participation is often linked more to structural factors than to motivation (McGivney, 2000). These issues were addressed by providing non-accredited learning opportunities in partnership with local providers enabling men to participate and build up their confidence in themselves as learners. This was achieved through the development of links with FEFC Non-Schedule 2 (NS2) work and a commitment to providing non-accredited learning opportunities in partnership as pre-entry courses for programmes offered through the project, thus developing greater synergy. Over three hundred learners accessed the NS2 provision piloted by the Progression Pathways Project and at least 50% have now progressed from these 'small bites' to accredited courses.

The success of outreach often depends upon the skills and personality of the tutors, since tutors must tailor their delivery to each particular group's needs. Not every tutor is successful in an outreach location. Research (Ideas for Inclusion, 2000; Lynn and Noble, 2001; Spedding and Gregson, 2000) suggests that tutors of the same gender and ethnic group, who have the same accent and background, are more likely to be trusted than those who haven't any characteristics in common with the outreach community. In general, outreach strategies are viewed as marginal and operated by part-time tutors on temporary contracts, who may occupy an ambivalent position in relation to their institutionally based colleagues. Indeed the desire to provide an effective learning experience is often incompatible with the structures and constraints of the learning provider. Unless institutional cultures and practices change in both FE and HE institutions, and outreach provision is viewed as an integral part of an institution's work, learners who do progress from outreach provision may withdraw or fail to achieve.

It is evident that the nature and structure of the course is important in encouraging progression. The Women's Studies modules incorporated an element of study skills and confidence building and were written specifically for the project and fully prepared the student for HE. This resulted in straightforward progression from FE to an HE module in Women's History, suggesting that a more culturally significant, tailor made curriculum will both interest and progress more learners from community provision. Art and Design FE modules were piloted at three locations and attracted large numbers of students. These learners have now progressed from Schedule 2D modules into Schedule 2A mainstream and it is hoped to further progress these learners into HE modules in Art and Design from September 2001.

The project did not significantly target minority ethnic communities, although in South Bank, working in partnership with the WEA, eight learners were recruited who embarked on an FE module in Community Research. However, in line with both national and local research findings, it is recognised that withdrawal rates are higher and achievement rates lower for some minority ethnic groups (McGivney, 2000). Indeed, of the eight students who enrolled for the community research module, all eventually withdrew from the formally assessed part of the module. The reasons for this are not fully clear but support played a part, which may suggest that providers need to look carefully at the level of support provided. More recently the project, in partnership with local providers, has provided childcare facilities and language support at Grangetown in Middlesbrough. However, in light of some of the numbers involved, the long term viability of provision poses a number of questions regarding sustainability; however some providers are prepared to run courses as 'loss leaders' to establish progression opportunities. Although the project was successful in recruiting non-traditional learners onto FE modules, preliminary research within the project suggests that it may be a number of years before such students have developed the confidence and skills to progress to HE provision, although the example of Grangetown demonstrates what can be achieved once provision is established.

Delivery of higher education learning in the community presents a number of challenges. Although students on HE modules have access to a range of University resources, including the Library, less use than expected was made of these facilities. This may be because students studying one module and often at some geographical distance from the campus are unable or unwilling to devote time and financial resources to travel to the main centre of the University. The teaching and learning styles adopted by HE tutors were also significant and suggest that different teaching methods designed to meet outreach students' preferred styles of learning are required. Learning can and should be fun, even at undergraduate level, and tutors must respond to a changing and more discerning and demanding student population. Students should be encouraged to become active participants in the learning process and guided to manage their own learning, which will effectively equip them for both HE and for life-long learning.

Assessment at the HE level remains a problem, with several students expressing a desire to move away from the essay as the only form of assessment. Although both the History and English sections responded to the element of 'risk taking' in assessment and demonstrated considerable flexibility, some students raised doubts about the length of the HE modules which initially earned six credits. Short modules were initially intended to maximise completion rates, but students were reluctant to buy textbooks that would only be used for seven weeks, which suggests that the tutor must make more resources available to the students. A number missed one or more classes for personal reasons, and most felt that topics had been rushed. The project has therefore responded to these concerns and new twelve credit HE modules were piloted in February 2001. Student evaluation forms evidenced that students had an enjoyable and rewarding learning experience, suggesting that larger modules of twelve credits are more feasible for students studying at higher education level in the community.

The project challenged a number of institutional values and structures, which can often limit, and even prevent, a genuine engagement with outreach students. Some within Higher Education find outreach both challenging and risky, viewing widening participation as possibly diluting quality. It is evident from the first stage of the project that some procedures, structures and practices in HE may be overly bureaucratic, for example the lengthy procedures to enrol students to HE modules and the submission of assignments demonstrating that widening participation requires the institution to change.

While it may often be relatively easy to engage learners, progression and retention may be more difficult to achieve. The profile of learners is quite diverse: more than one third of students come from recognised 'disadvantaged' postcode areas and 73 students were recruited primarily from the areas of Grangetown, Hemlington, Loftus and South Bank, areas of deprivation and social exclusion suffering higher unemployment. Progression rates, however, have been encouraging: over 10% of students progressed immediately from FE to HE provision, and the progression was both linear and upward. Two outreach students progressed onto part-time degree programmes on campus from February 2001 and three have progressed onto full-time programmes from September 2001.

The project has achieved a great deal in programme delivery. The FE/HE leadership of the project acted as a vehicle for raising issues of progression and ownership between partner institutions, and both students and learning providers have benefited from this. However, the first year highlighted a number of important issues which need to be addressed, perhaps most importantly the organisation, co-ordination and mainstreaming of such activity. Both local and national research (McGivney, 1996; Lynn and Noble, 2001; McGivney, 2000; Ideas for Inclusion, 2000) demonstrates that outreach provision must be viewed as an integral part of an institution's work and retention strategies must be improved to support those who progress to HE to minimise the likelihood of withdrawal.

Challenges in developing progression routes

The chapter has focused on three of the widening participation projects undertaken by the University of Teesside, illustrative of the institution's development of a holistic strategy towards developing progression. At the heart of the agenda is the development of successful partnerships for progression. A number of clear criteria emerge from the case studies that are of significance; these include: a shared identity and ethos, and shared and collective goals and objectives which provide benefits for each of the stakeholders whether they be the learner, the university, the college, the school, the student or pupils. Ownership will be developed if everyone stands to benefit. This is particularly evident in the work with schools where University students gain access to valuable work-related experience and where schools gain additional support to encourage and motivate pupils. For adult learners the Progression

Pathways Project has been very careful to ensure that all partners have a stake in the project and are clear about their respective responsibilities.

Partnership projects must build on the strengths of each partner and provide clear avenues of communication and coordination so that there is an understanding of how activities relate to each other. The range of activities and funding to support widening participation have increased rapidly in recent years and it is clear that coordination and inter-linkage and making sense of these linkages presents a major challenge for those running projects. The ability to develop projects that can be continued and are sustainable, not to start projects and switch them on and off according to different funding streams, is of considerable significance. A key aim of many of the projects in which the University is engaged has been to look at ways in which activity can be continued in the absence of further funding. This is particularly significant, for example, in the area of raising aspirations. If contact with the University ceases after several successful years this could have adverse impact on pupil attitude and aspirations which may take several years to re-establish.

Other criteria for successful partnerships involve sharing of workload and careful planning and attention to detail, so providing those involved with clear and accurate information that sets out aims and objectives. This can arguably be best achieved by establishing appropriate management arrangements which are effective, inclusive and representative of all partners. For example, on the Progression Pathways Project each of the partnership sectors is represented on the management committee, enabling one person to speak on behalf of their particular sector. An advisory group has also been established to provide the wider community with an opportunity to debate project aims and outcomes. These arrangements can undoubtedly be further enhanced through dissemination and the use of staff development events and conferences to raise understanding and awareness of the impact of initiatives in the region.

Further challenges

This discussion presents widening participation and progression work in a very positive light, but developing progression routes in a region like the Tees Valley also presents a significant number of challenges. A primary challenge is to create confluence and coherence and avoid confusion. The range of progression, widening participation and neighbourhood learning initiatives now evident in an area can lead to confusion not just for the partner but also for the participants. Securing partner involvement lies at the heart of success, where the objectives are shared and where different partner needs can be met. Confluence can be established through creating synergy with other initiatives, linking, for example, non schedule 2 activity with FEFC and HEFCE special funding initiatives; a major challenge has been to encourage partners to think in a collaborative rather than in a competitive way. Collaboration can be achieved through understanding relevant needs and involving individual organisations at the appropriate level within projects.

The second challenge concerns mainstreaming activity. Too often widening participation and special initiative projects remain marginalised within organisations. They are often led by committed individuals who take responsibility for the project and ensure the delivery of successful outcomes, but for impact to be sustained it is important that activities become a key part of an organisation's mission and objectives. This may result in difficult choices being required about whether engagement with a particular project should go ahead. Widening participation initiatives often put particular pressure on the organisation's or institution's capacity to respond (Dodgshon and Bolam, 2000). Questions that need to be asked include: Does participation in a project conflict with institutional pressures and priorities? How long will the impact last? What will happen when the funding ends? Will the lack of resourcing to support initiatives lead to their demise? These issues can clearly be overcome through attempts to embed the activity, to ensure that priorities are on the agenda and through recognising that initiatives have both direct and indirect benefits. This is particularly evident, for example, in the area of raising aspirations, where direct benefits may take ten or more years for full impact to be seen, particularly if work starts with very young pupils. Indirect benefits are many and include, for example, linkages with the community, and making parents more aware of the learning opportunities available. It is argued that it is these aspects that should be built upon and developed through the careful tracking and monitoring of outcomes so that the real impacts can be measured not just in the immediate short time-scale but also for the future. It requires in-reach into one's own organisation. McGivney (2001), for example, has argued that the process of widening participation must produce changes in institutional culture and practices. Without change, learners who move from community based learning into 'mainstream' may fail to achieve. This necessitates asking hard questions, what is the relevance to the organisation's mission? Is the activity tangential or is it central, and if it is tangential can it be made more relevant?

The challenges come together in the whole issue of sustainability. Initiatives must be embedded if they are to be sustained in the absence of future funding. There is a need to recognise the long lead-in time for many initiatives in order to sustain impact over a good number of years, and to consider what is the transferability of initiatives beyond the initial years of funding. Institutions and organisations need to be realistic in measuring the real impact in terms of time-scales and increased levels of participation. Many of the learners who are engaged in learning through widening participation projects may need considerable support and encouragement to continue on a lifelong learning path from their initial engagement. Herein lies one of the essential challenges of developing progression to learning: to create an environment of continued support and advice to open up clear pathways for learners but also to take a broad view of outcomes beyond immediate recruitment and education progression.

References

Baxter, L. and Hunt, L. (1999) *Widening Participation to Higher Education in the North East*, Universities for the North East.

Centre for Lifelong Learning (2001) *Developing Progression Routes for Lifelong Learning*: *Papers from the Conference held on 10 December 1999*, Centre for Lifelong Learning Publications No 1, University of Teesside.

CVCP (1999) *From Elitism to Inclusion: Good Practice in Widening Participation in Higher Education.*

Dodgshon, R. and Bolam, H. (2000) *Widening Participation across North East Universities: An Evaluation of Institutional Capacity*, Universities for the North East.

Fryer, R. H. (1999) *Creating Learning Cultures: Next Steps in Achieving the Learning Age: Second report of the National Advisory Group for Continuing Education and Lifelong Learning.* Ideas for Inclusion: An A to Z for Practitioners 2000

HEFCE (2001) *Strategies for Widening Participation in Higher Education: A Guide to Good Practice.* Joint Strategy Unit, Tees Valley 2001

Lynn, P. and Noble, M. (2001) *Developing Progression Pathways in the Tees Valley: Report of the First Year of the Progression Pathways Project*, University of Teesside.

McGivney, V. (1999a) *Informal Learning in the Community: A Trigger for Change and Development* NIACE.

McGivney, V. (1999b) *Excluded Men: Men who are missing from education and training*, NIACE: Leicester.

McGivney, V. (2000) *Recovering Outreach: Concepts, Issues and Practices*, NIACE: Leicester.

McGivney, V. (2001) *NIACE Briefing Sheet* 17, February.

Noble, M and Littlefair, D (2001) *Raising Aspirations and Achievement: An Initial Evaluation of the Meteor Scheme*, Centre for Lifelong Learning Publications No 2, University of Teesside.

Spedding, T and Gregson, M. (2000) Widening Participation a Missing Curriculum? – some observations on the Policy and Practice of Widening Participation in Further Education in the UK. Paper presented to British Education Research Association Annual Conference, Cardiff University, September.

11

The role of Community Colleges in promoting access to higher education for low-income students: the University of California at Los Angeles transfer program

Maureen Hoyler, Holly Hexter and Lorraine Casey

Introduction

The US community college system has been put forward as one model for promoting access and widened participation to higher education for low income groups. Community colleges offer 'sub-degree' level provision, two year courses which students have the option to top-up to a degree with a further two years study. It appears the UK is one country following the US example. At present a number of British institutions are piloting two year foundation courses which will also be convertible to a degree with extended study. Indeed, the UK Government is marketing these 'degrees' as comparable to the US system which it sees as a success (DfEE, 2000).

In fact, the record of community colleges has been 'mixed' (Jary et al, 1998), and the severest critique accuses them of offering previously under represented groups little more than a ' pretend degree' (Triesman,1996: 12). Consequently, the UK, and other countries following the U.S, should be cautious about how closely they adhere to this model. This chapter will detail the main shortfalls of community colleges and one university's successful attempt to overcome these and bring more low-income students into higher education. Through an appraisal of the University of California's Transfer System we conclude that success ultimately depends on effective collaboration.

The US context

In recent decades, enrollments in postsecondary education have risen among students of all racial and ethnic groups and socio-economic backgrounds in the United States. Nevertheless, despite such increases, significant disparities persist in high school graduation rates, college participation and completion rates by family income. Low-income students, taken here as those from families with incomes below 125 percent of the federally established poverty line, are less likely to participate and persist at each level. This correlation of probable college entry and family income holds across racial and ethnic groups, with the exception of Asian-Americans.

One-third of 18 to 24-year-olds from low-income families enroll in college in California, compared with 58 percent of those from high-income families (National Centre for Public Policy and Higher Education, 2000). Of that age group, 55 percent of those with parents who have some college education enroll, compared to 31 percent of those with no family college background.

Enrollment and transfer of low-income students in community colleges

Overall, about two-fifths of all first-time college freshmen in the US are enrolled in community colleges, institutions accredited to award the associate in arts or science as its highest degree (Foote, 1997). Evidence suggests that low-income students have become increasingly concentrated in public two-year colleges (McPherson and Schapiro, 1994). The public community college remains the point of entry to higher education for most first-generation, low-income students in the United States, a finding that Dougherty (1992) deems regrettable.

More positively, enrollment in a community college may be the first step toward academic and social advancement for these students;

however, it by no means leads directly to the baccalaureate degree. Although it is difficult to calculate a rate of transfer from two-year to four-year institutions, about one out of five community college students matriculates to a baccalaureate program, and that rate has not changed significantly in recent years (Cohen and Brawer, 1996). In other words, only 20 percent of students entering tertiary education via this route achieves a traditional degree level qualification.

Students in community colleges, and first-generation, low-income community college students in particular, are less likely to persist and to progress through the educational pipeline for many of the reasons associated with lower entry rates by low-income students generally: financial struggles, poor academic preparation, enrollment in vocational, technical or remedial programs, limited information and advising about transfer requirements, and personal doubts about their academic abilities (Striplin, 1999).

Some commentators have criticised community colleges more specifically, and argued that the 'two year institution has accentuated rather than reduced existing patterns of social inequality' (Brint and Karabel, 1989: 226). Community colleges have come to play an exclusionary role, 'cooling out' and 'managing ambition'. Despite these deficiencies, there are 'advantages' to the community college system but these will only be realised once good links are established with universities (Jary et al, 1998).

Issues of transfer and articulation, policies that facilitate movement between two- and four-year institutions, have remained prominent on the education reform agendas of educators, administrators and policymakers at the national level and in state governments. In the late 1980s, California and other states began allocating special monies for transfer-directed activities.

Demographic and policy changes impinge on access in California

In California, these issues have taken on special urgency because of a projected 'tidal wave' in the size of the traditional college-age cohort in the next 10 years. The state expects an additional 714,000 students to be 'knocking on the doors' of California's three public college systems in the next decade. Total enrollment at the California public colleges and universities is projected to rise from 1,998,000 students in 1998 to some 2,700,000 students by the year 2010, a 36 percent increase (California Postsecondary Education Commission, 2000).

Anticipating the increased demand, and recognising transfer as an important element of educational opportunity, the state in 1998 established ambitious community college transfer goals. The 'Partnership for Excellence' set numerical goals for additional transfers to California State University and the University of California annually by the year 2005 and has been augmented by memoranda of understanding between the California community colleges, CSU and UC.

The results of the systemwide agreements to increase student transfers from the public community colleges to the public four-year institutions have been mixed (California Postsecondary Education Commission, 2000). But transfer applications and admissions to some campuses in the public four-year systems have risen as a consequence of greater attention to 'lower-transferring' community colleges.

This chapter examines successful efforts by the University of California at Los Angeles to recruit and retain students transferring from the Community College District of Los Angeles and other area community colleges, with special attention to low-income and other under represented groups. Between fall 1989-9 and 1998-99 the total number of transfer students in the US did not alter significantly, but the number of transfers to the University of California rose by 24 percent (California Postsecondary Education Commission, 2000).

Community college transfer recruitment and retention at University of California in Los Angeles (UCLA)

UCLA in 1999 created an office under the Chancellor dedicated to community college outreach to increase the number of community college transfer students, who now constitute about 41 percent of all upper-division students in the university, and to strengthen the curriculum of community colleges. The core components of the transfer efforts at UCLA are as follows:

- The Community College Transfer Program (CCTP), which provides assistance to prospective transfer students at designated community colleges, with special emphasis on historically under represented students, during the academic year;

- The Transfer Alliance Program (TAP), an academic honors program at 33 community colleges that allows students completing a rigorous curriculum at the community college to transfer to UCLA as juniors;

- The Transfer Summer Program, a summer bridge program for community college transfer students who already have been admitted to UCLA, administered by the university's Academic Advancement Program;

- The Transfer Student Centre, an office that provides special support services for transfer students, and

- Summer Intensive Transfer Experience (SITE), an intensive one-week program that brings high school students who have been admitted to community colleges to the UCLA campus.

The **Community College Transfer Program** began 16 years ago as an effort to increase the application and admission rates of students from low-income backgrounds and under represented groups, including African-Americans, Chicano-Latinos and Native Americans. It is staffed by counsellors who visit the participating community colleges regularly during the academic year to provide workshops to community college students and to offer advice and assistance to transfer applicants throughout the application process.

UCLA gives highest priority in its transfer admissions to students from California community colleges and the University of California. It admits transfer applicants at the junior level who have attained a minimum grade point average and have completed most or all of the preparation coursework to enter as upper-division students, although the university will consider special circumstances, such as family responsibility or employment demands, that prevent applicants from meeting these academic standards.

UCLA has targeted community colleges in greater Los Angeles with low transfer rates. These institutions enroll predominantly Latino, Chicano or African-American students. At each of the more than 30 collaborating institutions, CCTP staff help motivate and prepare students by distributing information on financial aid, housing, and academic requirements for transfer. They advise students by review-ing individual transcripts and discussing course planning. CCTP also functions as the first step in a continuum of services for com-munity college transfer students; once they are admitted to UCLA they participate in the range of support services offered by the school's Academic Advancement Program (AAP) or other support service programs at UCLA.

The **Transfer Summer Program** is a six-week academic summer program that is designed to familiarise about 100 entering com-munity college transfer students with college life at UCLA. Students attending the residential program enroll in two university courses and receive advising in small group or individual sessions staffed by teaching assistants and tutors, with support from faculty and peer counsellors. This 'bridge' program provides a critical transition for students in acculturating them to the rigors of the university curri-culum and to campus ways generally.

Transfer students enrolled at UCLA can receive special services through the **Student Transfer Centre**, one of the many support programs and services offered under the umbrella of the Academic Advancement Program. AAP serves more than 6,500 students on campus as it provides tutoring, academic, personal and career counselling, graduate mentoring, scholarships, research oppor-tunities and stipends, science programs, and a computer lab.

The newest component of the university's outreach and retention programs aimed at low-income, under represented students in two-year programs, **Summer Intensive Transfer Experience**, or **SITE**, was added two years ago. Working with staff from high schools, community colleges and other undergraduate programs in the UC system, the program brings students preparing to enter community colleges to UCLA for an intensive one-week stay.

The objective of **SITE** is twofold-to increase participants' educational aspirations and to elucidate the academic path participants must follow to enroll in UCLA. The institutional goals of the initiative are to enhance access for under represented students and facilitate transfer from two-year colleges with track records of low transfer rates.

In the two years that **SITE** has been offered by UCLA, 350 students have participated – a cohort of more than 100 participants for each of the three one-week programs. The programs have involved UCLA faculty staff and students and faculty and staff from seven other UC campuses and six community colleges in the region.

Program outcomes
Due to its brief history, SITE has not yet produced quantitative outcomes that demonstrate its ability to increase the transfer rates of low-income, under represented students attending community colleges. Because students participate prior to entry into the community college, a lag of several years can be expected between participation in SITE and formal entry to the undergraduate admission process.

Nevertheless, taken as a whole, the programmatic efforts of UCLA to recruit low-income students, with special focus on transfer students, have yielded positive results. Between fall 1998 and fall 2000, the total number of transfer applications from community college students to UCLA rose by almost a quarter (23 percent), with Filipino, Latino, and Asian-Americans showing the most significant gains of all racial/ethnic minorities.

During that time, the total number of new transfers admitted to and enrolled in UCLA increased from 1,876 to 2,268. Although the average admission rate and yield (percentage of admitted students who register) remained unchanged, the admission rates of Chicano/Mexican American and Filipino students showed an increase.

Conclusion
The value of this transfer scheme lies in its long term approach and continuum of services and programs that track students from secondary to postsecondary education. Although it is too early to say if

this scheme has succeeded in transferring more low-income students to university, initial findings are positive.

This scheme tries to address criticisms of community colleges that see these institutions as 'confirming' class location and contributing to 'class reproduction' rather than to social mobility (Dougherty, 1987 in Jary *et al* 1998 p 88). Keen to improve access into higher education, this comprehensive transfer scheme provides a positive model of how successful collaboration between universities, community colleges and other partners, can increase the number of under represented students on university campuses. This model could prove particularly useful to the UK, at the present time, which is seen to be following closely behind the US system of higher education and expanding higher education provision in the further education sector.

Early criticisms of foundation degrees in the UK have included the short time frame in which these courses have been set up. Without adequate time, resources and student support dedicated to them, foundation degrees could easily fall into the same trap as community colleges and produce a low rate of transfer into higher education for low-income students. In order to avoid this situation, a number of principles must be adhered to. Students who enrol on these courses need to be aware from the very start of their choices once they have completed. They should also have the option of transferring to a degree programme in the final year. This transfer needs to be straightforward: foundation courses need to be articulated with degree courses and students need to have support available as their study environment changes. The key to success is long term and effective collaboration between the different stages of progression.

References

California Postsecondary Education Commission, (2000) 'New Community College Transfer Students at California Public Universities,' factsheet.

Cohen, A. M. and Brawer, F. B. (1996) *Policies and Programs that Affect Transfer.* Washington, D.C: American Council on Education.

Department for Education and Employment (2000) Foundation Degrees: A Consultation Document. www.dfee.gov.uk/heqe/fdcd.htm.

Dougherty, K. (1992) 'Community colleges and baccalaureate attainment', *Journal of Higher Education*, 63(2): 188-214.

Foote, E (1997) 'Community colleges: General Information and resources', *ERIC Digest* ED411929.

Jary, D., Gatley, D. and Broadbent, L. (1998) 'The US Community College' In Jary, D. and Parker, M. *The New Higher Education: Issues and Direction for the Post-Dearing University.* Staffordshire University Press: Staffordshire.

McPherson, M. S. and Schapiro, M. O. (1994) *College Choice and Family Income: Changes over Time in the Higher Education Destinations of Students from Different Income Backgrounds.* University of California at Los Angeles.

Striplin, J. J. (1999) 'Facilitating Transfer for First-Generation Community College Students,' *ERIC Digest* EDO-JC-9905.

The National Centre for Public Policy and Higher Education, (2000) *Measuring Up 2000: The State-By-State Report Card for Higher Education.* San Jose, CA

Triesman, D. (1996) 'Community challenges', *The Guardian Higher*, November 5.

12

Why collaborate? Initiatives for improving participation and completion for students with a disability in South Australia

Ann Noble and Gerry Mullins

Introduction

For many years the approach to disability issues in tertiary education has been rather 'ad hoc', with separate institutions engaging in often complex projects and initiatives, usually unrelated to each other (Ramsey, 1994). Despite continuing efforts, disability has remained a low priority, a poor sister to other targeted equity fields. However, attention to this field is important, given the characteristics which define the participation of students with a disability in tertiary education. Surveys conducted at the three South Australian universities between 1995 and 1996 confirmed studies elsewhere (Abbott-Chapman, Hughes and Wyld, 1992) that students with a disability are: more likely to be studying part-time; more likely to start/stop/re-start, change courses or withdraw; less likely to have clearly-defined academic or career goals; and unlikely to go on to postgraduate study.

Collaboration between institutions to improve the experience of students with disabilities has been encouraged over the last decade by a number of Australian government statements and frameworks. In 1990 the government stated its equity objectives: ' . . . to ensure Australians from all groups of society have the opportunity to participate successfully in higher education' (*A Fair Chance for All: higher education that's within everyone's reach*). The six designated equity groups included people with disabilities. Funds were provided to institutions through the Higher Education Equity Program (HEEP) to assist in the development of Cooperative Projects for Higher Education Students with Disabilities (CPHESD). This signalled the beginning of the collaborative initiatives to be outlined in this chapter. In 1992 the Commonwealth Disability Discrimination Act (DDA) gave further impetus to these developments.

The Martin Report (1994), *Equity and General Performance Indicators in Higher Education*, however, found that not only were students with disabilities under represented in the commencing and continuing cohorts, but once enrolled they performed less well than other students. Such a finding is not a purely Australian phenomenon. A University of Warwick project carried out between 1990-92 (Leicester and Lowell, 1994) highlighted how attention to disability came well behind other 'equal opportunity' initiatives (particularly race and gender) in relation to recruitment and curriculum development, and to 'success'.

The National Board of Employment, Education and Training (NBEET) report (1996), *Equality, Diversity and Excellence: advancing the higher education equity framework*, noted the continuing need for 'initiatives which focus on access and support mechanisms to improve success and retention of students with disabilities', and for 'programs to address the employment prospects' of these students (p. xviii). Interestingly, the report refers to the need to move the equity focus from individuals to systems, to address the systemic discrimination and disadvantage existing within educational cultures, a need highlighted in the literature of the mid-1990s (Porter, 1994). A further development at this time was the release of the *Guidelines for Disability Services in Higher Education* (NBEET).

The West Report (1998) *Higher Education Review* noted the continuing significant under-representation of rural and isolated students, and also students with disabilities. HEEP gave way to the Disabilities Initiatives Program in 1999, and the most recent Department of Education Training and Youth Affairs (DETYA) report, *Higher education: Report for the 2000-2002 Triennium*, refers to the continuing challenge of targeting, marketing to, and accommodating students from 'fringe' groups.

Why collaborate?

Given these federal government pronouncements, collaboration between institutions was imperative, though not always welcomed. What has been referred to as 'coercive federalism' was behind many equity programs (Bowen, 1994). However in several states there were a number of compelling 'local' reasons for collaboration. South Australia, for example, is a small state, with a population of slightly more than one million, and a tertiary education population of approximately 50 000 students. Students with a disability make up 3-4% of this number. Sharing resources and expertise makes sense when there is a limited market and limited resources (support personnel, 'extra' programs, Disability Liaison Officers [DLOs] etc) resulting from the limited funding available to, and available at, each institution.

Additionally, in South Australia the tertiary education providers exist in relatively close proximity, and so target overlapping markets. The three Adelaide-based universities are a matter of kilometres from each other; in one case campuses are adjacent. There are eight technical and further education colleges (TAFEs) which have amongst them approximately fifty campuses of varied sizes spread throughout the state, sometimes in close proximity to university campuses.

Collaboration also made sense because all tertiary institutions faced the need to address the requirements of the DDA (1992) and implement Disability Action Plans, a new and untested area of endeavour. Additionally, collaborative activity provided an opportunity to create consistency of practice across the tertiary education sector, with concomitant advantages for students, and to give legitimacy to an area traditionally hard to 'push' in tertiary education, and higher or university education in particular.

The joint projects undertaken involved a consortium of the three universities, and strategic collaborations with other further education providers, with staff in secondary schools, and with community organisations providing services to people with disabilities. Projects were initiated and overseen by an inter-institutional committee of staff and students, the 'Uniability' committee. The federally-funded Regional Disability Liaison Officer project was another important element in the collaboration. Much of the collaboration was between staff in agencies within institutions – staff developers, academic advisors and counsellors, equity personnel, and DLOs. However, collaboration was not always easy or straightforward. Collaborators worked in different locations and in different 'systems', and there were occasionally funding uncertainties, including changes in names of funding/oversight bodies, and in the nature of the funding conditions.

Some initiatives: their objectives and outcomes

The collaborative initiatives were designed primarily to attend to issues *after* access and lead to:

- improved retention and success rates

- consistency of practice across the sector

- a higher profile for learning and teaching issues

- better integration of students into tertiary 'life'

- more sophisticated support programs

- more inclusive learning environments (encompassing issues in curriculum development, teaching and assessment practices, and staff awareness).

The projects were many and diverse. Unfortunately only a small number can be described in this chapter.

Access to a Future is a 5-part radio program outlining tertiary options, and intended to encourage people with disabilities to aspire to tertiary study. Interviews with students, academic staff, support staff and a range of employers covered preparation for tertiary study, methods of entry, support systems, and pathways to careers.

Come and Try Tertiary Study is a 2 day 'experience' for secondary school students with a disability, held annually, and scheduled to coincide with tertiary institutions' 'Open Days'. This initiative grew from the recognition of the limitations of the 'staying at home to continue study' options often promoted to students with a disability. The experience is designed to make tertiary education options more relevant to a specific group, and the transition more manageable.

Employability is a resource kit designed to assist students to make informed decisions about entering the employment market. It includes information on skills sought by employers; how to 'research' the job market; preparing applications; preparing for an interview, with particular focus on 'disclosing' disability; disability and workplace legislation and 'rights'; advocacy and conflict resolution skills; and lateral and creative thinking skills.

Education, Registration and Employment is a project designed to address barriers which have traditionally existed for students with disabilities in entering certain professions, involving collaboration between university academics, professional registering bodies and employers in nursing, education, medicine and dentistry. The issues addressed include reasonable accommodations in the education setting; expectations of registering bodies regarding education and demonstrated competences/capabilities; and options for employment.

Three projects which demonstrate the very practical nature of these collaborations will be described in more detail: the pre-entry resource *Choosing courses and subjects at university: a guide for students with a disability*; the post-entry workshop *Speaking up; and a staff development resource Teaching students with a disability: guidelines for academic staff.*

Choosing courses and subjects at university: a guide for students who have a disability is a resource available in a range of formats which was widely distributed to secondary schools and colleges and community disability organisations. This initiative involved collaboration between student welfare officers, academic staff developers, and equity and school liaison personnel in one institution, and was designed to remedy the unsatisfactory high drop out rate of students with a disability.

There are many reasons why students fail to progress in their courses, or fail to complete them. Amongst these reasons the literature focuses on finance, family-related issues, changing goals, motivational and social factors, perceptions of institutional 'fit', and lack of academic preparedness (Astin, 1993; Tinto, 1993; 1997; McKenzie and Schweitzer, 2001). Failure to complete is sometimes a result of the unrealistic nature of students' expectations, and inappropriate course choice resulting from poor guidance from schools, inadequate institutional guidelines, or in the case of students with a disability, inaccurate or out-of-date information from community disability organisations. In Abbott-Chapman *et al*'s 1992 research, 33% of withdrawing students said that they had chosen the wrong subject(s). More recent research has found that in general applicants to university are poorly informed on 'key matters' including specific characteristics of courses of study (James et al, 1999).

A 1995 survey of students with a disability conducted across the three South Australian universities found that almost half the respondents had made changes to their study program in their first year – changing subjects, withdrawing from subjects (often because of workload, but also because of teaching or assessment issues) or moving to part-time status. Further information regarding the academic well-being and progress of students with disabilities was gathered in an Adelaide University survey (1996) which found that they: withdraw from subjects almost twice as much as other students; fail a greater percentage of the subjects in which they are enrolled than other students; have far fewer credit and distinction grades amongst their results and a greater number of 'withdraw not fail'; and change courses at the end of the first year more often than other students, essentially because of negative experiences ('It wasn't right for me').

Choosing courses and subjects does not give information about, or descriptions of, specific subjects. Rather, after an introduction which outlines the reasons why informed choices are so important to success, it engages students with some of the many issues relevant to preparation for tertiary study. Information is organised under the following headings:

- Think about your goals and interests

- Match goals and personal skills with subject choices

- Think about workload

- Think about teaching styles

- Think about assessment issues

- Use people who can help with course and subject decisions

- Other things to think about...

Informed choice will lessen the likelihood of failure and withdrawal. The advice given encourages students to acknowledge existing strengths, and consider how to accommodate or bypass their known limitations or areas of weakness.

Speaking Up follows on from the provision of appropriate advice related to course and subject choice to focus on orientation to the tertiary environment – and to sources of support. In one study of student progress (Abbott-Chapman *et al*, 1992) nearly a quarter of respondents indicated that they did not know who in the system to turn to for advice or support when they need it. Speaking Up is a one-day workshop for newly-enrolled students with a disability designed to promote familiarity with 'the system' and with some of the people in it. Because of institutional differences the workshop is of necessity institution-specific, but the core program is transferable.

An important adjustment issue for students with a disability coming to tertiary study is that they lose the support network they have relied on at secondary school (teachers and counsellors, disability organisations etc), and the feeling of safety inherent in everyone 'knowing' about their disability, and behaving accordingly. And while they are often well-equipped in an academic sense to succeed, they may be personally stressed by a lack of support, and by the relative impersonality of the tertiary environment. Not adapting well, and problems with staff (and peer) attitude and bias, are reasons frequently cited for withdrawal, particularly by students with a disability. Therefore, for these students, the way they disclose their disability, and discuss with staff its impact on their learning, may be crucial. Unfortunately, disclosure often results in students being made to feel 'more different' and therefore 'more difficult'.

Speaking Up covers the following topics:

- Understanding different approaches to teaching and learning

- Identifying personal learning strengths

- Developing new learning and communication skills (including self-advocacy)

- Knowing and negotiating the system

- Using support services and accessing support programs.

Workshop activities involve practising disclosure. Advocacy exercises use peers to promote feelings of identification and affiliation (Astin, 1993). Encouraging peer problem solving and support amongst students alleviates the potential problem of over-reliance on support services. This is particularly important given our knowledge that students who are overly-dependent on support services are likely to be patronised by both staff and other students, and experience demeaning and arbitrary treatment.

It is empowering for students when they know where they are in a system, where they stand in relation to other people in it, and when they are able to recognise situations and opportunities in which they might play some part in the decisions made about their academic experience. Tinto's (1993) model of institutional departure draws attention to the importance of students' early commitments and feelings of belonging, and decisions about whether or not to withdraw. Other studies highlight the role of staff in fostering student commitment and persistence (Abbott-Chapman *et al*, 1995). Students who feel that they are partners in, rather than receivers of, learning experiences, who feel acknowledged, known and 'integrated', who have 'networks', are more likely to persist (Thomas, 2000).

Teaching students with a disability: guidelines for academic staff follows on from these student-focused 'preparation for being in the system' initiatives, to focus on staff needs. It is a printed (and also web-based) resource, a set of six brochures providing guidelines which promote best teaching practice, and encouraging staff to consider changing conservative approaches to teaching and assessing. The project involved collaboration between academic developers and student learning advisers.

The main barriers to participation for students from non-traditional backgrounds might not be access as such, or support, but *what* is taught, and *how*. There is clearly a need, in order to create relevant and inclusive learning environments, for institutions to focus on refining the curriculum, introducing more relevant teaching and assessment activities, and raising staff awareness about diversity. It matters little what support systems are in place if teaching staff remain unaware of the issues involved in teaching students from a diversity of backgrounds.

Because over the last decade academics have faced increasingly complex issues arising from equity initiatives and consumer demands, focused staff development activity is important. Attitudinal barriers regarding disability are much harder to shift than physical or financial barriers, and in tertiary institutions there are still many practices which continue to disadvantage or marginalise those deemed different.

In the issue of transition and success at tertiary level, students already disadvantaged educationally are especially likely to regard aware and approachable lecturers as important to their persistence with study (Pascarella and Terenzini, 1991). But how are staff to become 'aware', and remain 'approachable'? Impressions gained from interviews with academics at Adelaide University suggested that they had relatively low expectations about the progress of students with a disability. They also indicated concerns about the extension of their traditional teaching role into the role of 'specialist'; about the increase in time spent accommodating the different needs of different groups; and about the perceived dilution of standards (see also McInnes, 1998; 2001).

There is a need for staff to move beyond merely complying with what they are legally required to do (Lissner, 1997) to understanding how better to manage 'difference' (Burbules, 1997). Any institution which seeks to address the limiting or discriminatory practices experienced by particular students, whether they be students with a disability, indigenous students, or students from other language or cultural backgrounds, will need to attend to ways of shifting the attitudes of staff and student peers (Elliott, in King *et al*, 2000), and challenging assumptions about the existence of 'usual' or 'mainstream' students.

Each brochure provides information specific to a particular type/category of disability, but each follows the same format. A general introduction to the disability 'type' is followed by information under a series of headings:

*   The impact of [the disability] on learning at university

*   Communicating with students with [the disability]

*   Teaching a group of students which includes students with [the disability]

*   Strategies for assessing students with [the disability].

Strategies considered under the subheadings 'Approaches to teaching which assist all students to learn include . . .' and 'There are some good assessment practices which help all students . . .' can be considered to be a revisiting of the principles of good teaching, and so relevant to *all* staff and *all* students.

Implicit in the brochures' focus on teaching and learning is that they should reflect the characteristics of good teaching as established in the literature (Ramsden, 1992); acknowledge that there are discipline differences and different contexts which students must juggle; and recognise that assessment is one of the most influential factors affecting how students learn (Boud, 1995; Nightingale *et al*, 1996; Ashcroft and Palaccio, 1996). The suggested strategies reinforce 'best practice' in teaching – awareness, appropriate language, and positive, professional interactions. The information is practical and to the point.

The brochures encourage teaching staff to engage with the ideas of difference and diversity, and fairness and equitable practice (Noble and Mullins, 2001), and to consider the need for consistency of practice. They also recognise the importance of finding appropriate language in this context, and so refer, for example, to teaching and assessment 'strategies' rather than 'adaptations' or 'adjustments', and to students with a disability rather than to disabled students. One of the goals of *Teaching students with a disability* was to encourage staff to think creatively beyond the old ideas of 'special provisions', 'students with special needs' and 'compensating' or 'accommodating'.

Issues relating to access and equity policy and practice
The problem of 'targeting' or stereotyping
There are significant problems inherent in 'grouping' minorities and assuming homogeneity because of those groupings. Groups are often marked out by stereotypes; stereotyping means that individuals within a group often have their interests and perspectives rendered invisible, their individual characteristics and differences overlooked. But within most groups, and particularly the 'disabled' group, there is a great diversity, not always apparent when the label is fixed. Consider, for example, the different needs and experiences of students who are blind or hearing-impaired from those who have a medical disability or a psychological disability. And within specific disability groups there are differences. For example in the hearing-impaired group there will be some students who are pre-lingually deaf, and those who have lost hearing gradually, over time. Their needs and approaches to learning will vary greatly. Some students may have multiple disabilities (for example a mature-age female from a different culture with cerebral palsy and a hearing impairment), and so are likely to experience multiple educational and social disadvantage, a situation often overlooked when a label is attached.

Difference and marginalisation
The fact that under represented groups have access to educational opportunities and educational facilities does not mean that marginalisation ceases. Further problems arise as a result of institutions' failure to acknowledge difference or to promote discussion

about diversity (Goodman, 1995; King et al, 2000). The continuing insistence on observing 'standard' qualifications and 'standard' forms of knowledge and ways of learning and 'standard' students undertaking 'standard' periods of study continues to marginalise many. A tension exists because tertiary systems are fundamentally designed to make people alike (a 'levelling' process), but now they also assert that they will serve the needs of an increasingly diverse student population. We need strategies which will move institutions beyond what Burbules (1997) refers to as 'sweeping claims' about difference, and about what is or is not possible educationally.

Where access and equity are 'managed'
Who initiates or manages the focus on difference in educational institutions? The business of equity and fairness is often left to non-teaching areas, to separate equity or disability or student affairs units. However equity issues are integral to, not separate from, teaching, and as such must become part of the academic development agenda, and of the agenda of all teaching departments. Only then is there likely to be a lessening of the marginalisation which occurs when learning and teaching issues for particular groups are dealt with by people outside the teaching/learning relationship. Having said all this, we realise that there is sometimes a downside to equity issues being 'mainstreamed' throughout institutions. When equity becomes everybody's business, it often ends up being nobody's. This is why a project such as *Teaching students with a disability* is so important. The guidelines reach all members of staff in all departments, which is essential given the increasing casualisation of the academic workforce.

Funding
Government policies related to access do not ensure that institutions have (or commit) the resources necessary to ensure equal access to the teaching/learning process, and equal participation after access. While equity programs have been largely successful in enabling access, they have been less successful in keeping students in the system.

This may be primarily a result of the paucity of funding directed to the area, but also because funding has traditionally been made available for short term projects rather than for the implementation of long term strategies. Ramsey (1994) noted that providing funding to often disparate and unrelated (though worthwhile) programs and initiatives resulted in staffing and structural arrangements which had several dysfunctional characteristics in terms of achieving longer term change. And as West (1998) pointed out, there are still few incentives for institutions to be innovative or to re-engineer traditional approaches to teaching and administration in order to capture particular groups.

Systemic change
Lasting systemic change (Taylor *et al*, 2000; Thanki *et al*, 2000) might result from more sustained and more encompassing initiatives, for example 'reaching back' initiatives which target schools and communities; initiatives which focus on the complex and controversial issue of 'alternative' assessment practices; and initiatives which encourage students with a disability into postgraduate study.

The relevance and benefits of tertiary education are not always clear to those who have suffered earlier educational disadvantage. Individual students need incentives and encouragement to move to the next level, but 'reaching back' initiatives should also target the 'significant others', families and teachers and counsellors in particular, who have an impact on the directions students take following the years of compulsory schooling. And there is much in the timing of such initiatives: targeting too late in the secondary years means that students may have cut off many options.

'Reaching back' initiatives are likely to be most successful when they are non-institution specific, and collaborative rather than individual and competitive. Likewise, in encouraging the development of initiatives which focus on the need for more relevant and appropriate methods of assessment (Noble and Mullins, 2001), collaboration between institutions can result in meaningful change and consistency of practice across the sector.

Conclusion

Some of the unresolved questions arising from our experience with collaboration include the following:

What happens after access?

Access is no longer a particularly pressing issue. Over the last decade it has been largely assured through a diversity of access programs. Real equity – in terms of teaching, assessment, and the provision of appropriate and relevant services to all students – must now be the focus of institutions' activities. Providing access is meaningless unless we can also point to indicators of retention and success, and eliminate the personally, socially, and economically costly 'revolving door' which catches so many 'at risk' students (Abbott-Chapman *et al*, 1992; Elliott in King *et al*, 2000).

How can the impact of collaboration be assessed?

Gauging impact is different to demonstrating outcome. The outcomes of these collaborative activities are clear: a range of useful and practical cross-institutional resources. But assessing their impact is a different matter. The response of staff and students to these various projects has been overwhelmingly positive: students have reported feeling better about the environment; staff report feeling more aware, and better-equipped to respond to different requests. How do we know, however, that these improvements are the result of specific projects – or of a combination of them – or of something outside our understanding or control?

Does collaboration change institutional cultures?

Compliance with legislation is one thing; but changing systems and attitudes so that we move from the notion of disability as being simply about deficits in individuals is another. There is some change in institutional approaches to diversity, but it is impossible to know whether this is an outcome of collaboration, or of the passage of time, or the influence of other factors. And there is still evidence, unfortunately, of a general lack of commitment in many institutions to the principles of equal access and equal opportunity. And we need to acknowledge that, in an increasingly competitive, market-driven tertiary environment where institutions must develop and capitalise on individual strengths, and diversify their roles, collaboration is not always realistic.

Is the notion that collaboration is a 'good thing' myth or reality?
Collaboration between institutions is common in many areas – with regard to credit accumulation and transfer, for example, or the 'sharing' of courses. But arguments for the need for institutions to collaborate to boost the factors which encourage the participation of equity groups are rarely supported by a theory or model. The economic benefits of collaboration in a small state where there is limited funding and a limited market are clear, but beyond that, we have yet to see the long term changes which it was hoped collaborative activity would deliver, and it remains to be determined whether innovation is indeed more likely with collaboration.

The questions raised during the course of, and by, these collaborative projects do not have immediate or easy answers: how do we ensure a continuing dialogue between students, academics, administrators and employers to facilitate change across the sector; how do we ensure that academics respond positively to increasingly complex ideas about alternative assessment; how do we measure 'success' – both of programs/projects, and of students? However, the strategic collaborations described in this chapter, and the policy and pedagogical issues raised, represent both an achievement and a challenge in this rather neglected area of tertiary education.

References

Abbott-Chapman, J. Hughes, P. and Wyld, C. (1992) *'Monitoring Student Progress'* Hobart: National Clearing House for Youth Studies.

Abbott-Chapman, J., Easthorpe, G, and O'Connor, P. (1995) 'Post-compulsory participation of students with disabilities: the importance of perceived personal control' in *Australian Educational Researcher*, vol 22 (1): 67-83.

Ashcroft, K. and Palaccio, D. (1996) *'Researching into assessment and evaluation in colleges and universities'* London: Kogan Page.

Astin, A. W. (1993) 'What Matters in College? Four critical years revisited' San Francisco: Jossey-Bass.

Australian Commonwealth Government (1992) *'Disability Discrimination Act'* Canberra: Australian Government publishing service

Boud, D. (1995) 'Assessment and learning: contradictory or complementary?' in Knight, P. (ed) *Assessment for learning in higher education* London: Kogan Page.

Bowen, M. (1994) 'Mainstreaming equity activities in universities: the next challenge' in *Australian Universities' Review*, vol 37 (2): 19-23.

Burbules, N. C. (1997) 'A grammar of difference: some ways of rethinking difference and diversity as educational topics' in *Australian Educational Researcher,* vol 24 (1): 97-116.

Commonwealth of Australia (1990) 'A fair chance for all: higher education that's within everyone's reach' Canberra: Australian Government Publishing Service.

Department of Education Training and Youth Affairs (DETYA) (2000) *'Higher Education: report for the 2000-2002 triennium'* Canberra: Australian Government Publishing Service.

Goodman, D. J. (1995) 'Difficult dialogues: enhancing discussions about diversity' in *College Teaching*, vol 43 (2): 47-51.

James, R., Baldwin, G. and McInnes, C. (1999) *'Which university? The factors influencing the choices of prospective undergraduates'* Canberra: Australian Government Publishing Service.

King, R., Hill, D. and Hemmings, B. (Eds) (2000) *'University and diversity: changing perspectives, policies and practices in Australia'* Wagga Wagga: Keon Publications.

Leicester, M. and Lowell, T. (1994) 'Equal opportunities and university practice: race, gender and disability. A comparative perspective' in *Journal of Further and Higher Education*, vol 18 (2): 43-51.

Lissner, L. S. (1997) 'Legal issues concerning all faculty in higher education' in Hodge, B. M. and Preston-Sabin, J. (eds) *Accommodations – or just good teaching? Strategies for teaching college students with disabilities* Westport: Praeger.

Martin, L. (1994) *'Equity and general performance indicators in higher education. Volume 1: Equity Indicators'* Canberra: Australian Government Publishing Service.

McInnes, C. (2001) 'Researching the first year experience: where to from here?' in *Higher Education Research and Development*, vol 20 (2): 105-114.

McInnes, C. (1998) 'Change and Continuity in Academic Work' Department of Employment, Education, Training and Youth Affairs (DETYA), *Higher Education Series Report No:3.* Canberra: Australian Government Publishing Service.

McKenzie, K. and Schweitzer, R. (2001) 'Who succeeds at university? Factors predicting academic performance in first year Australian university students' in *Higher Education Research and Development*, vol 20 (1): 21-33.

National Board of Employment, Education and Training (NBEET) (1996) *'Equality, Diversity and Excellence: Advancing the higher education equity framework'* Canberra: Australian Government Publishing Service.

Nightingale, P. *et al* (1996) 'Assessing learning in universities' Sydney: University of New South Wales Press.

Noble, A. and Mullins, G. (2001) 'Teaching and assessing students with a disability: providing guidelines for academic staff' in *International Journal of Academic Development* (in press).

Pascarella, E. T. and Terenzini, P. T. (1991) *'How college affects students'* New York: Jossey-Bass.

Porter, J. (1994) 'Disability in higher education: from person-based to interaction-based' in *Journal on Excellence in College Teaching*, vol 5 (1): 69-75.

Ramsden, P. (1992) *'Learning to teach in higher education'* London: Routledge

Ramsey, E. (1994) 'Managing equity in higher education' in *Australian Universities' Review*, vol 37 (2): 13-18.

Taylor, S. and Henry, M. (2000) 'Challenges for equity policy in changing contexts' in *Australian Educational Researcher*, vol 27 (3): 1-15.

Thanki, R. and Osborne, B. (2000) 'Equal opportunities monitoring: policy and practice for students' in *Higher Education Quarterly*, vol 54 (1): 88-98.

Tinto, V. (1993) *'Leaving college: rethinking the causes and cures of student attrition'* (2nd ed) Chicago: University of Chicago Press.

Tinto, V. (1997) 'Classrooms and communities: exploring the educational character of student persistence' in *Journal of Higher Education*, vol 68 (6): 599-623.

Thomas, S. L. (2000) 'Ties that bind: a social network approach to understanding student integration and persistence' in *Journal of Higher Education*, vol 71 (5): 591-615.

West, P. (1998) *'Higher Education Review'* Canberra: Australian Government Publishing Service.

13

'College wouldn't touch me with a barge pole': a collaborative educational development programme for ex-offenders

Lucy MacLeod and Jan Tunnock

Introduction

This chapter describes the reasons why collaboration between community and educational partners has proved successful in widening participation for ex-offenders, who make up one of society's most challenging excluded groups. 'Think Again' is a thirteen-week pre-access course designed to address the barriers facing ex-offenders who wish to return to study in college or university. The project is led by Napier University in partnership with Apex Scotland and Jewel and Esk Valley College. It aims to raise awareness of educational opportunities, develop personal and study skills and increase self-confidence and motivation.

Drawing upon the experience of the Think Again programme, this chapter argues that collaboration makes a radical difference in a number of different ways. It reports on the policy and research rationale for the programme; the course team's findings relating to the impact of the programme on participants and on widening participation; the learning for each of the partners involved; the unique benefits that collaboration can bring; key learning points about the reality and challenges of collaborative working across sectors; and issues of future development and sustainability.

Rationale

Think Again was developed against a policy background that includes, not only the Scottish Executive's and UK government's national objectives in relation to widening participation in higher education, but also in relation to the reduction of crime rates in disadvantaged areas. Both objectives feature as key milestones in the government's social justice agenda (Social Inclusion: opening the door to a better Scotland, Scottish Executive, 1999). Ex-offenders are also recognised as a priority group within the government's policies in relation to social inclusion and by the European Union through its European Social Fund Objective 3 programme. Both acknowledge that:

> a criminal record, and especially a prison record, is a barrier to participation in mainstream society for those offenders who wish to mend their ways (*Social Justice – a Scotland where everyone matters, Scottish Executive*, 1999).

The European Social Fund (ESF) Objective 3 Operational Programme estimates that in Scotland around 9,000 ex-offenders re-enter the community each year, the majority of whom are male. Ex-offenders often lack previous work experience and certified qualifications and commonly experience negative employer perceptions and discrimination. They can also lack personal and work-related skills and competences and this can result in low motivation, low self-confidence and self- esteem. The 'benefits trap' also affects ex-offenders, who often feel limited to low paid jobs where the financial gain from entering employment will be minimal in comparison with welfare benefits. The result is commonly long term unemployment and re-offending. Jobless ex-offenders are three times more likely to re-offend than those who gain employment or move onto training or further education opportunities (Scottish Executive, 2000).

The Scottish Prison Service Annual Report 1999-00 (Scottish Prison Service, 2000) states that the average cost of keeping an individual in prison is £26,000 per annum. It is important not only for the individual but also for mainstream society to offer offenders pathways back into legitimate activities. The overall aim of the Think

Again programme is therefore to provide participants with access to further training and education that improves their employment prospects.

Napier University has a long track record in attracting non-traditional students and this has been reflected in its strategic planning. Research carried out at the University (Tunnock, 1999), which included in-depth interviews with teaching staff and voluntary organisations, recommended that Napier should seek to build closer links with community and voluntary organisations working with socially excluded groups, because of their expert knowledge of the barriers facing socially excluded groups, their skills in working with individuals from those groups and their ability to use their contacts and networks for recruitment. Subsequently, Napier was successful in its application to the Scottish Higher Education Funding Council for Wider Access Development Grant assistance. This addressed a range of actions designed to widen participation through partnerships bringing greater expertise in working with new client groups facing specific barriers in accessing further and higher education. One of these partnerships has been with Apex Scotland, a leading national organisation working with ex-offenders and Jewel and Esk Valley College of Further Education.

The Think Again partners
Established in 1987, Apex Scotland is a leading Scottish training organisation specialising in work with ex-offenders. Since it was set up, over 35,000 individuals have used Apex services with 40% gaining employment, 28% moving on into further education and training and 25% undertaking further training with Apex: only 5% have re-offended (Apex Scotland Annual Report: 1999/2000). This compares with a national recidivism rate of 86% within two years of release from prison. Think Again was designed to appeal specifically to ex-offenders who wished to explore opportunities for further study, and, in particular, to raise aspiration and awareness of routes into higher education through both further education colleges and university.

The course utilises Apex's expertise and knowledge of this target group and the barriers they face in accessing education and employment opportunities. The bulk of the course takes place at Apex premises which offers a familiar, non-institutional setting. As well as bringing expertise in working with participants with offending backgrounds, Apex staff provide specialist input to the course on conviction relevance and disclosure, relevant legislation and equal opportunities. The link with Apex also enables the partnership to access new networks, such as social work and the voluntary sector, for recruitment of course participants.

Jewel and Esk Valley College is a local further education college with considerable experience of access level provision that offers qualifications at a range of levels. It has a strong track record in working and delivering in community settings. A further education partner was always recognised as essential to the programme because it was anticipated that the majority of course participants would be likely to find this route into education more achievable as a next step.

Napier is a post-92 university with a strong vocational tradition and a commitment to widening participation and lifelong learning. As mentioned above, the Think Again programme was made possible through successful application for grant funding to the Scottish Higher Education Funding Council and the European Social Fund. Napier is responsible for the overall project and financial management. Part of the programme is delivered at the University involving staff from a range of teaching and support departments. The purpose of adopting a tripartite approach is to ensure that all course participants get a taste of both college and university environments, that they are exposed to teaching staff and methods in further and higher education and gain knowledge of the opportunities offered by both sectors. Underpinning the whole experience is the aim of altering perceptions and raising aspirations, demonstrating educational progression routes for those with low or no previous formal qualifications. Napier has developed formal agreements with 12 local further education colleges that facilitate collaboration, especially articulation between HNC/D programmes in the colleges into levels 2 and 3 of degree programmes respectively.

The partnership grew out of contacts made initially on an advisory group of external organisations set up to guide Napier's research on community links. The University's Vice Principal had invited representation from voluntary and community sector organisations with strong reputations for providing education and training opportunities for excluded groups. He also chaired meetings of the group. As well as Apex Scotland, the Workers' Educational Association, Lead Scotland (Linking Education and Disability) and Volunteer Development Scotland were amongst the membership, as was the Community Links Co-ordinator from Jewel and Esk Valley College. From this formal network, University Wider Access Team staff developed more informal contacts which have led to a number of ideas for joint working to be identified. The Think Again programme was one of these.

Over a period of several months, Napier Wider Access staff met with Apex personnel and the Community Links Co-ordinator from the College on a regular basis to develop the idea and eventually put together an integrated programme, which met each partners' strategic objectives. A key worker from each organisation was identified to take the project forward, engage appropriate staff from their organisations and organise the programme. So, all three partners have had a direct input to programme content and design, delivery, pre-course support and ongoing careers guidance, counselling and evaluation.

Marketing and recruitment
A collaborative approach to marketing and recruitment ensured that all key agencies were targeted, especially via Apex contacts within social work departments, other Apex offices and the Scottish Prison Service. This joint marketing strategy resulted in the production of a promotional leaflet which incorporated a number of elements to engage the target group of ex-offenders. These included clear, appropriate use of language, conciseness of text, a colourful style and an outline of the benefits of the programme. Another real benefit of partnership working here was the input of Apex staff who made sure that the tone and content of the leaflet would appeal to their clients.

Recruitment was conducted via an Open Day and individual interviews conducted by the key workers. Although the programme is open to both men and women, the vast majority of people who have expressed an interest have been male. This is not surprising given that the bulk of the ex-offender population in Scotland is male. However, it appears that lack of resources to provide childcare facilities is proving a barrier to female participation. Investigations are underway to try to address this issue.

The Think Again programme and approach
The programme was designed to run for 13 weeks for 3.5 days per week. This format enabled the students to continue to claim unemployment benefit or Job Seeker's Allowance. All the students, when questioned, would not have been able to take part if the programme had not kept within the 16-hour rule. While the programme was based at Apex in Leith, North Edinburgh, the students spent two-week blocks at the College and the University as well as visiting for project activities at other times.

The skills development content of the course covered working with others (including a team challenge involving planning, scripting and directing a short video); goal setting and action planning (looking ahead, making changes, reflection and evaluation); personal presentation (self-assessment, preparation and confidence building); communication skills (use of language, listening, tone of voice, body language, assertiveness, passive and aggressive behaviours, writing skills); use of information technology (familiarisation, use of the internet and world wide web, web site building); creativity (art and design and use of video); study skills and learning strategies (information and library skills, reflective and analytical skills); and health awareness (fitness, drug and alcohol issues, personal health and fitness planning).

At a fairly early stage, the students were encouraged to explore their understandings of the culture of further and higher education and the barriers that these perceptions presented in terms of their own participation. The aim of the facilitators in these sessions was to address these issues and to promote discussion about potential benefits that continuing study can bring in terms of personal and career development. Presentations on practical issues such as student finance were included, as well as individual support sessions and careers guidance. Each individual student received a full employability assessment using diagnostic tools developed by Apex. Later in the programme, job search skills, including interview techniques, telephone skills and CV preparation, were addressed. Personal challenge elements led by physical education staff in Napier's Student Services department encouraged group coherence and self-confidence as well as developing problem-solving skills. Visits to a football stadium (as part of an exploration of issues relating to hooliganism and racism and society) and to a go-karting stadium and bowling alley (to have fun) built upon the communication and teamworking development that had taken place earlier in the course.

In addition, sessions led by Apex staff covered issues of especial relevance to ex-offenders in relation to the labour market: equal opportunities, how to deal with discrimination, planning and using leisure time, dealing with authority and conflict, dealing with the past, conviction relevance, techniques for conviction disclosure and preparation of individual disclosure letters, and knowledge of the Rehabilitation of Offenders Act 1974 and the Police Act 1997.

Throughout the programme, ongoing support and guidance was provided by the key workers, with additional input from careers advisory service staff from the College and from Napier. Each Friday morning, a full feedback session took place where students filled in weekly diaries and were encouraged to speak openly with the key workers about the past week's experiences. This time also allowed for individual students to receive one to one support with particular aspects of their coursework. The diaries consisted of a set of simple feedback sheets asking participants to list individual activities undertaken during the week and give their comments. Participants were then invited to raise any points as part of a group discussion and, in addition, any individual concerns were addressed confidentially as necessary. The group discussions encouraged participants to talk, to develop skills of framing questions and listening to others and to gain confidence from being an equal part of the course development process. The key workers observed positive changes in individuals' level of participation in group discussion, in the degree of mutual support and affirmation amongst participants, in self confidence and in the ability to express opinions in more considered ways, in other words, an increase in participants' skills of reflection. Indeed, many of the issues that came up in the early stages of the diaries and discussions related to lack of confidence and self-esteem and lack of recognition of existing skills and abilities.

Student experience and outcomes

The first course ran from February 2001 with twelve male students aged between 21 and 57 with the majority of the group aged between 29 and 34. Their entry qualifications ranged from none, through some school level qualifications to one with an Open University degree studied in prison. Many expressed negative school experiences due to bullying, overcrowded classes or being labelled as disruptive. Several had learning difficulties that had not been identified. In informal discussions, some course members described their experience of the education offered in prison as poor, with an emphasis on basic education (literacy and numeracy) and, sometimes, positive discouragement of those who wished to undertake higher level study. The Think Again course aimed to change their perceptions of education, building on the fact that they had all come forward prepared to explore new options and consider moving forward in their lives.

Many of them had very chaotic backgrounds and lifestyles, which affected their ability to sustain their commitment to the programme. Nevertheless, 50% of participants fully completed the course, all achieving key elements of national Scottish Qualifications Authority (SQA) modules in Communication. Their next steps included the following further study in further education colleges: HND (Higher National Diploma) Health and Fitness, HND Environmental Studies and SQA qualifications in Computing, Communications and Catering. These were very positive outcomes. However, they do not totally reflect the full extent of the distance the students travelled during the thirteen week programme. They became a cohesive group, demonstrated excellent problem-solving skills, grew in terms of self-confidence and levels of motivation and learnt to communicate more effectively. By the end of the programme all had made at least two presentations, had prepared CVs and action plans and undergone interview training with local employers. Three of the students attended a visit to Napier University by the Lord High Commissioner to the Church of Scotland and two presented at the 10th EAN Conference in Glasgow in June 2001. Four of the students came to the open day for the second course to act as role models and promote the course to potential applicants. We will return below to the need to develop different techniques for measuring these softer indicators.

In end-of-course feedback forms, the students expressed a high level of satisfaction with the overall content and format of the course and with the tutor input. The time spent at the University and the College were highly rated, despite initial apprehension. The main change suggested was having an additional team building event at the University earlier on in the programme (to provide an early opportunity to develop group identity) in addition to the session time-tabled during their block at Napier later in the course. There were also some concerns about the structure of the input on drugs and alcohol awareness. It had been too lecture-based, with not enough opportunity for interaction. Both of these issues have been addressed in the programme for the second course which started in September 2001. Comments made in the feedback forms included the following:

> *'It is a good course for building self-confidence and breaking down mental barriers that can stop you from applying yourself.'*

> *'I enjoyed visiting the college and university to see that people of all ages could study harmoniously together and blend in with tutorial staff.'*

> *'If you had told me before I started the course that I would end up being accepted for an HND at college, I just wouldn't have believed you.'*

Future growth and sustainability

A repeat course is underway with ten male participants. This has been made possible through joint funding from the Scottish Higher Education Funding Council and the European Social Fund (ESF). The outcome of a renewed application to ESF is awaited. This would allow a further two programmes to run in both 2002 and 2003. Closer links are developing with the Scottish Prison Service and other institutions in Scotland with the aim of establishing additional partnerships to enable the programme to be delivered in other locations. This work is clearly in line with current policies in relation to social inclusion. Its future will depend on continued commitment from the government and at senior levels within the educational institutions.

On the basis of past experience, the development team have been able to focus marketing activities more carefully. This has resulted in a greater number of more appropriate referrals from other agencies and in a build-up of potential clients for future programmes. The programme is growing in order to take account of different levels of educational need within the group, especially in terms of qualifications in Communication and IT. This will affect the structure of the students' experience during their block at college. For some students, additional, higher level expectations are being introduced into some of the programme project work and into the reflective diaries in order to enable them to test and develop their writing skills more fully.

Conclusions: learning from collaboration

Our conclusions fall into two principal groups – those related to the nature of the programme and those concerned with the experience of collaboration. First, the team approach to programme design and delivery, support and guidance proved to be a very effective one. It enabled the programme to access a range of skills in teaching, group-work and guidance. It also meant that it was possible to offer the participants a wide range of taster experiences in college, university and local community settings. The team was experienced in allowing the students to progress at their own pace, while moving them forward from the 'safer' environment of Apex into the unfamiliar and apparently intimidating surroundings of the institutions. The team members were also able to provide each other with support and feedback. Key workers were helping course members to deal with personal issues including homelessness or life in supported accommodation, lack of any family support or complex, demanding family relationships, managing drug and alcohol problems and failures in job applications, plus dealing with their knowledge of the nature of some of the offences.

The team brought a range of perspectives to bear on the programme as it progressed allowing agreed adjustments to be made as needed. The establishment of good communication channels was of crucial importance at both an operational level (phone calls at eleven o'clock at night were not unknown) and an executive level (for example, to resolve queries relating to financial management).

The observation of the course team was that, at the outset and in the early stages of the course, participants were clearly feeling very insecure, frightened and powerless, which could lead some to appear aggressive and disrespectful of other members of the group. The weekly feedback sessions proved to be essential in encouraging the students to provide open and honest feedback, enabling problems to be picked up very quickly. The understanding that their views would be listened to and acted upon was, in our view, one of the factors which helped to build self-esteem and develop confidence. The sessions helped to build relationships between the key workers and the students engendering a strong sense of team spirit with the learners being part of the team.

The key workers provided briefing to all other staff members who were involved in programme input. On one occasion, early on in the programme, when this was not carried out thoroughly, inappropriate and judgmental remarks from one tutor (e.g. that they might be carrying transmittable diseases) directly caused at least one person to leave the course to the great disappointment of the team and the rest of the group. As a result, more detailed briefings are provided for all staff who will be in contact with the group on visits. In fact, all the staff from the institutions have come forward to contribute to the second programme and many have expressed how much they have enjoyed the experience of working with this group.

As mentioned before, we need to find better ways to measure the 'soft' indicators of project success in order to assess how far participants make progress in terms of personal development. For the second course, use of the Rickter Scale has been introduced. This is a motivational and assessment evaluation tool developed by Hutchison and Stead in 1994, widely used in Canada and the US and increasingly in the UK, which looks at the positive and negative aspects of clients' lives. One of the Apex key workers has undergone specific training in its use and will be employing it as part of programme evaluation at both the start and end of the course to measure distance travelled.

The importance of adequate aftercare and support cannot be underestimated. Many of the course participants remain clients of Apex who are providing ongoing back-up as they progress with their chosen pathway. This level of aftercare could not be achieved by the education providers working alone. The participants also have access to the key workers from the College and the University, who, if there is sufficient demand, intend to offer other opportunities, such as additional help with Maths (using a maths support programme developed by Napier that includes both distance learning packs and tutorial support sessions). Unfortunately, participants' enquiries about courses of study have revealed limited experience within the partner institutions in dealing with issues relating to the disclosure of convictions and in applying equal opportunity policies in relation to ex-offenders; these are issues that need to be addressed.

In conclusion, the experience of the Think Again programme has confirmed that collaborative working takes time to develop. Partners approach any project of this sort from different perspectives and need to agree common objectives and ways of working which may require adjustment from accepted norms. It has been shown to be essential to engage staff who are open to change and willing to share, and who understand the processes involved in so doing. The task of building partner relationships which acknowledge and respect differences in approach, and can accommodate change, is a complex and demanding one, which means that all involved have to be prepared to devote time to nurturing the partnership. We have striven to arrive at a clarity of goals and objectives and to bring these together in a written partnership agreement. This is important but, on a day to day basis, much depends upon the trust that develops between the key workers.

As has become apparent, much has depended on the skills of the key workers and continuity of their input was crucial. However, each of the partners has been very much aware of the problems that can arise in the event of staff illness, for example. The delivery of the programme is dependent on particular individuals who know the group and how each individual is progressing; it is almost impossible to bring in new key workers once a programme is established. A related issue is the importance of providing the key workers with adequate support, in what is a considerably challenging and, occasionally, distressing role. However, it is also the joint view of the Think Again partners that the programme could not have recruited so successfully, offered the range of learning experiences or delivered the positive outcomes which it has without working together and adopting a collaborative approach. As well as building on these findings to explore with Apex the scope for offering similar programmes elsewhere in Scotland with other HE and FE partners, the model used for Think Again – of engaging in joint working with relevant voluntary agencies and local college partners – is one which appears to be capable of replication in attempting to engage with other under-represented groups.

References

Scottish Executive (1999) *Social Justice – a Scotland where everyone matters.* HMSO.

Scottish Executive (1999) *Social Inclusion – opening the door to a better Scotland.* HMSO.

Scottish Executive (2000) *Scottish Objective 3 Operational Programme 2000-2006.*

Scottish Prison Service (2000) *Annual Report and Accounts 1999-2000.* HMSO.

Tunnock, J. (1999) *Building Community Partnerships – fostering Napier's commitment to wider access.* Internal publication: Napier University.

14

Academics and first-year students: collaborating to access success in an unfamiliar university culture

Jill Lawrence

This chapter argues that the contemporary Australian university constitutes a new and unfamiliar culture for the increasing numbers and diversity of students accessing it. Traditional approaches have viewed language development and literacy acquisition as key factors in dealing with this diversity, conceptualising disadvantage in terms of scholastic deficits and a lack of academic literacy. Inherent in these approaches is the assumption that there is one mainstream discourse and that languages and literacies other than those of the dominant mainstream represent a deficit or a deficiency on the part of students who do not possess them. An alternative approach, utilising Critical Discourse Analysis (CDA) and cross-cultural communication theory, re-conceptualises the contemporary university as a dynamic culture, subject to ongoing and rapid change and encompassing a multiplicity of diverse cultures and sub-cultures. The students' transition to it is then re-positioned as one of gaining familiarity with, engaging and mastering the new culture's multiple discourses and multi-literacies. I argue that the use of key socio-cultural competences constitutes the means by which students can achieve this familiarity, facilitating their successful transition to university culture. Also that academics have a responsibility in this process, collaborating with students to help them access and negotiate the unfamiliar discourses.

The contemporary university

During the last decades of the twentieth century, the 'elite-mass' and 'investment-cost' paradigm shifts irrevocably changed the nature and purposes of university education in Australia. While the first shift widened the participation of the student body, the second shift redefined the parameters of responsibility for this participation. The wider participation rates have meant, for example, a corresponding increase in the diversity of the student body signifying 'the expansion in participation of the critical mass of identifiable subgroups that were formally significantly under represented in universities' (McInnis and James, 1995). The 'investment-cost' shift depicts the changes to Federal Government policies and funding arrangements since the mid-1990s. According to the Department of Education, Training and Youth Affairs (DETYA, 1999) these changes have increasingly shifted the responsibility for higher education expenditure from public (state) to private (individual) funding.

Universities are also beginning to exhibit the tensions embodied in these shifts – in the dramatic and ongoing pace of change. The literature on higher education, for example, documents the difficulties experienced by the increasing diversity of students. A National Board of Employment, Education and Training (NBEET) funded study, *Towards Excellence in Diversity*, for example, found that 'a clear trend is the lack of progress of the socio-economically disadvantaged and people from rural and geographically isolated areas' (Postle *et al,* 1997, p.xii). The literature also documents the responses developed to explore and overcome these difficulties (Postle et al, 1996 and Beasley, 1997). Postle *et al* (1996) argues that these approaches emanate from two main research focuses. The first research strand has concentrated on the determination of socially or culturally inappropriate curricular and teaching methods: how programmes and services might be more responsive to the cultural academic needs of students (see for example NBEET, 1995). The second research strand has attempted to understand how programmes and services could assist students to better adapt to the demands of university education (Beasley, 1997; Postle, Sturman and Clarke, 2001).

While both approaches help students adjust to university requirements and demands, their underlying assumptions remain essentially
unchallenged. These include assumptions about the political,
economic and cultural contexts impacting on both higher education
and the experiences of students; assumptions about the nature of
university languages, practices and policies; and the assumptions
made by academics about their roles as university teachers. Long-
held assumptions about the nature, characteristics and abilities of the
'typical' university student in the early stages of the twenty-first
century as well as the tensions inherent in the contrast between
lecturers' perceptions of the traditional 'elite' student and the
'actual' student, for example, remain largely unexplored. The current
approaches also reflect the pedagogical or curriculum focus
assumed by much of the research literature; the focus on policies,
programmes, systems and organisational support. Positioning the
debates within a theoretical context, however, might present alternative ways of conceptualising the experiences of the diversity of
students participating at university.

Critical discourse analysis

Critical Discourse Analysis (CDA) provides a theoretical frame that
is useful in re-positioning the experiences of students participating
at university. CDA is appropriate as it is able to reveal the discursive
practices that operate as power relationships in an educational context, focus attention on the role of discourses[1] in constructing and
maintaining dominance and inequality in society, and connect local
texts and cultures, theoretically and empirically, to power and
ideology configurations operating in the broader society (Fairclough, 1995). As such CDA has the capacity to provide a systematic
means of linking the students' experiences to the wider external
forces which operate on and influence both the localised site (the
university) and the students who inhabit it.

CDA is able to contextualise the tensions rising, for example, from
the ideologies currently informing and driving higher education in
Australia. These are evident in the confrontation between traditional
scholarly ideals and entrepreneurial, corporate, business practice
(see Coady, 2000). The economically driven political agenda has

meant that the university is now operated from an economic rationalist platform, which is market and outcome driven, prioritising managerialism and consumerism (McInnis, 2000). This has resulted, for example, in increased budget constraints, the demands of which are currently and increasingly dictating pedagogical decisions. Quality control measures and strategies designed, for example, to help make explicit, and more transparent, the expectations of markers and the 'hidden' curriculum have been eroded. This situation is compounded by the fact that, at the same time as strategies designed to empower students have been eroded, pressures have increased on those staff who are most in a position to support students new to the university culture. McInnis (2000), for example, documents the increasing casualisation of staff involved in first-year teaching. Students too are under pressure. McInnis et al (2000), for example, report that the most striking difference between the 1994 and 1999 snapshots of the first year at university in Australia was the increased proportion of students who are enrolled full-time and engaged in part-time work, and the increase in the average number of hours students are employed. At the same time, outcomes and throughput, in minimum time, are prioritised. These pressures also provide consequences for student retention. McInnis *et al* (2000) found, for example, that one-third of the students in their snapshot of the 1999 cohort seriously considered deferring or withdrawing during their first semester.

CDA is also able to contextualise the ideologies currently informing the debates about equity in education, about the role of 'social justice' and about the nature and meaning of higher education in Australia. Much of the rhetoric emanates from the Federal Government's move to transfer the responsibility for the 'infrastructure of learning' from the state to the individual: from public to private funding (DETYA, 2000). There are the changes to government funding to universities, to the Higher Education Contribution Scheme (HECS) and to AUSTUDY regulations; changes that reinforce the idea that higher education had entered 'hard times'. Emanating from the 'investment-cost' paradigm shift, this 'public-private' shift also redefined the meaning of both social justice and educational equity in the higher education context (Postle, Sturman and Clarke, 2000:16). In 1990, *A Fair Chance for All: Higher Education That's in Everyone's Reach'* (Department of Employment, Education and Training, DEET, 1990) reflected the notions that educational disadvantage constituted a social/public responsibility and that the links between social positioning and educational disadvantage were pivotal. However, in Howard's Liberal Government, the funding arrangements for higher education are becoming increasingly delineated as a 'cost' (see Coady, 2000 and DETYA, 2000). Under this mindset, educational disadvantage is reshaped as the fault/responsibility of the individual and unrelated to social positioning. A failure to realise potential represents a loss to the individual only. While the difference in the redefining of equity is subtle, the results may be 'profound for those in society who are most disadvantaged, especially during their first year of study when nurturing and concerted support remains critical to retention and ultimate success' (Postle, Sturman and Clarke, 2000:18).

CDA also unveils the role of discourse in constructing and maintaining dominance and inequality in society (Van Dyjk, 1997: Fairclough, 1995). By providing insight into the fact that language is not only socially shaped, but that it is also socially shaping or 'constitutive', it encourages an investigation of the ways in which subjects are constituted and reconstituted through discourse (Fairclough 1995, p.132). CDA thus provides a means of understanding the familiarity or lack of familiarity some groups have with university culture. Critical researchers (for example, Bourdieu and Passeron, 1977; Connell, 1994; Scheurich, 1997; and Young, 1998) see the relationship between education and social positioning as pivotal. The social and cultural capital of some groups, they argue, helps them endow their children with the cultural knowledge and discourses more in tune with mainstream university culture. These include the shared preferences, beliefs and attitudes which families transmit to their children as well as the ways in which parents help define and shape the future of their children. There is the time spent reading with children and beliefs in the importance of education as well as the encouragement of critical and analytical thinking skills. These groups, also, may be more prepared to invest in their children's education, for example, by investing in private schooling. This may be significant, as there is an emerging body of research in Australia correlating types of schooling with the likelihood of university participation (Jamrozik, 1991 and Beasley, 1997).

Alternatively the experiences, beliefs and values of other groups may be less in tune with mainstream university culture, and may even 'marginalise' them – exemplifying the consequences of a social positioning which can act to exacerbate educational disadvantage. Some groups, for example, may have a cultural aversion to the accumulation of debt (a characteristic which becomes more critical as students themselves become more responsible for funding their tertiary education), have negative experiences of school, poor study habits/facilities and lack the family/peer reference groups which have knowledge of and value tertiary education. These groups may de-value education and the benefits of education generally. This is demonstrated in my own research (PhD thesis, ongoing):

> 'My mother and father both left school early and have grown up with the belief that schooling is generally economically 'useless'! My mother would praise me for doing well at school but was unlikely to take a day off from work to watch me take part in school performances while my father showed very little interest towards my schooling. My parents encouraged me to secure a job as soon as possible, even if this meant leaving school before my senior schooling was completed. They believed that securing a job was much more important for my future than a high level of education. I realised early on in my high school education that because of my parents' values and beliefs, I would not be attending university. This idea was simply ridiculous as to them, university was 'a pure waste of time and money'. I found that this affected my schooling and I left high school half-way through year 12.' (Low SES student)

> 'My uncle and aunt say I am mad, 'What are you doing, you will never be able to pay it off? What do you want a job for, you'll just start working and you'll be married with kids'. My family thinks you don't need any education. (23 year old rural student)

The lack of cultural familiarity displayed by the diversity of students attempting to access the new university culture is woven through the literature on the first year experience (see, for example, Williams, 1987; Connell, 1994 and Postle *et al*, 1997). Beasley (1997: p29) argues 'universities have cultural values and norms to which new students must adjust, and students come with their own unique but varied cultural values'. This literature echoes that of the critical theorists. For example Gee (1990) contends 'the ways of communicating within an academic setting are not easily grasped and are often more difficult for students whose backgrounds seem to differ from, or even conflict with, the ways of writing, knowing and valuing favoured within a university context'. Students themselves verbalise this notion; 'it's a society which is totally different from what most of us are used to' (cited in Beasley, 1997, p182).

The question of how this lack of familiarity is dealt with thus becomes pivotal if these groups are to persevere and succeed at university. CDA also helps here as it can uncover and address the power relationships that operate in and guide the choices made, for example, by academics in university contexts. Fairclough (1995) argues that not only is education itself a key domain of linguistically mediated power, but it also mediates between other key domains for learners. So how is diversity perceived and dealt with by Australian academics? The most recent study of 2,609 academics in fifteen Australian universities reported that 'high proportions of academics' were reportedly negative about the calibre of students, with 69% of respondents considering the provision of academic support a major cause in the increase in staff work hours (McInnis, 2000: p24). The fact that there were 'too many students' with 'too wide a range of abilities' was delineated as a 'problem'. Other studies have found that, while most staff in tertiary institutions acknowledged the benefits of having the diversity of students entering courses at their institution (altruism, social justice, student diversity) they demonstrated little knowledge about these students (Postle *et al*, 1996 and Beasley, 1997). Postle *et al*'s (1996) study, for example, revealed that the staff interviewed believed that these students should be treated no differently from other students and that existing academic support mechanisms should be resourced to provide any remediation that was deemed necessary. That the staff gave very little support and credence to value-added teaching as an indicator of good teaching involving these students also reinforces the ascendancy of the deficit approaches to dealing with diversity. Such attitudes reinforce the dominance of the mainstream academic discourses resonating through them. Inherent lies the assumption that there is one mainstream academic culture, with one mainstream discourse, operating within an unchanging, static and consistent organisational context.

This mindset provides implications for both higher education and for the students attempting to access it. The first is the recognition that higher education institutions, particularly in times where government policies are driven by liberal/individualist ideologies, are inherently conservative, demonstrating an unwillingness to examine their policies and attitudes as a first step in initiating changes that could serve to facilitate students' success. The second is that the institutions in themselves may not be able to redress inequalities in society, given that their policies and practices currently not only do not question the sources of inequality but in fact can be perceived to be maintaining them. The third implication is that, under this mindset, students who do not succeed or who have difficulties in accessing and mastering the mainstream academic discourses are labelled, perhaps 'blamed', as being under-prepared or 'intellectually deficient', revealing a 'sink or swim' approach to the issue of diversity. It is accepted that it is the students' responsibility if they fail, with academics perceiving that they have little role in, as well as little responsibility for, the retention and ultimate success of students.

Rethinking diversity: the 'deficit-discourse' shift

The New London Group (1996: p72) argues that such deficit approaches involve 'writing over the existing subjectivities with the language of the dominant culture'. They are representative of models of pedagogy that emerged from the idea that cultures and languages other than those of the mainstream represent a deficiency, a shortcoming. Further, they deny the implications provided by the existence as well as the potency of the concept of the multiple linguistic and cultural differences. An alternative approach, incorporating the notion of meta-literacies or multi-literacies, characterises the university as a dynamic culture embodying a multiplicity of subcultures, each imbued with their own discourses, literacies and practices. Students' transition to the new culture can, then, be re-conceptualised as one of gaining familiarity, and ultimately mastery, of these discourses. Lankshear *et al* (1997) contend that, to feel comfortable in and perform with competence within a culture, means becoming literate in that culture – becoming familiar with and engaging the multiplicity of new discourses within the culture. As Bartholomae (1985: p134) argues:

> Every time a student sits down to write for us he or she has to invent the university for the occasion – invent the university, that is, or a branch of it......The student has to learn to speak our language, to speak as we do, to try on the particular ways of knowing, selecting, evaluating, reporting, concluding, and arguing that define the discourse of our community. Or perhaps I should say the various discourses of our community.

CDA thus provides the grounds, the rationale and the impetus for re-theorising both the transition to university and the first year as processes. Processes which intrinsically involve the familiarisation, negotiation and mastery of the discourses and multi-literacies of a new, often unfamiliar, dynamic and rapidly changing university culture.

However, the approach provided by CDA also has limitations. CDA, as a form of analysis, is able to identify the (hidden) discourses in institutional/organisational communication. This is an important first step in helping students raise their awareness of the power relationships operating in that context as well as in alerting them to the importance of engaging and mastering the languages/discourses of the institution. However CDA, in itself, with its emphasis on analysis, is not able to provide a recipe for actively changing organisational behaviour, for actively empowering students. It doesn't encompass the capacity, for example, to develop strategies which students can utilise to help them access, engage and master the unfamiliar discourses of the university. A further theoretical perspective, that provided by cross-cultural theory, may be able to provide the means by which these aims can be accomplished.

Cross-cultural communication theory

If, as this chapter argues, the contemporary university is re-conceptualised as an unfamiliar, dynamic and often fragmented culture, encompassing a multiplicity of sometimes inconsistent and abrading subcultures, each with their own discourses and languages, then a second theoretical perspective may be applicable: cross-cultural communication theory. The use of this theory, facilitating as it does a means of making a transition into an unfamiliar host culture, may be able to provide an action framework that can be utilised by students negotiating their transition to the new university culture. Its use also provides implications for academic staff whose roles and responsibilities in helping students access success in the new culture gain momentum.

Cross-cultural communication theory is usually applied, in a university context, to international or English-as-a-second language students adjusting to an unfamiliar host culture (Barker, 1993; Volet and Tan-Quigley, 1999; Mak and Barker, 2000). The literature contends that in order to reap maximum benefits from an unfamiliar educational system, international students need to establish interpersonal relations and communicate effectively with mainstream students and teachers: an adjustment similar to that demanded of the diversity of local students entering an unfamiliar university culture. Boekaerts (1993) sees that adjustment involves learning processes which refer to the ways in which individuals acquire knowledge and skills, essentially enlarging their personal resources to cope with the new context. Involved is the students' self efficacy, the belief that they can successfully perform or complete social behaviours in academic and everyday situations and thus master the relevant discourses and literacies of the culture (Bandura, 1986).

Bandura's (1986) social learning model is utilised as the basis of a cross-cultural communication programme called *ExcelL: Excellence in Experiential Learning and Leadership* (Mak, Westwood, Barker and Ishiyama, 1998). ExcelL is an experiential, skills-based, practice-focused programme, which 'enables people who have recently arrived in a new culture to be competent and effective in dealing with members of the host culture' (Mak *et al*, 1998: p4). The significance of this programme is twofold. It not only establishes the grounds for prioritising the role of socio-cultural competences in helping students adjust to an unfamiliar university culture; it also provides a theoretical frame for prioritising particular socio-cultural competences – specifically those of seeking help and information, participating in a group, making social contact, providing feedback, both positive but particularly negative feedback, expressing disagreement and refusing a request.

The efficacy of these competences has been firmly established, validated by a number of studies conducted in Canada, the United Kingdom, and Australia (Shergill, 1997; Mak, Barker, Logan and Millman, 1999; Pearson, 1999; Mak and Barker, 2000). Their application is however wider than their use in the programme. Firstly, that they are validated as facilitating a successful transition to the unfamiliar university culture for international students reinforces their efficacy in other cross-cultural situations in the university context. For example, in the case of the diversity of local students now participating at university: low socio-economic or rural and isolated students engaging an unfamiliar university culture; mature-age students negotiating unfamiliar academic literacies; and alternative entry students confronting unfamiliar discipline discourses. Secondly the competences also possess daily currency – we all use them, to varied effects, in our personal, social and work lives. Students do not necessarily have to undertake a programme to utilise them effectively. Their significance is reinforced however by the fact that they are able to provide students with a means of engaging and negotiating the multiplicity and diversity of the new discourses and specific literacies that are crucial to their success – for example, communication technologies, referencing systems and research methodologies. Students themselves acknowledge the difficulties of accessing these new discourses and literacies:

> One difficulty was how to research because what I am used to and what the expectations are here are two separate things.

> (My) mathematics was not up to the standard required. It was very difficult and the course content was not explained before I embarked on it. (cited in Yorke, 2000, p38)

These competences are also able to facilitate more meaningful exchanges and dialogue between the many different cultural groups present within the culture (for example, locals, staff, older people and younger people, people of different cultures, different socio-economic levels and different genders).

An essential feature of the competences is that they are socio-cultural: that they are socially and culturally appropriate or attuned to the particular culture, subculture or discourse being engaged. The specific verbal and nonverbal means of asking for help or refusing a request differ, for example, from culture to culture, from subculture to subculture, from discipline area to discipline area. Observation – listening and watching – and reflection (for example in relation to the specific verbal and nonverbal practices of a culture or discourse) are essential features of the competences. Observation and reflection are also inherent in the theories developed, for example, by Giddens, when he discusses enhanced reflexivity, and by Fairclough, who argues for a critical awareness of language. Giddens (1994: p90), for example, emphasises the ability to study and reflect on the social, cultural and educational practices of each culture or subculture, to engage in a consistent monitoring of them, and as a consequence, accumulate new and better understandings of them. Fairclough, (1995: p220) talks about the importance of critical language awareness – which he argues has the capacity for reflexive analysis of the educational process itself, including 'the capacity to promote social awareness of discourse, to encourage critical awareness of language variety and to promote practice for change'. Observation and reflection form the basis of the socio-cultural capacity of the competences. Utilising them is a first step in enabling students to not only fine tune the competences to the specific culture or subculture being engaged, but also to achieve new understandings about the new discourses and cultures they are confronting. The socio-cultural competences thus provide students with the means to encompass the diversity present within the evolving and often fragmented university culture.

The role of socio-cultural competences in facilitating transition to an unfamiliar culture

Seeking help and information

The ability to seek help and information, for example, is a crucial socio-cultural competence that needs to be consistently demonstrated by students in and across a variety of university cultures and sub-cultures. Students need to be able to canvass a wide range of resources and be able to determine which one will best meet a specific need for specific discipline areas. They need to be able to access for themselves, locating, utilising and assessing, for example, information gleaned from handbooks, booklets and websites, as well as discipline specific assistance such as peer assisted learning programmes, consultation with tutors and lecturers, library and computer support services, and study skills sessions. They need to know how to access learning enhancement support and the personalised coping mechanisms to help them negotiate the bureaucratic infrastructures in a variety of departments and faculties. There is also the help and support available from a plethora of support staff: careers, peer and clinical counsellors. Pearson (1999) argues that accessing these kinds of remedial and crisis oriented intervention is essential in supporting students in reaching their goals or in repairing the devastation that occurs when failure is experienced as a total loss of confidence in personal and cultural identity (cited in Mak and Barker, 2000). These kinds of support can make the difference between retention and withdrawal. It is one prioritised by the participants in my research:

> 'The ability to ask for help is 60 – 70% of passing a unit of study.'

> 'The skill of seeking help would be the highest priority, crucial.'

Further:

> 'Asking for help is the basis for study because if you can't get help then what are you doing? If you don't understand, what have you learnt – nothing.'

> 'My advice to someone starting university is to go and ask questions, what do I need to know, how does the university operate, what do I do. The mechanics of the university are more important than the

225

study. In the first semester the mechanics of the university are subjects in themselves.' (a mature-age female)

Another student of mature age who had been in the military, comments:

> 'One thing the military did bash into me was the ability to ask for help. After you are taught the first time around they are going to ask you to do it within three minutes. For example, with a weapon you really have to ask if you don't understand. So I have transferred it to here and it has been helpful. I think I will transfer it to the rest of my life as it actually saves you time in the long run, it helps speed up the learning curve, rather than waiting until a problem becomes too big and uncontrollable.'

Although this socio-cultural competence is considered to be crucial in cross-cultural adjustment (see, for example, Mak *et al*, 1998) it is not as straightforward as it seems. The cultural belief systems or values underlying an individual's use of this skill are many and varied. Some students may consider it to be a sign of weakness, for example, or equate help with 'remedial' intervention or a 'loss of face'. They may feel they may not have the 'right' or lack the confidence to ask, especially as they make their transition to the new culture. For example:

> 'I don't feel confident enough to speak to my lecturer or tutor about the essay question because they might think I am stupid or something.'

There are also problems related to the under-utilisation of support services by some students, as well as the implications consequently provided for retention. These are issues which are beginning to be addressed in the literature (see for example Coles, 2001) and are also reflected in the development of a number of early warning intervention programmes. Shiplee and Wilson, from the University of West Florida, and Dietsche, Flether and Barett, from Humber College, Canada, presented papers on this issue to *The Fourteenth International Conference on the First Year Experience* held in Hawaii in July 2001.

Making social contact and conversation

Also pivotal is the ability to make social contact and social conversation, in socially and culturally appropriate ways, across a multiplicity and diversity of cultural groups. This competence is crucial as it facilitates the development of study groups, writing groups or learning circles, as well as study partners, mentors and friends, and perhaps, the support of a 'significant other'. The literature surveying student retention argues, for example, that social isolation is the major factor determining student withdrawal (McInnis and James, 1995; Tinto, 1995). McCann (1996) argues that social isolation plays a significant role in causing difficulties in transition. The features she sees as significantly contributing to student participation and success include academic support strategies, access programmes and social networks (McCann, 1996). Benn (2000) maintains that the 'presence of a significant other' was the most significant variable facilitating continued perseverance at university in Britain while a study conducted by Watson, Teese, Polesel and Golding, pinpoint alienation as one of the main reasons for dropping out in Australia (cited in Illing, 2000). McInnis and James (1995, p.118) also contend that there are differences in academic performance between those students who interact with other students and those who do not. They suggest that particular reference should be paid to the role and significance of the social context of learning as 'successful learning and the development of a positive view of the university experience did not occur in a social vacuum'.

> First-year students' orientation towards learning is in a formative stage and inextricably linked to the pursuit of identity and self-efficacy developed in a peer group (p119).

There is also their finding that 'personal connection with other students and academics was far more important than a lot of people imagine' (cited in Illing: 1995, p47). Clulow and Brennan (1996, p33) argue that there is a positive relationship between personal support and persistence with study and that there is a significant correlation 'between a group of people never spoken to and withdrawal or failure in a subject.' Kantanis (2000) argues that, without friends, students have fewer resources at their disposal to assist them in the process of transition. Students themselves confirm the importance of the competency:

> 'The most helpful support at university were the friends I made.' (Rural and isolated student)

> 'Friends are crucial in getting the best out of yourself.' (Alternative entry student)

> 'At first I was completely confused doing full time study but I wanted to be a teacher and Brian was emotionally very supportive – I absolutely couldn't do it without him. Also I made a good group of friends and we often met at the coffee shop to talk over things and help each other along.' (A female, mature-age student who won a university medal)

Participating in a group or team
The ability to participate in a group or team is another socio-cultural competence pivotal to perseverance and success at university. This ability can generate feelings of confidence and belonging in a diversity of classroom settings and contributes to the critical and questioning engagement essential to academic success. Students themselves acknowledge the importance of this competency in developing feelings of confidence and connection:

> 'Every single time I have been involved in a study group, I have achieved a distinction or high distinction. Just talking about the objectives or an assignment for an hour a week reinforces key points and examples in your memory. They are definitely well worth the effort.' (Mature-age female student)

> 'We push each other to learn from each other and I found that quite useful and helpful.'

> 'I just did x unit and hated it. There were no tutorials at all and it was horrible....I didn't have people around that I could talk to and complain to and this affected my confidence and study.'

The importance of this socio-cultural competence is reflected in the efficacy of learning communities, peer collaboration or peer cohorts, all of which are gaining in popularity and credence, particularly in the United States (see *Program and Proceedings: The Fourteenth International Conference on the First Year Experience* held in Hawaii in July 2001).

Seeking and giving feedback

In the transactional model of the communication process, feedback is integral. A crucial socio-cultural competence includes the two-way feedback process, again in culturally and socially appropriate ways as providing negative feedback, in particular, is often a 'risky' behaviour when used in relation to a high status professor for example. This competence hinges on the ability to both solicit constructive feedback and give negative criticism, and conversely, give constructive feedback and solicit negative input. For example students need to be able to ask lecturers for advice on how to improve a draft plan or the structure or body of an assignment. At the same time they need the skills of explaining the difficulty of anticipating the lecturer's requirements in the absence of a Marking Criteria Sheet. Or being able to ask for guidance about research sources, while providing, in a socially and culturally appropriate way, negative feedback, for example in relation to the quality of the learning environment – illegible transparencies, lack of constructive feedback on assignments or the use of unexplained technical language. The ability to give and receive feedback is integral to perseverance:

> 'Thank you for taking the time to look at and give me feedback on my drafts and assignments. Your support and advice was crucial to my understanding and to my development as a student but best of all helped me to attain better marks. The emphasis you placed on understanding what was expected and sticking to the topic assisted my interpretation of the question. As a first-year student it was difficult to know if I was on the right track so your help reduced my fears and guided my actions.'

> 'In one unit I am studying there are no lecture notes and the examples that are given aren't explained in a way that relates back to theory. I am having difficulties learning and so are most of the other students. There is no student evaluation form so next year's students will experience the same things.'

Expressing disagreement and refusing a request

The final key competence concerns to the ability to express disagreement or to refuse a request, again in socially and culturally appropriate ways. This is vital, for example, in organising a time-table, in maintaining discipline, in being assertive and in preventing stress in a variety of contexts and situations. It is also an essential ingredient in fostering flexibility, an important feature when an increasing number of students are working part-time. A mature-age female notes:

> 'I had a few dramas organising a few things next semester because academics in different departments don't communicate with each other. I got a letter saying I couldn't do five units but when I questioned this they let me (this student completed a double degree within two and a half years by doing five rather than four units each semester and by studying during summer term, semester three).'

These are then the specific and key socio-cultural competences, which, if utilised by students, enable them to construct a more effective means of negotiating and mastering the unfamiliar discourses of the new university culture. They enable students to demonstrate the appropriate inter-cultural competences and specific literacies necessary for perseverance in the new university culture and, in particular, they empower them to exhibit the knowledge and characteristics which successful students possess and display.

The Role of the Academics: collaborating to facilitate students' transition to an unfamiliar culture

The re-theorisation of university transition, however, also demands responses from the other party involved in the communication process – the academics. A possible first response is to re-think university beliefs and practices in relation to diversity, to re-conceptualise diversity as a 'resource' rather than as a 'problem'. Such a re-positioning could result in a shift in focus from the deficit view to one which takes into account the ways in which academics can help facilitate students' familiarity, or overcome a lack of familiarity, with the culture and its discourses and multi-literacies.

The re-definition of diversity raises a number of questions about the nature of university practices. Questions, for example, about the potential 'blame' attached to students who are considered 'inadequate' or 'under-prepared' by teaching staff immersed in the dominant academic discourse. Questions, also, about the roles of

230

university teachers in terms of their responsibilities as educators, as communicators. Involved here, firstly, is the need for academics to accept and embrace their responsibilities in terms of student retention. They also need to acknowledge that they teach students as well as, or perhaps instead of, teaching subject matter. A further responsibility for academics is to acknowledge that successful students are those who are 'expert' at being students. This involves the understanding that the students most likely to succeed are those who actively seek to become enculturated into the teaching/learning styles, life, procedures and practices of the new university culture (Kantanis, 2001). This chapter would argue, in fact, that 'expert' students are those students who utilise, in socially and culturally appropriate ways, the socio-cultural competences outlined above. Academics can assist them in this process by not only raising the students' awareness of the importance of these competences, but also by actively facilitating their use. For example, raising the importance of utilising student consultation times, on-line discussion groups, e-mail and news groups, telephone tutorials, video conferences, study partners and study groups, learning communities and learning circles which can constitute resources of help and information as well as sources of feedback. The use of icebreakers, group exercises, networking opportunities, dialogue across cultures, problem-solving activities and role plays, and opportunities for class interaction also helps students develop their abilities to participate in a group or team and to make social contacts and connections. On the other hand, the incorporation of feedback loops and different forms of evaluation, as well as the encouragement of the use of consultation times, can provide students with the opportunities to voice their concerns and, simultaneously, enhance their membership of the learning community.

Pivotal, however, is the need for academics to make their discourses explicit. To not only explain and make clear the rules, but also to make explicit the hidden agendas, the covert or hidden curriculum, the implicit expectations as well as the expected (but not stated) behaviours intrinsic to students achieving success in their discipline (Benn, 2000). Boud (cited at the Researching Widening Access: International Perspectives Conference, held in Glasgow in June

2001) argues that academics have expectations, but fail to articulate them and then make judgments about students who fail to demonstrate them. Model or sample assignments, formative assessment related to structure and process, constructive feedback, marking criteria feedback sheets and draft proposals constitute ways in which academics can make explicit their expectations. Assessment targeted early, both to provide students with a gauge about the degree and speed of their adjustment and to implement early warning strategies, is also important (Kantanis, 2001).

The key to teaching/learning, for academics, is, then, as much the 'process', as it is the 'content', with an acknowledgement by academics that retention relies in part on what the academic does in the classroom, as a professional educator. An important thread can therefore be woven into the philosophy of university teaching. It lies in recognising, participating in and facilitating the processes by which students learn to negotiate and integrate a number of competing discourses and multi-literacies – the university, faculty, department and discipline discourses they are engaging. Pivotal is the need for academics to actively seek and look/listen for feedback about the effectiveness of their curriculum planning and teaching strategies. Also important is the need to develop a more coherent university-wide teaching and learning framework, including the development of policy in relation to the first year experience, transition and diversity. The 'deficit-discourse' shift thus reinforces a further driving impetus of this chapter; that academics have a vital role in the process whereby students learn to negotiate the multiple linguistic and cultural differences of the university – a process which is central to their abilities to persevere and succeed in a new, and often unfamiliar, university culture.

Conclusion

This chapter has applied CDA to illuminate the ideologies that are currently informing the higher education community in Australia and to analyse the power relations that maintain their influence. It focused attention on how these power relations are realised through the university discourses, both to challenge the assumptions of deficit which underpin many of the responses to the increasing diversity of the student body, and to establish the potency and applicability of the role of multiple cultures, multiple discourses and multi-literacies in the university context. This analysis made possible, even imperative, a re-theorisation of the transition to the new university culture by first year students. It provided the grounds, the rationale and the impetus for its re-theorisation as a process of gaining familiarity with the unfamiliar discourses of the university. The chapter then challenged both the students and the university. It challenged students to recognise that to demonstrate mastery of these discourses, the use of key socio-cultural competences must be evoked. It also challenged academics to collaborate with students: to identify and make explicit their discourses – the university discourses and multi-literacies that the students need to master in order to succeed.

References

Anderson, L.E. (1994) A New Look at an Old Construct: Cross-cultural Adaption in *International Journal of Intercultural Relations*, 18, 293-328.

Austin, A. (1993) *What Matters in College? Four Critical Years*. San Francisco, Jossey Bass,

Bandura, A. (1986) *Social Foundations of Thought and Action: A Social Cognitive Theory*, Englewood Cliffs, New Jersey, Prentice Hall.

Barker, M (1993) *Perceptions of Social Rules in Intercultural and Intracultural Encounters, PhD thesis, School of Psychology*, University of Queensland, St Lucia, Queensland.

Bartholomae, D. (1985) 'Inventing the University' in M. Rose (ed) *When a Writer Can't Write*. Guildford, New York: 34-165.

Beasley, V. (1997) *Democratic Education: An Examination of Access and Equity in Australian Higher Education*, a thesis submitted for the degree of PhD, University of South Australia.

Benn, R. (2000) *Exploring Widening Participation in Higher Education: Targeting, Retention and 'Really Useful Knowledge'*, Seminar Presentation, Toowoomba, Queensland:15 March.

Boekaerts, M. (1993) Being Concerned with Wellbeing and Learning, *Educational Psychologists*, 28, 149-178.

Boud, D. (2001) Keynote Presentation given to the Researching Widening Access: International Perspectives Conference, Glasgow Caledonian University, Scotland 29June – 1 July 2001.

Bourdieu, P. and Passeron J-C., (1977) *Reproduction in Education, Society and Culture*, London, Sage Publications.

Cartwright, P. and Noone, L., (1996) Abrasions: dilemmas of doing a critical literacy pedagogy with first year students within/against the academy' in James, R. and McInnis, C. (ed) *Transition to Active Learning, Centre for the Study of Higher Education,* University of Melbourne.

Clulow, V. and Brennan, L. (1996), 'Its not what you know – it's who you know: student relationship constellations and their impact on study success and persistence' in James R. and McInnis C. (ed) *Transition to Active Learning,* University of Melbourne.

Coady, T. (2000) *Why Universities Matter: a Conversation about Values, Means and Directions,* Sydney, Allen and Unwin.

Coles, A. S. (2001) *Student Services at Metropolitan Universities*, Paper delivered to the European Access Network Conference 'Can Collaboration Widen Participation? Examining the Evidence', held in Glasgow, Scotland, in June 2001.

Connell, R. W. (1994) *Equity through Education: Directions for Education*, Sydney, Australian Centre for Equity Through Education.

Crouch, M. (1996) 'New Students and Old Teachers: in Transition Together', in James, R. and McInnis, C. (ed), *Transition to Active Learning*, Centre for the Study of Higher Education,

Dearn, J.M., (1996), 'Enhancing the First Year Experience: Creating a Climate for Learning' in James, R. and McInnis, C. (ed) *The Transition to Active Learning,* Centre for the Study of Higher Education, University of Melbourne.

Department of Employment, Education and Training (1990), *A Fair Chance for All: Higher Education that's within Everyone's Reach*, Canberra, DEET.

Department of Employment Education and Training, Higher Education Division (1995), *Selected Higher Education Student Statistics*, Canberra, AGPS.

Department of Education, Training and Youth Affairs, (1999) *Transition from Secondary to Tertiary: a Performance Study, Higher Education Series*, Report No. 36, September.

Department of Education, Training and Youth Affairs, (2000) *OECD Thematic Review of the First Years in Tertiary Education*, Occasional Paper Series, March.

Department of Education, Training and Youth Affairs, (2000) *Demographic and Social Change: Implications for Educational Funding*, Occasional Paper – OOB.

Department of Education, Training and Youth Affairs, (2000) *Students 1999: Selected Higher Education Statistics.* Canberra, Department of Employment Training and Youth Affairs, February.

Fairclough, N. (1992) ' The Appropriacy of Appropriateness' in *Critical Language Awareness,* London, Longman.

Fairclough, N. (1995), *Critical Discourse Analysis: the Critical Study of Language*, London, Longman.

Fan, C. and Mak, A., (1998) 'Measuring Social Self-efficacy in a Culturally Diverse Student Population' in *Social Behaviour and Personality*, Vol 26, 131-144.

Gee, J P., (1990), *Social Linguistics and Literacies: Ideology in Discourses*, Bristol, Taylor and Francis.

Giddens, A., (1994), *Institutional Reflexivity and Modernity, The Polity Reader in Social Theory,* Cambridge, Polity Press.

Gudykurst, W. B. and Hammer, M. R. G. (1988) 'Strangers and Hosts: an Uncertainty Reduction based Theory of Intercultural Adaptation' in Y. Y. Kim and W. B. Gudykurst (Eds) *Cross-cultural Adaptation: Current Approaches,* Newbury Park, Sage:105-139.

Gudykunst, W. B. and Kim Y. Y. (1984) *Communicating with Strangers,* Reading, Addison Wesley.

Hofstege, G. (1980) *Culture's Consequences: International Differences in Work Related Values,* Beverly Hills, CA, Sage.

Illing, D. (1995) 'External Students Need Connectedness' in *The Australian Higher Education Supplement,* 13 December: p1.

Illing D., (2000) 'Tertiary Drop-outs Prompt Survey', *The Australian,* 2 February: p37.

Jamrozik, A. (1991) *Class, Inequality and the State; Social Change, Social Policy and the new Middle Class,* South Melbourne, McMillan.

Kantanis, T. (2000) 'The Role of Social Transition in Students' Adjustment to the First-Year at University' in *Journal of Institutional Research,* 9 (1):100-110.

Kantanis, T. (2001) Transition to Self-directed Learning: Issues Faced by Students in Adjusting to the First-Year at University, Paper presented to *The Eight International Learning Conference,* held in Spetses, Greece, July 4-8.

Kuh, G. (1995) 'The Other Curriculum', *Journal of Higher Education,* 66 (2).

Lankshear, C., Gee, P., Knobel, M. and Searle, C., (1997) *Changing Literacies, Buckingham,* Open University Press.

Lankshear, C. and McLaren, P. (eds) (1993) *Critical Literacy; Politics, Praxis and the Postmodern,* Albany, State University of New York Press.

Lawrence, J. PhD thesis (ongoing) 'Journeys of Transition: Alternative Entry Students and Their Means'.

Lee, A. (1996) *Working Together: Academic Literacies, Co-production and Professional Partnerships,* Keynote Address, First National Conference on Tertiary Literacy: Research and Practice VUT.

Luke, A. (1999) 'Critical Discourse Analysis' in Keeves J.P., and Lakomski, G., (eds) *Issues in Educational Research,* Amsterdam, Pergamon.

Mak, A.S., M.J. Barker, M.C., Logan, G. and Millman, L, (1999) Benefits of Cultural Diversity for International and Local Students: Contributions from an Experiential Social learning program (The ExcelL Program), in D. Davis and A. Olsen *International Education: the Professional Edge,* Sydney, IDP Education:: 63-76.

Mak, A. S. and Barker, M.C. (2000) 'The ExcelL Program for International Students' in *Proceedings of the 2000 Conference, Transcending Boundaries: Integrating People, Processes and Systems,* held at Griffith University, Brisbane, Sept.

Mak, A.S., Westwood, M.J. Barker, M.C., and Ishiyama, F.I., (1998), *The ExcelL Program: Excellence in Experiential Learning and Leadership,* Lyonco, Brisbane

Mak, A.S., Westwood, M.J. Barker, M.C., and Ishiyama, F.I., (1999) 'Optimising Conditions for learning Socio-cultural Competences for Success' in *International Journal of Intercultural Relations,* 23 (1): 77-90.

Mak, A.S., and Barker, M.C., (2000) 'The ExcelL Program for International Students' in Sheehan, M., Ramsay, S. and Patrick, J. (2000) *Transcending Boundaries: Integrating people, Processes and Systems, Proceedings of the 2000 Conference,* Griffith University, Brisbane.

Marginson, S., (1993) *Education and Public Policy in Australia,* Cambridge, Cambridge University Press.

McCann, H. (1996) From the Regions to the Centre: 'How Student Diversity may Change Universities', in James, R. and McInnis, C. (ed) *Transition to Active Learning,* Melbourne University.

McInnis C. (1996) (ed) *Transition to Active Learning, Centre for the Study of Higher Education,* University of Melbourne.

McInnis, C., (1996) 'Change and Diversity in the Work Patterns of Australian Academics', *Higher Education Management* 8 (2), pp.105-117.

McInnis, C., and James, R., (1995), *First Year on Campus – Diversity in the Initial Experiences of Australian Undergraduates,* Centre for the Study of Higher Education, University of Melbourne.

McInnis, C., (2000) *The Work Roles of Academics in Australian Universities,* AGPS, Canberra

McInnis, C., Hartley, R., and James, R. (2000) *Trends in the First Year Experience, Centre for the Study of Higher Education,* University of Melbourne

McInnis, C., Hartley, R., Polesel, J., and Tease, R. (forthcoming) Non-completion in Vocational Education and Training and Higher Education, AGPS, Canberra.

Meek, L. (1994), 'Higher education policy in Australia' in L Goedegeboure, F. Kaiser, P. Maassen, L. Meek, F. van Vught, and E. de Weert (Eds) *Higher Education Policy: An International Comparative Perspective,* Oxford, Pergamon Press.

Moodie, G. (1995) 'An Instrumentalist Approach to Equity', in *Journal of Institutional Research in Australasia,* 4 (2).

Muspratt S., Freebody, P. and Luke, A. (1997), *Constructing Critical Literacies: Teaching and Learning Textual Practice,* St Leonards, Allen and Unwin.

National Board of Employment, Education and Training (1995), *Advancing the National Framework for Student Equity in Higher Education Canberra,* NBEET.

National Board of Employment Education and Training (1996) *Equality, Diversity and Excellence: Advancing the National Framework for Higher Education Equity Framework,* Canberra.

Pearson, H (1999) 'Joining Forces to Increase Student Success: The Social Cultural Competences Project', *College and Institute Counsellors' Association of British Columbia Newsletter.*

Postle, G. Taylor, J., Bull, D., Hallinan, P., Newby, L., Protheroe, W., James, T., (1996) Successful Alternative Entry Students: Overcoming Potential Barriers to Academic Success, Unpublished Study, USQ., Toowoomba.

Postle, G.D., Clarke, J.R., Skuja, E., Bull, D.D., Batorowicz, K. McCann, H.A., (1997), *Towards Excellence in Diversity,* Toowoomba, USQ. Press.

Postle, G., Sturman, A and Clarke, J., (2001) *Widening Access to Further and Higher Education – an International Evaluative Study.* Toowoomba, USQ. Press.

Scheurich, J. J. (1997) *Research Method in the Postmodern*, London, Falmer Press.

Shergill, A. (1997) An Evaluation of the Social Cultural Competency for Success Training program for the Acquisition of Intercultural Interpersonal Competency Skills Among Health Care Trainees, Unpublished doctoral thesis, University of British Columbia.

Skilbeck, M. (1993), *Opening Address: The Transition from Elite to Mass Higher Education*, Canberra, DEET.

Smith R., (1993), *The Transition from Elite to Mass Higher Education Systems in Conference proceedings*, Canberra, DEET.

Stuart Hunter, M. (1996), 'Much a do about Something' in James, R. and McInnis, C. (ed) *Transition to Active Learning, Centre for the Study of Higher Education*, University of Melbourne

The New London Group, (1996), 'A Pedagogy of Multiliteracies: Designing Social Futures' *Harvard Educational Review*, 66, (1): 60-92.

The Fourteenth International Conference on the First Year Experience, held in conjunction with the Fifth Pacific Rim First Year in Higher Education Conference, Hawaii, July 2001.

Terenzini, P. T. (1993) *In and Out of Class Experiences*, Paper presented to Study of Higher Education Association.

Tinto, V. (1995) *Learning Communities and the Reconstruction of the First Year Experience*. Keynote address, Inaugural Pacific Rim, First Year Experience Conference, Brisbane, July.

Van Dijk, T. A (1997) *Discourse as Social Interaction,* London, Sage.

Volet. S. and Tan-Quigley, A. (1999) Interactions of South east Asian students and Administrative Staff at Universities in Australia' *Journal of Higher Education Policy and management,* 21: 95.

Ward, C., 'Acculturation' in D. Landis and R. S. Bhagat (Eds) *Handbook of Intercultural Training*, Sage, Thousand Oaks: 124-147.

Williams, T. (1987) *Participation in Education*, Australian Council of Educational Research (ACER), Hawthorn.

Yorke, M. (2000) Smoothing the Transition into Higher Education: What can be learned from Student Non-completion in *Journal of Institutional research*, 9 (1): 35-47.

Young, M. F. D. (1998) *The Curriculum of the Future from The New Sociology of Education to a Critical Theory of Learning*, London, Farmer Press.

Notes

1   I mean discourse in its most open sense to include all forms of talking and writing. By critical discourse analysis I mean analysis of any of these forms of discourse, at research which involves looking critically at language and texts in order to understand the meanings, social relations and cultural processes underlying them.

15

Inter-university collaboration – a regional approach

Algirdas Vaclovas Valiulis and Edmundas Kazimieras Zavadskas

Introduction

BALTECH, the University Consortium in Science and Technology, was created in 1998. It is an autonomous non-governmental non-profit organisation which consists of partner universities interested in creating a solid base for closer partnership and co-operation in the Baltic Sea Region within the areas of natural and engineering sciences, technology development and industrial management.

BALTECH was founded by seven universities from four Baltic Sea Region countries: Tallinn Technical University, *Estonia*; Riga Technical University, *Latvia*; Kaunas University of Technology and Vilnius Gediminas Technical University, *Lithuania*; Linköping University, Lund University/ Lund Institute of Technology and the Royal Institute of Technology, *Sweden*. BALTECH is open to other universities of the Baltic Sea Region and in 2001 two more universities from Finland and Denmark reinforced the consortium: Helsinki University of Technology and the Danish Technical University (Copenhagen). The *aim* of BALTECH is to develop stable and trusting relationships between its partners, which will lead to closer co-operation, based on respect for each country's educational system and cultural heritage. In the long term, the aim of BALTECH is to create a virtual Baltic Sea Region University of Science and Technology as a strategic resource for the long term development of education and research in accordance with the needs of region, sustainable development and further integration into the European Union. The quest for knowledge by its nature ruptures boundaries, crosses frontiers and discovers new paths.

The basic objectives and priorities

According to its statutes, the BALTECH consortium has the following basic objectives:

- to play an active role in the development of the policy for higher education and science in the Baltic Sea Region countries,

- to provide the highest quality scientific expertise and to give expert advice on principal questions of technology development in Baltic Sea Region countries,

- to assure integration into the European education and research system,

- to develop novel study programmes and courses in various fields of science and technology,

- to support the integration of higher engineering education, research and technology development,

- to develop efficient methods of training engineers and technologists,

- to promote innovation in engineering and technology education,

- to participate in international assessments of study programmes and research projects,

- to support the mobility of academic and administrative staff and students,

- to strengthen the development of relations between universities and industry and to consider the requirements of industry with regard to engineering and technological education,

- to develop new approaches in the management of engineering and technology education,

- to promote the continuing and distance education of engineers and technologists,

- to promote the awarding of joint degrees.

The following are the BALTECH priority areas: *energy-related technology, environmental technology, industrial business administration and management, industrial engineering and product development, information technology, materials science and technology.*

BALTECH's resources consist of funding from member universities, subsidies, which may be granted by various states, regional or local authorities, subsidies that might be granted by European or other international bodies, subsidies or subscriptions from individuals or institutions accepted by the Consortium Board.

Pilot activities

One of the first steps of the consortium was to initiate co-operation within the area of **Industrial Engineering and Management** by developing courses and programmes to be given at the Baltic Partner Universities as companies today have a great need of development managers. The work was carried out with major contributions from all the partner universities. The programme launching mechanism was as follows:

- initially, the need for the programme was discussed at an international workshop organised by representatives of industry, business and the academic community from the four countries participating in the consortium;

- the second step was the joint preparation of separate modules. The representatives of each university held a one-week seminar devoted to the content, scope, materials, literature, etc. of the module;

- finally, the graduates' theses will be approved by an international committee consisting of representatives of Swedish and the Baltic countries' academic staff.

This programme has to provide the future graduates with specialised knowledge (the basics of business administration, general and operations management, product and process management) for successful practical activities. It contains both engineering and management sections. The engineering sections depends on the specific field the student has studied previously (electrical, civil, mechanical engineering, etc.). The management section includes subjects intended to provide the future specialist with knowledge and experience in the field. The contents and objectives of the programme were discussed with successful companies, because the main aim is to prepare specialists for companies in the role of *development* or *technical managers* with an emphasis on international business. As every country has its specific tasks in the field, the target is not to introduce a unified programme for all universities. The working programme in each country has similar objectives based on similar principles. The nominal study period of the programme is *2 years – 80 credits. Admission requirements are: a bachelor's degree in Industrial Engineering, Mechanical Engineering, University diploma or a diploma from a polytechnic-type higher educational institution. The degree awarded is: Master of Engineering (M. Eng.)*

The programme is made up of a number of compulsory blocks: general and basic studies necessary for management and business studies (Operations Analysis, Statistical Analysis, etc.), technology (Product Design, Design for Quality, etc.), management (quality, productivity, personnel, etc.), the fundamentals of business and finance and finally a master's thesis. General studies cover 4.5%, basic studies 15.5%, core studies 18.5%, special studies 27.5% and the master's thesis 34% of the study time.

Each university participating in the programme has some modules in which it plays the leading role:

Operations research (Tallinn) 3.5 credit points (CP)

Optimisation. Linear planning. Mathematical planning. Nonlinear planning. Optimal management. Methods of global optimisation.

Statistical analysis (Linköping) 3.0 CP

Simple linear regression and correlation, multiple linear regression, analysis of variance, general factorial experiments, the 2k factorial design, fractional factorial designs.

Industrial production (KTH, Stockholm) 4.0 CP

Production systems, product manufacturing, MRP, planning, production chains. Logistics.

Total quality management (Vilnius) 2.0 CP

Definition of total quality management. Urgent problems of production quality and quality management. The main factors in the quality management system and its development. The industrial quality management system. Economic, legal, technological, social aspects of the total quality management system.

Information systems of production management (Vilnius) 2.0 CP

Definition of the information systems of production management. Information technologies and their development. Functions of production management. Peculiarities of the information systems of industrial production management. The creation of information systems. Economic, legal and technological aspects of information systems of production management.

Some fields for topics for the final thesis are the following:

– *management decisions, operations research and information systems*

 (models of mathematical programming, their analysis and application in improving the organisation of practical activities; processes of mass service, their modelling and methods of decision making; the creation of information systems to improve the practical activities of an enterprise; the creation of production management decision information systems to improve the practical activities of an enterprise);

- *competition* (analysis of competitors and the competitiveness of markets and the means of maintaining stability; preparing the strategy for products' competitiveness);

- *product quality management* (analysis of product quality and the perfection of management in large and medium-sized production; the content of quality management, its analysis and improvement in small and medium-sized enterprises, etc.);

- Other spheres: *business management, statistical analysis, manufacture planning, industrial marketing, productivity management, small and medium-sized businesses, production efficiency, international business management, supply management, industrial manufacture, international industry.*

Quality review

The international programme management committee has foreseen the need for a careful quality review of the programme, a review with the following objectives:

- to identify activities leading to the improved and/or maintained quality of the programmes

- to identify activities leading to the low and/or diminishing quality of the programmes;

- to increase the awareness of quality issues and stimulate internal quality work by giving those involved in each programme evidence and support for the improvement and development of the programme;

- to broaden the views on quality issues by referring to equivalent non-domestic programmes;

- to provide Rectors with information on the quality of their programmes as a basis for their decision-making;

- to investigate and assess the influence of research and technical development on the education.

The review process will be realised in two steps: *self-assessment* and *external assessment* by the Evaluation Group (Peer Group) consisting of representatives from each of the participating universities. Self-assessment has the following aims:

- the stimulation of internal quality control through the analysis of strengths and weaknesses;

- internal preparation for the visit of the Evaluation Group;

- the provision of basic information for the Evaluation Group.

The self-assessment should be the result of an open discussion within the institution that involves groups of teachers, administrative staff and students. Such discussion should analyse the strengths and weaknesses of the institution. Self-assessment will be carried out with the aid of a questionnaire. The evaluation group will make their assessment on the basis of extensive interviews with programme management, teachers, and students. The textbooks and supporting literature, written examinations and graduate theses will be reviewed as well.

New programmes

Two new master degree programmes were agreed recently at the consortium board meeting. One of them 'Environmental Management and Cleaner Production' will be started in the academic year 2002/2003, and the other – an MSc – programme in 'Regional Development Management' – in 2003/2004.

Access

Each programme places great emphasis on promoting democracy, intercultural contacts, helping students to make new friends and to educate themselves for the better utilisation of the countries' resources.

As regards Vilnius Gediminas Technical University, it is making efforts to create the conditions for wider access to these study programmes which have a limited number of places. National minorities have no access limitations and are, thus, represented in all study groups. Students with a lower level of family income have some opportunities for mobility exchange as they receive support (including travel, accommodation and maintenance expenses) from the University and the Consortium. A more difficult task is to create the infrastructure for disabled people. The modernisation of access to laboratories and classrooms is very expensive and complicated, particularly in centuries' old buildings. New or renovated buildings, on the other hand, are provided with the necessary facilities; for instance the modern university library has been equipped with all the necessary devices, but very large parts of the premises are still difficult for people with movement disabilities to access.

Conclusions

The academic networks help to promote democracy and intercultural contacts, and enable students to educate themselves for the better utilisation of the countries' resources.

The response of the university to growing business, cultural co-operation, manpower mobility, and new communication capabilities is more effective if it is enforced by the joint efforts of different universities in different countries.

From the launching of these study programmes, strong emphasis should be laid on widening access for different youth strata.

16

Interdisciplinary collaboration: its role in widening participation in Higher Education

Jocey Quinn

This chapter presents a rather different perspective on the question of collaboration to that of the rest of the collection, and its concerns are primarily conceptual rather than practical. Whilst collaboration is normally discussed in terms of partnerships and structures, fore-grounding the ways in which different types of institutions can work together, I want to argue that collaboration should apply to knowledge generation itself. Through working across disciplines, collaboration can be a way of thinking new thoughts, commensurate with the challenges posed by widening participation in Higher Education. It is not enough to simply act in the sphere of access, we need to understand what is or is not happening, and why: looking beneath the patterns of exclusion from HE. Widening participation implies a deconstruction of the university, a transformation, not only of surfaces and structures, but of knowledge itself. As Taylor argues, in the contemporary UK university 'the tyranny of established disciplinary canons disintegrates' under the weight of attack from both postmodernists and vocationalists, whilst at the same time traditional educational divisions are buttressed by Research Assessment and Quality Assurance mechanisms 'based entirely upon traditional, conservative disciplinary divisions.'(2000; 69) It is a contradictory situation in which interdisciplinary working holds enormous potential but may not be easily facilitated. Although lifelong learning has been characterised as a 'moorland' (Edwards, 1997), an uncharted and developing territory where intellectual crossings of academic borders are common, the extent to which different academic fields are actually working collaboratively together, rather than temporarily meeting on crisis – crossing paths, seems very limited. Nevertheless, collaboration in the sphere of intellectual ideas remains just as urgent for the contemporary university as working effectively with schools and further education providers.

The notion of pragmatism, of identifying what will and won't work, how to be effective within the bounds of institutional constraints, clearly has its place, but has it been over privileged in the access discourse? Activity cannot exist outside the realm of ideas. Pragmatism in itself is an inadequate response to widening participation. We cannot act unless we know why we are acting and we need to have a conscious conceptual base on which to place our activities, otherwise they are empty. Moreover, as Hughes has recently argued, concepts themselves shift in meaning, and 'we need to develop our levels of conceptual literacy so that, whilst we do not simply assume that we, and those whom we research, are all speaking the same language, we are also not prevented from being able to talk to each other at all.'(2001; 612) In this chapter I want to illustrate how interdisciplinary collaboration can help us to understand and address some complex and material issues: firstly, why some people don't participate in Higher Education, and, secondly, how to deal with the pedagogical conflicts generated by widening participation. In doing so I hope to illustrate the intellectual and practical benefits that can accrue when those researching and working in the field of access to HE work and think collaboratively with other academic fields.

Reconceptualising widening participation
Widening participation must be conceived as far more than a set of activities to get people into Higher Education. Developing a richer and more intellectually engaged access discourse can be fostered by collaboration at a theoretical and pedagogical level. As widening participation happens, it generates new landscapes and problems. In this chapter I want to introduce two concrete examples of inter-

disciplinary collaboration which can illuminate both patterns of access and questions of teaching and learning. In other words, they may help both in getting new kinds of students into the university and in dealing with them effectively once they are there. Interdisciplinary collaboration presents infinite possibilities but I want to focus on two examples which particularly interest me: collaboration between Educational Research and Human Geography and collaboration between the fields of widening participation and feminist pedagogy.

Interdisciplinary collaboration between human geography and educational research

I want to begin by considering the scope for collaboration between the fields of Educational Research and Human Geography, a possibility which has been interestingly raised by Tamboukou (1999) but which, as yet, is not well developed. Why should we even want to consider such a collaboration, what are the potential benefits for widening participation? The usefulness of this collaboration lies in its ability to help us understand space and who enters into it; in this case the space of the university or college of HE. Rational barriers to entry, such as finance, can well be understood. It is easy to comprehend why potential students resist large burdens of debt and why families believe they cannot afford HE. How do we approach barriers that are less easy to quantify? There are other reasons why people feel they cannot enter the university space, and do not belong there: reasons bound up in questions of subjectivity and identity. HE must be understood, not only as a bounded material space, but also a symbolic one. The university is not just a place that exists, although its material limits are important; but it is also an imagined space in people's heads, both for those inside and outside the university. Indeed its symbolic meanings may be more important than its actual ones.

To illustrate how HE can function in this way as a symbolic space, made meaningful by its emotional topography, I can draw on my own doctoral research (Quinn, 2000). This research studied women students as the first successful wave of widening participation in the UK. Numerically women students have moved from being very much the minority to being a slight majority amongst under-graduates. My research considered whether HE, and in particular its curriculum and culture, had changed in response to this very shift. One of the significant findings of the research was that, in spite of what still appeared to be male dominated structures, curricula and classrooms, which seemed to leave women a marginalised majority, women saw the university as a protected space where they felt they belonged. It was a space away from various forms of threat. For example, it offered protection from abusive partners, not only a physical, but a mental refuge with a communal identity, which, significantly they could draw on when not actually there. It also offered protection from emotional demands which were placed on them in their roles as carers of children, partners, parents. It was also a protection from the expectations of others: a space with freedom to imagine new possibilities and identities. The meaning and signi-ficance of the university space lay not in what it was, but in what it represented to them.

However, it is also apparent that the university can be perceived, quite legitimately, as a dangerous space, embodying difference and threat. How do we help those who perceive it in this way to access HE? How can we use spatial concepts to break down this sense of threat and address its material causes? How might access to HE be placed within broader patterns of the use and avoidance of space? Sibley's concept of the 'geographies of exclusion' (1995) illuminates how those who are particularly marginalised within our culture, such as homeless people and people who are experiencing mental illness, will home in on spaces shared by others in the same situation, feel-ing comfortable in such spaces and avoiding others. Thus their marginal positionings are both created by, and recreate, geographies of exclusion. This concept can be turned to the question of widening participation. Among the spaces such groups may avoid, lies the university, and this in turn re-enforces exclusion: particularly since access to HE is increasingly portrayed as a base line requirement for social participation. Understanding this process reveals that measures which focus on the university alone cannot break what is a systemic pattern of use of space. It also highlights the uncomfor-table truth that the discourse of widening participation can even multiply exclusion. However, Human Geography can also provide illuminating visions of the potential of space and its meanings. One such influential concept is Rose's 'paradoxical space... a space imagined in order to articulate a troubled relation to the hegemonic discourses of masculinism' (1993;159) In this configuration a dominant space creates the conditions whereby it is, paradoxically, possible to imagine alternatives of freedom born both of and against the dominant order: imagined spaces of possibility. The university is in an excellent position to generate such paradoxical space, and indeed seems to have done so for the women students in my research. By application of Sibley and Rose's concepts to the access debate it is possible to see how the university can be both exclusionary and liberating at the same time, and that, in both senses, it is the function of HE as a symbolic space which matters most and which needs to be addressed. My argument is that access needs to be contended at the level of the symbolic and the imaginary if the concrete aims of the pragmatists are ever to be fully realised.

Space for Lifelong Learning: an example of interdisciplinary fusion

Interdisciplinary research is needed which simultaneously interrogates marginalised perspectives on the symbolic space of the university and uses them to create improvements in the sector. One such example is research currently planned by the Institute for Access Studies at Staffordshire University, working with three groups who have been identified as experiencing exclusion from HE: people with mental health problems, rural working class men, Bangladeshi women. This diverse participation hopefully provides a multifaceted picture of exclusion and rich conceptualisations of HE as a space and geographical concepts will be mobilised to explore how these participants imagine HE as a space, and how barriers can be overcome. Part of the process would be to reconfigure HE in a positive way, drawing on the experiences of successful learners: with the ultimate goal of helping institutions improve their provision to excluded groups. The research would explore how people from these three groups imagine HE, and whether this imagined space fosters their exclusion from lifelong learning. It would be particularly interested in the relationship between both subjective and material barriers. By also involving students from these categories, who have overcome exclusion to become successful learners, the research would also explore how far the university can offer protection from the threats they commonly experience in 'everyday' space. Underlying the project is the fundamental question: can the interdisciplinary fusion of educational research and human geography provide a new way of understanding patterns of exclusion from lifelong learning? Widening participation initiatives will never fully succeed unless they understand how marginalised groups configure educational space. The solution involves both simultaneously addressing their perceptions and changing our processes: in a genuine bid for 'conceptual literacy'(Hughes, 2001) The proposed research forms a useful exemplar of how this might be approached.

The collaboration of widening participation and feminist pedagogy

I now want to move to another fruitful area of interdisciplinary collaboration: that between widening participation and feminist pedagogy. As the student body becomes more diverse within HE, new pedagogical issues arise, and teachers face new dilemmas. Feminist pedagogy has already confronted, if not resolved, these dilemmas. Some of the concepts with which it has engaged are not unique to feminist pedagogy, but it is useful to consider what has been learned from an international debate which has been sustained amongst feminist teachers over the past twenty years.. This international debate stems from twenty years of practice and theory in Women's Studies, trying to create new kinds of classrooms which meet the needs of a student body which has been particularly diverse in terms of age, race and class. Although any short summary is inevitably over-schematic, three key areas can be identified. The first relates to questions of 'voice' and the problematising of the notion of 'giving someone a voice'. Feminists such as Kenway and Willis (1998) in Australia have challenged the idea that there is any such thing as a person's 'authentic' voice, still less that a teacher is in a position to release it. Lewis (1993), writing from Canada, stresses the importance of listening to silence. She argues that silence, may not always connote powerlessness; it may rather be revolt, a refusal to engage in normative practices. Within feminist pedagogy there has been a crucial turn from 'speaking for' to 'speaking with' (Spivak, 1988).The second key concept is that of 'difference' and the importance, not of exploiting, but valuing, and utilising, the different life experiences and cultures which diverse students bring to the class room. This debate was sparked by black feminists such as Lorde in the USA (1984) who argued that it is neither possible nor desirable to create a homogenous classroom with unified goals. There are different power relations amongst students: these have to be acknowledged, they cannot be erased or made to disappear by wishful thinking. However, different knowledge is of vital importance as a resource, but this has to be approached with care lest the 'different' student be exoticised as a 'native informant'(Hooks, 1994; 43).The third concept, and the one which underlies all three, is that of empowerment. Empowerment has become a highly contested notion in feminist pedagogy. Ellsworth (1992) has deconstructed the vision of the teacher as disinterested power-giver. The teacher has their own interests and allegiances which they do not give up on entering the classroom. Moreover, power can only be produced not handed over as a possession. Students come with their own power, which manifests itself in different ways. They are not empty vessels, simply because they do not possess formal qualifications. As Letherby and Marchbank (1997) have demonstrated in the UK, students may choose their own vision of what is empowering, and not be confined by the tutors vision of what is worthwhile or valid.

If we apply these critiques to the rhetoric of widening participation we can see that feminist pedagogy has attained a level of sophistication which the access arena may lack. How often is the notion of 'voice' unproblematically invoked in access conferences and papers without any recognition that it is, at the least, a loaded concept? Access discourse tends to the humanistic and individualistic, it can be simultaneously narrow in its focus and naïvely optimistic. In drawing on the lessons which Women's Studies has been forced to learn, we can more fully respond to the challenges raised by widening participation. These lessons can be encapsulated as a need for greater reflexivity and responsibility on the part of teachers teaching more diverse students. They teach us that idealism and naïve assumptions of sharing, caring classrooms must be replaced by a more rigorous thinking through of what both teachers and students bring to the HE arena. Moreover, this catalytic Women's Studies classroom only exists because the subject itself poses a question as to what is valid knowledge. My research indicates that such questions are not yet widespread within the mainstream curriculum (Quinn, 2002). If widening participation is to be at all meaningful, such curricular questions must also take centre stage.

Conclusion

I wish to end with what is perhaps a contentious claim, that despite international conferences and collections such as this one, the field of widening participation can sometimes be narrow and parochial. The tendency to simply repeat and exchange 'what works' leaves us in danger of neglecting more far-reaching questions. Although achieving positive outcomes is clearly important, sometimes it is necessary to step back and reflect, find new ways of thinking about the issues. In this chapter I have tried to demonstrate how collaboration can exist on a conceptual level. Interdisciplinary collaboration can help us to rise to the challenge of widening participation, understanding more acutely the meanings and potential of the university space and the learning possibilities which exist within it. At the same time, it can solve some very practical problems which as yet elude us, such as how to provide access to HE for some of the most excluded groups in society and how to best teach and learn from them once they are there.

References

Alasuutari, P. (1998) *An Invitation to Social Research*. London: Sage

Edwards, R. (1997) *Changing Places? Flexibility, Lifelong Learning and a Learning Society*. London: Routledge

Ellsworth, E. (1992 Why Doesn't This Feel Empowering? Working through Repressive Myths of Critical Pedagogy. *Harvard Educational Review,* 50 (3), pp297-234

hooks, b. (1994) *Teaching to Transgress*. London: Routledge

Hughes, C. (2001) Developing Conceptual Literacy in Lifelong Learning Research: a case of responsibility. *British Educational Research Journal*, Vol 27,No 5,601-615

Kenway, J. and Willis, S. (1998) *Answering Back: Girls Boys and Feminism in Schools.* London: Routledge

Lewis, M. G. (1993) *Without a word: Teaching beyond women's silence.* London: Routledge

Letherby G. and Marchbank, J. (1997) I don't want to be empowered, just give me a reading pack: student responses and resistance to different forms of teaching and assessment. Paper presented at Equal Opportunities and the Curriculum Conference, Oxford Brookes University, September

Lorde, A.(1984) *Sister Outsider.* Trumansberg New York: The Crossing Press

Mason, J. (1996) *Qualitative Researching.* London: Sage

Quinn, J. (2000) Powerful Subjects: Women Students, Subjectivity and the Higher Education Curriculum. Unpublished PhD thesis, Lancaster University

Quinn, J.(2002) (forthcoming) *Are Women Taking Over the University?* Stoke: Trentham Books

Rose, G. (1993) *Feminism and Geography: The Limits of Geographical Knowledge.* Oxford: Polity Press

Sibley, D. (1995) *Geographies of Exclusion.* London: Routledge

Spivak, G. (1988) *In Other Worlds: Essays in Cultural Politics.* London: Routledge

Tamboukou, M. (1999) Spacing Herself: women in education. *Gender and Education* Vol 12, No 2 pp183-195

Taylor R, (2000) Concepts of self-directed learning in Higher Education: re-establishing the democratic condition, in *Stretching the Academy* ed J. Thompson Leicester: NAICE pp68-80

17

Putting partnerships into practice

Sarah Williams

Introduction

Encouraging collaboration across the sectors is invaluable and should be encouraged, definitely! (Steering Group member from a well-established partnership).

T his chapter is based on findings drawn from research commissioned by HEFCE to examine collaboration, or co-operation between higher education institutions (HEIs) and further education colleges (FECs) (plus other education institutions, community groups and regional agencies) in attempts to widen participation in higher education by students who are currently underrepresented (Thomas *et al*, 2001). Research was conducted in the 25 regional partnerships funded as part of a widening participation special funding programme. In particular, the research focused on the initial one-year research projects and, where applicable, subsequent second phase projects. The research critically examined the processes of co-operation and the impact of collaboration, including an examination of monitoring, evaluation and tracking procedures and explored the significance of a regional approach to widening participation. In addition it sought to identify and explore good practice amongst partnerships. Although the findings are drawn from research based in England it is likely that they can be generalised to other countries both inside and outside the UK.

The overwhelming response from the partnerships participating in the research was that collaboration is an effective way to widen participation. In addition, with only one exception, survey respondents felt that collaboration was an effective use of funding, avoiding '*duplication of effort*', facilitating '*shared good practice*' and '*providing better quality output than if FEIs get funding direct*'. Our research suggests that regional partnerships do have the potential to widen participation. However, there are a number of ways in which the collective efforts of partnerships can be made more effective. This chapter is primarily concerned with discussing aspects of collaboration that have been highlighted by the participating partnerships in our research. It is our hope that some of these discussions will be of value to institutions contemplating collaboration or to those currently involved in a partnership but requiring guidance or information on how other partnerships are developed and managed. The chapter is in five sections which examine some of the key issues raised during our research: creating an effective partnership; building coherence; management and administration; sustainability; and monitoring and evaluation. It concludes with a summary of our research recommendations for collaborating and developing an effective partnership.

Creating an effective partnership

The research addressed the question of how partnerships were initially formed. The predominant mode for identifying partners appeared to be serendipity, and once partners were agreed, and then the focus of the partnership was determined, rather than vice versa. Although there were many informal links between partners, most partnerships were formed in response to an invitation to tender for funding. However, our research illustrates that problems can occur when there is no clear purpose to the formation of a partnership (other than to secure funding). It demonstrates that partners should be selected carefully to take account of the aims and objectives of the project to be embarked upon and they should be clear about what it needs to achieve and how it will proceed.

> One of the things I've learned is that discussion about the nature of the partnership should be had early on. So people are clear with one another

what they expect from it both in terms of institutions and how it was going to work as a partnership that would allow people to be honest and demarcate the boundaries. (HE Project Officer)

All the partnerships that participated in our research are led by HEIs, and FE is rarely a full partner. Where FE are partners, they are often 'used' for their 'grass roots' experience but are not perceived as organisations that offer the partnership anything on a more strategic or managerial basis. This can cause problems in how FE perceive their role in the project and effect the contributions they want to make to it's overall success. Partnerships should be encouraged to involve FE as full partners, and not to make assumptions about what they can contribute and how they can benefit from collaboration. Perhaps involving FE in project development from the beginning could be included as a pre-requisite to obtaining funding by funding bodies.

Furthermore, community representation is often excluded from partnership management, research and implementation. Community members are rarely included on the steering and advisory boards. This is in part due to difficulties experienced in getting people from the community to become involved in formal meetings. However, the often bureaucratic systems that can be inherent in educational organisations may also be opposed to, or at odds with, the more informal methods of community communication and cultures. If HE and FE can develop more familiar methods of communicating with the community around them then a less hierarchical partnership may be developed. One partnership who were attempting to develop a more participative outreach model, described working with the community in the following terms:

It's about finding an equitable way of doing things that overcome political sensitivities. (Steering Group member)

If funding bodies could encourage partnerships to work with a range of partners and possibly members from other regional networks, then the real needs of the community might be recognised and addressed more fairly and widening participation within the region could be increased. However, involving too many organisations that have the same catchment area and needs to recruit can be problematic. It is commonly acknowledged that tensions exist between collaboration and competition for those within partnerships (see Thomas, in this volume), described by a Steering group member as: '*At the heart of widening participation are sensitive competitive issues around recruitment...*'

Building coherence

Partnerships involve multiple partners who often have different motivations and interests and it is therefore necessary for partnerships to consider how they are going to build levels of coherence through the organisations involved. Three approaches to developing coherence were identified during our research (which have also been suggested by Chataway *et al*, 1997): achieving a shared vision, sharing good practice within the partnership and creating a bridging organisation.

The importance of shared vision was frequently reiterated:

> *Partnerships are always the agony and the ecstasy, every single partnership goes through some agony but what keeps them together is some kind of common vision and common commitment.* (Steering Committee members)

A true partnership needs to have a shared vision of what the aims and objectives of the project are and a sense of ownership over their role within the project, otherwise deadlines may not be met, confusion may be felt about what each partner is supposed to be doing and ultimately the project could fail to function correctly. To achieve shared vision there needs to be early debate and agreement on the aims and parameters of the partnership which are agreed by all partners. Time needs to be spent early in the partnership formation to identify a clear mission statement. A member of a well established partnership described the importance of having common goals for their partnership:

> *We have a common purpose to help raise awareness, to help under achievement – we do this in many other ways to, with other groups but that is what we are doing, that's what we want to do and we come together and we do it. Widening participation is not about people's ability, but about barriers and we recognise that. We are part of the process that may create*

some of those barriers and I think all of us recognise that this massive underachievement in terms of engaging the vast population of [name of region] – we're part of the problem and part of the solution. We all agree that we can do something about it and agree that we must do something about it and we all share that. (Member of the Steering Group)

As well as a clear mission, partnerships seem to work best when they have something on which to focus, a project around which to build. To establish what the mission is and what part each partner has within achieving it, the roles and responsibilities of each member should be agreed, preferably in writing, by the partnership: this helps communication and determine what is expected from each individual. Formal agreements which lay out the tasks required to be undertaken by each member and which can be 'signed off' by each organisation, could help to achieve this

The importance of sharing good practice with others was also foregrounded. The partnerships generally felt they had been given little guidance from the funding body in how to build effective partnerships. They felt that it was beneficial to have information about what other partnerships were doing and to share their experiences and learn from other organisations. Such learning took place in more or less formal ways and with differing consequences.

Firstly, learning "what not to do" and avoiding duplication of activities and services was essential:

...people are informed about what FE's doing, what HE's doing, it allows us not to duplicate. (Project Officer, non-lead HEI)

Secondly, "ad hoc learning" took place informally between partnership members and this was used to improve their own practice,

I didn't have to reinvent the wheel. the bicycle was there for me to get on and ride. (Project Officer, HEI, non-lead institution)

In terms of more organised learning, mechanisms were set up within some of the partnerships which initiated inter-institutional learning. These included: working groups, meetings, seminars, conferences. It appeared that workshops and other more formal mechanisms need to be flexible to meet the requirements of different partners, but they can be very useful to the communication within the partnership. Few partnerships established standard practices for all partner members but where they have, they can ensure a consistency of services or activities for the learners throughout the region or sub-region.

In order that good practice can be shared there needs to be a high level of trust between members. Only then can partnerships become the antidote to competition, which potentially is progressive for the learner. Within the funding strand, partnerships should be encouraged to develop mechanisms for sharing good practice. To further encourage good practice, the funding body can also facilitate inter-institutional/partnership learning e.g. through organising regional seminars.

The third approach for establishing coherence within partnerships is the creation of a 'bridging organisation' (Brown, 1991). The majority of regional partnerships tried to create bridging organisations, in other words set up a new organisation. For example a number of partnerships tried to create a new identity by creating a name for their partnership which signifies that it is more than a collection of educational providers. In at least one case, the partnership devised it's own web site, stationary and premises, as well as employing its own staff:

> Obviously [name of bridging organisation] as the umbrella organisation has helped, and that we've got these premises here is good. I think because we've taken a regional approach this has helped individual organisations trust each other a bit more.

Creating a bridging organisation can provide a more comprehensive and coherent set of activities to widen participation, but it can also limit the amount of power the lead partner has over other partners. During our research we discovered that bridging organisations, if used appropriately, can be very effective and wherever possible partnerships should be encouraged to examine their structure and determine if a bridging organisation would be of benefit.

Management and administration

Our research also highlights the need for a clear management structure within partnerships, which is non-hierarchical and facilitates open and transparent decision making. If decision making is not transparent then individuals may not feel committed and the role of the partnership may be perceived as a waste of time and even opposed to the process of widening participation. As one Senior Manager commented:

> You've got to play it dead straight though, you can't try to pull the rug from under people otherwise they just won't collaborate with you again. So when we put together the [partnership] bid we said you will have some money to employ a project officer, so they're not employed by us. In the past when universities got money they tried to hang on to it which is understandable... (Senior Manager, lead-HEI)

It was also apparent from our research dedicated central administration is advantageous, and so funding bodies should be encouraged to provide for the creation and development of autonomous partnerships. A partnership's central administration can be well informed about all aspects of the partnership and therefore provide a focal point for facilitating and co-ordinating projects and assisting communication.

Communication has to be effective across partnerships within institutions and within the region or sub region. We feel that partnerships could benefit from developing a communication strategy at its conception. However, we discovered that one of the most important components of effective communication within partnerships is enthusiasm and a genuine commitment to widening participation. Where this exists there are greater benefits and better working relationships between organisations, which in turn enhances efforts to widen participation.

Sustainability

Collaboration is extensive and time consuming and there is a danger that where initiatives to widen participation are short term the benefits do not last beyond the funding period, so genuine change cannot be achieved. As one, long term partnership member states:

> Hang on in there!! It's the stuff that goes on over years – the partnership takes time, it takes will and persistence really and there will be peaks and troughs. And also to keep driving forward. (Steering Committee member from a well-established partnership)

However, there is a mismatch between the process of having to bid for funding and developing long term approaches to widening participation. It would thus be beneficial for partnerships to have access to more secure sources of income. It is also useful to be forewarned of forthcoming funding initiatives, which allows partnerships to propose more fully developed projects. This can ensure more commitment is given by each of the members and real results can be achieved for the target groups.

Short term commitment and lack of funding can also harm widening participation. Funding is crucial to the development of any partnership and for the implementing of project activities: if there are insufficient resources then the full aims of the project may not be possible to achieve. In turn this may affect how the target group of students perceive entering into education. Furthermore it is important that widening participation staff have greater employment security and career development opportunities, otherwise they will not continue to work in the field.

> I am very keen to continue in widening participation after this project, so if anything can be fed back to [funding body] it is don't leave it till the eleventh hour because we have people on contract and they start to get to the end of their contract they start looking elsewhere. But we could retain some very good staff if we knew in advance of additional funding or projects in the pipeline. (Project officer)

Some partnerships have managed to sustain themselves by focusing on more than one project at a time, and not allowing one project be so exclusive that it cannot aid the development of another when its funding comes to an end. Other factors that have aided sustainability have been the sharing of good practice and learning from each other to benefit their own organisations. Through our research it became apparent that partnerships must build sustainability into their strategic planning. Moreover, original funding proposals should address this issue, or alternatively provide an 'exit strategy' that will allow the project to come to an end without damaging the target groups involved.

Monitoring and evaluation

One of the findings from our research has been the lack of fully developed systems for monitoring, evaluation and tracking students' progression within the projects. It would appear that monitoring and evaluation are often not activities that are given much attention. This, however,is not a new discovery. Previous research carried out by Thomas (1998) identified five barriers to monitoring and evaluation: poor understanding of what monitoring and evaluation is; lack of incentive; costs; lack of skills and guidance from external bodies; lack of time. Another barrier highlighted by our research was a lack of data and appropriate methodologies with which to evaluate.

For widening participation to be successful it is vital that monitoring and evaluation processes are in place before the project begins, thus project funding proposals should address specific questions about monitoring, evaluation and tracking and funding should be explicitly provided for such activities. Funding bodies could provide guidance about monitoring and evaluation systems, and training about possible approaches to monitoring and evaluation could also be available to practitioners and steering committee members *before* projects commence. Monitoring, evaluation and tracking tools could be developed by an external body and used and adapted by partnerships and institutions to assess the impact of their widening participation policies and practices.

Conclusion

Whilst we are aware that our research does not address all the issues surrounding institutional collaboration, it has revealed that developing partnerships can help individual organisations complement each other and also assist in widening participation. However, it is important that funding bodies are aware of some of the difficulties in providing partnerships with short term funding. For partnerships to truly develop they need to be secure in the knowledge that they can sustain their activities effectively and maintain a good team of staff to ensure that they meet their aims and objectives. A significant part of this process is how the partnership is initially established. Funding bodies should use selection and evaluation criteria that ensure partnerships are formed which take proper consideration of how the community will benefit, thus widening participation. The criteria could stipulate that partnerships need to select a good cross section of organisations involved at partnership management level. Additional funding should also be provided for the development and communication needed to build an effective partnership. Funding for the general running of the partnership is another important consideration, as this administrative responsibility often falls as an additional task for employees already involved with the lead organisation.

For a partnership of any kind to work effectively it is important that functions are fulfilled correctly, and a partnership between organisations is no exception. Our research highlights the fact that it is crucial to the development and sustainability of partnerships that solid communication structures are implemented and agreed between all members and a clear goal of what the partnership needs to achieve is understood throughout the partnership.

References

Brown, L.D. (1991) Bridging Organisations and Sustainable Development, *Human Relations*, vol. 44, no. 9, pp.807-831.

Chataway, J., Hewitt, T., Johnson, H. and Thomas, A (1997) From public sector to public action in *Capacities for Managing Development*. Global Programme in Development Management. Milton Keynes: The Open University

Thomas, E., Quinn, J., Slack, K., Williams, S. (2001) Widening Participation: Evaluation of the collaboration between higher education institutions and further education colleges to increase participation in higher education. Bristol: HEFCE

Thomas, E. (1998) Conceptualising the role of evaluation in small voluntary organisations, PhD Thesis, University of Sheffield

Index

Abbott-Chapman, J. 188
academia: freedom 52;
   networks 246; staff
   188-9, 190, 222;
   support 127-9; tuition
   117
academics: and first year
   students 213-33; role
   230-2
Access Summer School
   141-2, 146, 148
Action on Access 39-40
Action Group on Access 60
Adelaide University survey
   (1996) 188
admission profile 122
admission and recruitment
   policies 112
African-American students
   85-6, 88
African-Caribbean males
   114
Afrikaans-speaking white
   institution 100
Ambrose, P. 34
American Indian students
   88
anti-discrimination
   legislation 66
Apex Scotland 199, 201
Asian-American students 88
Association for Higher
   Education Access and
   Disability (AHEAD)
   54
Association of South
   African Historically
   Disadvantaged
   Institutions
   (ASADHI) 106
Australia 4, 6, 14-15;
   government 183-4;
   Melbourne 11-12, 19,

21, 23, 40; universities
   215-35; Victoria
   University of
   Technology 11

baccalaureate degree 175
Bachelor of Arts
   BA/Science (BSc)
   133, 134
Balloch, S. and Taylor, M.
   32
BALTECH: 239-246
Baltic Sea Region 239
Bandura, A. 222
Bangladesh: 114, women
   251
barriers: abolishing 14
   attitudinal 189
   financial 189
   geographical 154
   psychological 152
   subjective and
   material 253
Bartholomae, D. 221
Blackburn: England 132
Boekaerts, M. 222
Boud, D. 231-2
Bowers, B. and Geneeb, H.
   34
Brennan, L. and Clulow, V.
   227
British Telecom 113
Burbules, N.C. 192
Bury: England 132

California 172, 176
California State University
   7, 174
Canada 209
Careers Service 148
Chaplaincy 148
City and Guilds 44

Clancy, P. 51; and Wall, J.
   51, 55
Clulow, V. and Brennan, L.
   227
co-operation and alliances
   106
co-ordination 32, 45
collaboration 10, 16-18, 24-
   25, 47 with
   community 111-38;
   impact 194; inter-
   university 239-246;
   internal 40; learning
   from 208-11; long
   term impact 96-7;
   models 6-12; multi-
   lateral 20-1;
   promoting 36-41;
   reasons 46; typology
   6; vertical 20
collaborative approaches
   16-18, 25, 47, 184-91,
   195
collaborative educational
   programme 199-11
collaborative structure 15-
   16, 25
college: access 85-97;
   access programmes
   75-6; preparatory
   course 96; public two-
   year 172
College Intranet 129
college network: clearing
   house 91; pathways
   85-97; pathways
   social context 95-6
Commonwealth Disability
   Discrimination Act
   (DDA) 184
community 130 engagement
   89; learning 159;
   location 117

Community College
    Transfer Program
    (CCTP) 7, 175, 176
comparative analysis 12-20
competition 36, 42-3, 45,
    244
compulsory courses 242-4
Connell, H. and Skilbeck,
    M. 5, 55
Consortium 246
Cooperative Projects for
    Higher Education
    Students with
    Disabilities
    (CPHESD) 182
cost-effectiveness 13-15,
    19-20
Council on Higher
    Education (South
    Africa 2000) 102
counselling 148
courses: 127-9
credit system 115
Critical Discourse Analysis
    (CDA) 213, 215-20
cross-cultural theory 213,
    221, 222-4
culture 213, 218, 222
curriculum 130, 254

deficit-discourse shift 220-
    21, 232
Denmark 239
Department of Education
    Training and Youth
    Affairs (DETYA) 182-
    83, 214
disability (AHEAD) 55, 65;
    multiple 191
Disability Action Plans 183
Disability Liaison Officer
    (DLO) 183, 184
disabled students: South
    Australia 181-95
disadvantage: criteria 146-7
Disadvantaged Fund 53
Dougherty, K. 172
'Dual Admissions' Scheme
    19, 23
Dublin Institute of
    Technology Act
    (1992) 53

Dundee University 141,
    148-53
Durham University 162

East Cleveland: England
    161
education 185; attainment
    levels 115; ex-
    offenders 208-11;
    framework 232;
    parental experience
    123; reformers 95
Education Resources
    Institute (TERI):
    Boston; 88
educational research 249-51
Ellsworth, E. 253
England: higher education
    (HE) 29; North West
    132; policy and
    practice 29-47; see
    also individual
    universities
enrollment 172-3
equality of opportunity 62-
    68, 217
equity 100; groups 64-5,
    Lithuania, 79-84,
    policy and practice
    191
Equity and General
    Performance
    Indicators in Higher
    Education 182
Estonia 239
European Council (EC) 83
European Social Fund
    (ESF) 118, 202, 207
European Union 20, 240
Evaluation Group (Peer
    Group) 244-5
evaluation studies 59-60
Evans, P. 34
Everton 118
ex-offenders: education
    199-211
Excellence in Experiential
    Learning and
    Leadership (Excell)
    224-5

Fairclough, N. 221, 226
family: Asian 114; Black
    114; framework for
    learning 113-14;
    minority 114, 121;
    support 128; working
    class 114
feminist pedagogy 249,
    252-4
Ferrier, F. and Heagney, M
    38
Fife: Scotland 143
Fife Wider Access
    Partnership (FWAP)
    144
Finland 239
formative evaluation
    findings 93-5
foundation degrees 178
Free State University (South
    Africa) 103
From Elitism to Inclusion
    (CVCP report 1999)
    155
Fryter, R.H. 155
funding 20, 41, 193-5

Gee, J.P. 219
Geneeb, H. and Bowers, B.
    34
graduation exams 81 reform
    81, 82
Granby/Toxteth Task Force
    116, 135
Grangetown:
    Middlesborough 166
growth and sustainability
    207-8
Gutteridge, R. 38-9

Harrison, R. 37
Heagney, M and Ferrier, F.
    38
higher education: modules
    167; reasons for
    entering 126-7;
    system 100
Higher Education Authority
    (HEA) 50, 56, 59, 67-
    8

Higher Education
  Contribution Scheme
  (HECS) 216
Higher Education Equality
  Unit (HEEU) 55
Higher Education Funding
  Council for England
  (HEFCE) 30-1, 36-7,
  39, 40, 42, 155, 170
Higher Education Reform
  in Lithuania (HERIL)
  81
Higher Education and
  Research Committee
  (HERC) 83
Higher Education Review
  182-3
Higher Equity Education
  Program (HEEP) 182
Higher National Diploma
  (HND) 44, 206
historically black
  institutions (HBIs) 99
historically white
  institutions (HWIs) 99
Hodge, M. 30
Hughes, C. 248
human geography 249-51

Industrial Engineering and
  Management 241
Information Technology
  (IT) 50; resources
  129; Services 148;
  skills 130
Initial Strategic Statements
  31
Institute for Access Studies:
  Staffordshire
  University 42
Institute of Sport 148
institutional autonomy 23-4,
  52
institutional cultures 194-5
institutional equality 66-7
institutional mergers 102-4
integration 23-4
inter-organisational
  relationships 33
inter-partner
  communication 92

interdisciplinary
  collaboration 247-54
introductory courses 76
Ireland 4, 6, 9-11, 18, 20,
  21, 22, 49-69
demography 49
education policy 49
legislative context 50,
  52-3 third level
education 50

Jewel and Esk Valley
  College 199, 201, 202,
Job Seeker's Allowance 204
Joint Funding Councils
  Group 4

Kantanis, T. 227
Kennedy, H. 37
Kenway, J. and Willis, S.
  254
key workers 208-9, 211

Lankshear, C. 221
Latino students 85-6, 88
Latvia 239
Layer, G. 40
Lead Scotland (Linking
  Education and
  Disability) 203
learning continuum 13-14
Leith, H. and Osborne, R.
  55, 58
Letherby, G. and
  Marchbank, J. 253
Lewis, M.G. 252
lifelong learning 122, 155,
  167, 248, 250
Lithuania 241; Constitution
  80; equity problems
  79-84; Parliament 83-
  4
Lithuanian Association of
  the Institutions of
  Higher Education
  (LAMA) 82
Liverpool City Council:
  Parent School
  Partnership 113
Liverpool Hope University
  113, 114, 116, 120,

  135; Deanery of Hope
  133
Liverpool Pathway Areas
  113
local access partnership:
  rationale 142-3
Local Education Authority
  (LEA) 148-9, 156;
  Parent School
  Partnership Service
  116
Lorde, A. 253
Los Angeles 7
Lund University (Sweden)
  72

McCann, H. 227
McGivney, V. 156, 171
mainstreaming 60, 170
management 169, 192, 243
Manchester 132
Marchbank, J. and Letherby,
  G. 253
marketing 35, 203-4
Melbourne: Australia 11-12,
  19, 21, 23, 40
merger 103-6
Merseyside 115
Merseyside Open College
  Network 120
Meteor Plus 161, 162
Meteor Scheme 160-3
Middlesbrough College 163
minority groups 66, 191-2
ML Sultan Technikon 102,
  105
motivations 34-5
Multicultureel Instituut of
  Utrecht 8

Napier University 199, 201
Natal Technikon 102
National Board of
  Employment:
  Education and
  Training (NBEET)
  182, 216
National Exam Centre
  (NEC) 81
National Exam Centre of
  Slovenia (RIC) 81

National Vocational
Qualification (NVQ)
158
National Working Group:
South Africa 102
Netherlands 4, 6, 18 Utrecht
'Bridge' 8
New London Group 222
New Public Management
32
North University (South
Africa) 103
Northern Ireland 30

Occidental College: Los
Angeles 88, 92-3
Open College Networks 115
open learning techniques
117
Open University (UK) 206
operations research 242,
243
Organization for Economic
Co-operation and
Development (OECD)
countries 49-50
Osborne, R. and Leith, H.
55, 58
outreach 147-8

parents 89, 123
part-time degree provision
124-5
partnership 25, 42-6, 113,
130, 133-4, 138, 141,
151, 160, 169, 210
Pearson, H. 225
personal skills 129-30
personal tutors 152-3
Personalised Access and
Study Scheme (PAS)
11-12, 15, 40-1
Planning and Resources
Operations Group for
Equal Access Summer
Schools (PROGRESS)
150-1
Points System (Hyland) 55
Police Act (1997) 207
policy implications 26-7
policy makers 5, 27-8

Position of Students (HERC
1995) 83
post-compulsory education
3, 43
Postle, G. 219
pragmatism 35, 154, 248,
251
preparatory year: extended
75
Preston: England 132
Progression Pathways
Project 163, 169
PSP 127-9
Public Speaking 130

Qualifications (Education
and Training) Act
(1999) 53

Ramsey, E. 193
REACHOut 111-38
recruitment 120, 203-4;
broader 74; delegation
74; focus 25; over
136; policy 72-3
recruitment measures:
active 73
Regional Technical Colleges
Act (1992) 53
Rehabilitation of Offenders
Act (1974) 205
'request for proposal'
process 88
retention 25, 136
Richter scale 209
Robinson, D. 33, 34, 35
Ronayne, J. 12, 41
Rose, G. 251

schools 95, 149-50;
disadvantaged leavers
56, 57
Scotland 4, 30, 143, 200,
203; Fife 143
Scottish Examination Board
(SQA) 81
Scottish Funding Councils
3-4
Scottish Higher Education
Funding Council
(SHEFC) 147, 202,
207

Scottish Prison Service 207;
Annual Report (1999-
2000) 200
Scottish Qualification
Authority (SQA) 206
selection process 76-7
Sibley, D. 250
Single Regeneration Budget
(SRB) 136
Sixth Form Colleges 156
Skilbeck, M. 61-2, 68-9 and
Connell, H. 5, 55
Social Inclusion Partnership
(SIP) 144
social learning model 222-3
social participation 256,
227, 250
socio-economic
disadvantage 9, 65
South Africa: history of
Higher Education 99-
108; mergers 100-1;
Ministry of Education
101; national plan
101-2; proposed
strategies 104-5;
Province of
Mpumalanga 101;
Province of Northern
Cape 101
South Australia: disabled
students 181-95
Soviet Union 79
Staffordshire University
253; Institute for
Access Studies 42
Stockport 132
Storan, J. 37
Strategies for Widening
Participation in
Higher Education
(HEFCE 2001) 155-6
student achievement 132-3
African-American 85-
6, 88; aims 125-6;
American Indian 88;
Asian-American 88;
characteristics 121-2;
competence 223-4;
with disabilities 57-8;
educational
experience 122-4;

experience and outcome 206-7; information interview selection 145; Latino 85-6, 88; leaders 152-3; low-income 173-80; mature 52, 57, 66; mentors 162-3; part-time 66; 'perpetual' 79; progress study 187; support 152-3; tutoring 147; typical profile 124; under-represented 85-97
Student Advisory Service 148
Student Ambassador Scheme 161-2
Student Shadowing schemes 147
Student Transfer Center 176
Students' Association 148
study: guidance 74-5, 118-19
Study of Non-Completion in Undergraduate Courses 56
sub-cultures 213, 222
Summer Intensive Transfer Experience (SITE) 7-8, 175, 176-78
sustainability 37, 169
Sweden 239; cyber university 77-8; government deliberations 71-8; Open University (draft bill 2001) 78; Swedish language courses 76

Tamboukou, M. 249
Targeted Initiatives 2001: proposals 60
targeted initiatives: evaluation 58-9
Taylor, M. and Balloch, S. 32
Taylor, R. 247
Technikon South Africa 103-5

Tees Valley: building progression pathways 155-71
Teesside University 156, 159, 163, 168
Think Again: pre-access course 199-11
Thomas, E.A.M. 35, 37, 42
Tinto, V. 188
Transfer Alliance Program (TAP) 7, 175
Transfer Student Center 175
Transfer Summer Program 175, 176
transferability 12-13
tripartite system 15-16

under-represented groups 3-4, 5
United Kingdom (UK) 209, 247, 253; government 171
United States of America (USA) 4, 6, 209, 228; community college 171-8; Department of Education 85; Education Resources Institute (TERI) Boston 88; education system 86; K-16 system 86, 89, 91; Pacific territories 95; students and college access 85-97
Universities Act (1997) 53, 61
university: contemporary 214-15; courses 185-6; culture 213-33; equality policies 61-3; space 254
University of California 7, 13, 16, 17, 21, 22, 23, 176, 178; transfer programs 171-8; transfer recruitment and retention 174-7
University of South Africa 103-4
Usdan, M. 86

Utrecht 'Bridge' Netherlands 8, 20, 21

Victoria University of Technology: Australia 11
Vilnius Gediminas Technical University 245
Vista 103-4
Volunteer Development Scotland 203

Wales 30
Wall, J. and Clancy, P. 51, 55
Warwick University 182
West, P. 193
White Paper 3 (South Africa 1997) 100
White Paper on Adult Education (2000) 55
widening participation 111-38, 250-1
Wigan 132
Willis, S. and Kenway, J. 252
women 65-6, 121; Bangladesh 251; feminist pedagogy 249, 252-4; students 249-50
women's studies 165, 252
Woodrow, M. xv-xxv, 3-4, 34
Woods, M. 60
Worker's Educational Association (WEA) 156, 203